Practical Explainable AI Using Python

Artificial Intelligence Model Explanations Using Python-based Libraries, Extensions, and Frameworks

Pradeepta Mishra

Apress®

Practical Explainable AI Using Python

Pradeepta Mishra
Sobha Silicon Oasis, Bangalore, Karnataka, India

ISBN-13 (pbk): 978-1-4842-7157-5   ISBN-13 (electronic): 978-1-4842-7158-2
https://doi.org/10.1007/978-1-4842-7158-2

Managing Director, Apress Media LLC: Welmoed Spahr
Acquisitions Editor: Divya Modi
Development Editor: James Markham
Coordinating Editor: Divya Modi
Copyeditor: Mary Behr

Cover designed by eStudioCalamar

Cover image designed by Pixabay

Distributed to the book trade worldwide by Springer Science+Business Media New York, 1 New York Plaza, Suite 4600, New York, NY 10004-1562, USA. Phone 1-800-SPRINGER, fax (201) 348-4505, e-mail orders-ny@springer-sbm.com, or visit www.springeronline.com. Apress Media, LLC is a California LLC and the sole member (owner) is Springer Science + Business Media Finance Inc (SSBM Finance Inc). SSBM Finance Inc is a **Delaware** corporation.

For information on translations, please e-mail booktranslations@springernature.com; for reprint, paperback, or audio rights, please e-mail bookpermissions@springernature.com.

Apress titles may be purchased in bulk for academic, corporate, or promotional use. eBook versions and licenses are also available for most titles. For more information, reference our Print and eBook Bulk Sales web page at www.apress.com/bulk-sales.

Any source code or other supplementary material referenced by the author in this book is available to readers on GitHub via the book's product page, located at www.apress.com/978-1-4842-7157-5. For more detailed information, please visit www.apress.com/source-code.

Printed on acid-free paper

I dedicate this book to my late father, who always inspired me to strive hard for the next level, to never settle, and to keep moving. Love you, dad; you would have felt proud of this book.

To the three ladies in my life, my wife, Prajna, and my daughters, Aarya and Aadya, for always supporting me and loving me. Completing this book would not have been possible without their support.

Table of Contents

About the Author

Pradeepta Mishra is the Head of AI Data Products at L&T Infotech (LTI), leading a group of Data Scientists, Computational linguistics experts, Machine Learning experts, and Deep Learning experts in building Artificial Intelligence-driven features for Data products. He was awarded "India's Top – 40 Under 40 Data Scientists" by *Analytics India Magazine* for two years in a row (2019, 2020). As an inventor, he has filed five patents in different global locations currently in pending status. He is the author of four books published in different languages including English, Chinese and Spanish. His first book has been recommended by the HSLS Center at the University of Pittsburgh, PA, USA. His latest book, *PyTorch Recipes,* was published by Apress. He delivered a keynote session at the 2018 Global Data Science Conference, CA, USA. He has delivered over 500 tech talks on data science, ML, DL, NLP, and AI at various universities, meetups, technical institutions, and community-arranged forums. He is visiting faculty for AI-ML in M. Tech for an AI course and a cyber security course at Reva University, Bangalore, India and at various other universities. He has mentored and trained over 2,000 data scientists and AI engineers in the last nine years.

About the Technical Reviewers

Abhishek Vijayvargia works as a data and applied scientist at Microsoft. Previously, he worked at many startups related to machine learning and IoT. He developed AI algorithms to handle various problems in the cybersecurity, IoT, manufacturing, shipping optimization, and transportation domains. He is also an expert and active researcher in explainable AI and ML System design. He is a data science author and research paper reviewer, and he has presented his ideas at many AI conferences.

Bharath has over ten years of experience and is currently working as a Senior Data Science Engineer Consultant at Verizon, Bengaluru. Bharath has a PG Diploma in Data Science from Praxis Business School and a M.S in Life Sciences from Mississippi State University, U.S.A. He worked as a research data scientist at the University of Georgia, Emory University, and Eurofins LLC. At Happiest Minds, he worked on AI-based digital marketing products and NLP-based solutions in the education domain. Along with his day-to-day responsibilities, he is a mentor and an active researcher. He is particularly interested in unsupervised and semi-supervised learning and efficient deep learning architectures in NLP and Computer Vision.

Acknowledgments

This book is based on the research conducted on the available frameworks around model explainability for making black box-based artificial intelligence models into white box models and making the decisions made by AI models transparent. I am grateful to my friends and family for encouraging me to start the work, persevere with the work, and get to the final step of publishing it.

I thank my wife, Prajna, for her continuous encouragement and support in pushing me to complete the book, helping me to prioritize the book over vacations, taking care of the kids, and allowing me enough time to Complete the book.

I thank my editor, Divya, who has been a continuous support throughout writing the book, being flexible with timelines and giving me enough time to complete this book.

I thank my editorial board and Suresh for believing in me to write about the complex subject of model explainability and giving me the opportunity to write on the topic.

Finally, I thank my daughters, Aarya and Aadya, for loving me and supporting me in completing this book.

Introduction

Explainable artificial intelligent (XAI) is a current need as more and more AI models are in production to generate business decisions. Thus, many users are also getting impacted by these decisions. One user may get favorably or unfavorably impacted. As a result, it's important to know the key features leading to these decisions. It is often argued that AI models are quite black-box in nature because the AI model's decisions cannot be explained, hence the adoptability of AI models is quite slow in the industry. This book is an attempt at unboxing the so-called black-box models to increase the adaptability, interpretability, and explainability of the decisions made by AI algorithms using frameworks such as Python XAI libraries, TensorFlow 2.0+, Keras, and custom frameworks using Python Wrappers. The objective of this book is to explain the AI models in simple language using the above mentioned frameworks.

Model interpretability and explainability are the key focuses of this book. There are mathematical formulas and methods that are typically used to explain a decision made by an AI model. You will be provided with software library methods, classes, frameworks, and functions and how to use them for model explainability, transparency, reliability, ethics, bias, and interpretability. If a human being can understand the reasons behind the decision made by the AI model, it will give much more power to the user to make amendments and recommendations. There are two different kinds of users: business users and practitioners. The business user wants the explainability in simple language without any statistical or mathematical terms. The practitioner wants to know the explainability from the computational point of view. This book is an attempt at balancing both needs when generating explanations.

This book begins with an introduction to model explainability and interpretability basics, ethical considerations in AI applications, and biases in predictions generated by AI models. Then you will learn about the reliability of AI models in generating predictions in different use cases. Then you will explore the methods and systems to interpret the linear models, non-linear models, and time series models used in AI. Next, you will learn about the most complex ensemble models, explainability, and interpretability using frameworks such as Lime, SHAP, Skater, ELI5, and Alibi. Then you will learn about model explainability for unstructured data and natural language processing related to text classification tasks. Examining model fairness also requires a simulation of what-if scenarios using the prediction outcomes. You'll cover this next. Then you will read about counterfactual and contrastive explanations for AI models. You will explore model explainability for deep learning models, rule-based expert systems, and model-agnostic explanations for prediction invariance and for computer vision tasks using various XAI frameworks.

Today we have AI engineers and data scientists who train or build these models; software developers who put these models into production and thus operationalize the models; business users who consume the end result or outcome generated by the models; and decision makers who think about the decisions made by the models. The leadership in driving AI projects/products think, "Is there any way to have clarity around the models and predictive modelers?" Bio-statisticians of course think how explain the model predictions, etc. The expectation is to develop an explainability framework that caters to the needs of all stakeholders involved in this process of making AI work in real life. Again, this book strikes a balance between multiple stakeholders. It leans towards data scientists, because if a data scientist is at least convinced about the explainability, they can explain further to the business stakeholder.

Making AI models explainable to the business user in simple, plain language will take some time. Perhaps some new framework will come along to address this. At this moment, the challenge is that the data scientist who built the model doesn't have complete clarity about the model's behavior and lacks clarity in explaining the AI model. Newly trained data scientists or graduating data scientists will get a tremendous benefit from this book. Similarly, other AI engineers will also benefit from this book. This is an evolving area; this book's explanations were current in July, 2021.

## CHAPTER 1

Model Explainability and Interpretability

In this book, we will begin with an introduction to model explainability and interpretability basics, ethical considerations in AI applications, and biases in the predictions generated by AI models. We will cover the reliability of AI models in generating predictions in different use cases. Then we will cover the methods and systems to interpret the linear models that are used in AI, such as non-linear models and time series models. Next, we will explore the most complex ensemble models, explainability, and interpretability using frameworks such as Lime, SHAP, Skater, ELI5, and more. Then we will cover model explainability for unstructured data and natural language processing-related tasks.

Establishing the Framework

Tremendous progress has been made in last few years in the area of machine learning and deep learning in creating artificial intelligence (AI) solutions across different sectors, spanning retail, banking, financial services, insurance, healthcare, manufacturing, and Internet of Things-based industries. AI is the core of many products and solutions that are coming up with rapid digitalization of various business functions. The reason why AI is at the root of these products and solutions is that intelligent machines are now powered by learning, reasoning, and adaptation capabilities. Experience is scarce. If we can leverage the rich experience gained by intelligent people and reflect it using a learning, reasoning layer through machines, that can go a long way in bringing a multiplication factor to the learning element. By virtue of these capabilities, today's machine learning and deep learning models are able to achieve unprecedented levels of performance in solving complex business problems, thereby driving business outcomes.

© Pradeepta Mishra 2022
P. Mishra, *Practical Explainable AI Using Python*, https://doi.org/10.1007/978-1-4842-7158-2_1

If we look at the last two years, there are plenty of AutoML (Automatic Machine Learning) tools, frameworks, low code, and no code tools (minimum human intervention), which is another level of sophistication that has been achieved by AI-enabled systems. This is the epitome of near-zero human intervention required in terms of design, delivery, and deployment of solutions. When the decisions are completely made by machines and because humans are always at the receiving end, there is an urgent need to understand how the machines arrived at those decisions. The models that power the AI systems are often referred as black box models. Hence there is a need for model explainability and interpretability in order to explain the predictions made by the AI models.

Artificial Intelligence

Artificial intelligence refers to the design of a system as a computer program that automatically makes decisions on behalf of human beings, with respect to some task, without explicitly being programmed. Figure 1-1 explains the relationship between machine learning, deep learning, and artificial intelligence.

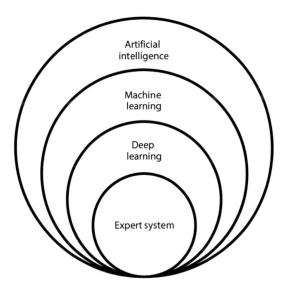

Figure 1-1. *Relationship Between ML, DL, and AI*

Artificial intelligence is a system designed using a computer program where intelligent inferences can be drawn with respect to a problem statement. In the process of deriving intelligence we may use machine learning algorithms or deep learning algorithms. Machine learning algorithms are simple mathematical functions used in the process of optimization using input and output data combinations. Further, the functions can be utilized to predict the unknown output using new input. For structured data we can use machine learning algorithms, but when the data dimensions and volume increases, such as image data, audio data, text and video data, the machine learning models fails to perform better, hence a deep learning model is required. An expert system is designed as a rule-based system that helps in getting inferences. This is required when we do not have enough training data to train machine learning models or deep learning models. Overall the construction of an artificial intelligence system requires a combination of expert systems, machine learning algorithms, and deep learning algorithms to generate inferences.

Machine learning can be defined as a system where the algorithm learns from examples with respect to some task defined earlier, and the learning performance increases as we feed more and more data to the system. The tasks can be defined as supervised, where the output/outcome is known beforehand; unsupervised, where the output/outcome is not known beforehand; and reinforcement, where the actions/outcomes are always driven by a feedback layer and the feedback can be a reward or a penalty. So far as the learning algorithms are concerned, they can be categorized as linear algorithms, deterministic algorithms, additive and multiplicative algorithms, tree-based algorithms, ensemble algorithms, and graph-based algorithms. The performance criteria can be defined as per the selection of the algorithm. Explaining the decisions of an AI model is called explainable AI (XAI).

Need for XAI

Let's have a look at the reason for calling the AI models as black box models. Figure 1-2 explains the classical modelling scenario where the set of independent variables is passed through the function, which is predetermined to produce the output. The output produced is compared with the true output in order to make an assessment of whether the function fits the data or not. If the function does not fit well, then we must either transform the data or consider using another function so that it can fit to the data, but the experiment is quite manual and every time there is a data refresh, there is a need for statisticians or modelers to recalibrate the models and again see if the data fits the model. This is why the classical way of predictive model generation for inference processing has human dependency and is always subject to more than one interpretation. At times it is difficult for the stakeholders to trust the model as all variants proposed by many experts may sound good in a sense, but there is no generalization. Hence the classic system of model development as shown in Figure 1-2 is difficult to implement in the world of artificial intelligence systems, where every moment data is on the run. It keeps on changing. Human dependency on calibration is a bottleneck; hence there is a need for a modern system of inference generation dynamically using dynamic algorithms.

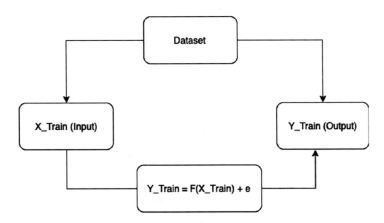

Figure 1-2. *The classic model training system*

Figure 1-2 shows the classic model development scenario, where the model can be captured through an equation and that equation is easy to interpret and simple to explain to anyone, but the existence of formula-based interpretation is changing in the AI world. Figure 1-3 shows the structure of exploring the best possible functions that produce the output using the input. Here there is no constraint to limit the model to a particular function like linear or non-linear. In this structure, the learning happens through many iterations and using a cross validation approach the best model gets identified. The challenge with AI models is interpretability and explainability as many algorithms are complex and so it's not easy to explain the predictions to everyone.

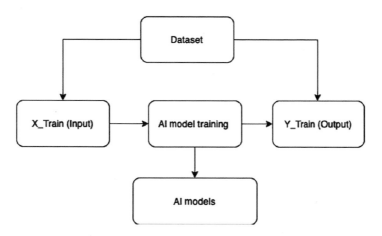

Figure 1-3. *AI model training process*

With the advancement of computer programs and algorithms, it became very difficult for developers to search for different kinds of functions such as linear and non-linear, and the evaluation of such functions also became extremely difficult. ML or DL models take care of the search for appropriate functions that fit the training data well. Figure 1-3 explains that the machine identifies the final model that provides better performance not only in terms of accuracy but also stability and reliability in generating predictions. When the functional relationship between input and output is clearly defined, there is less ambiguity and the predictions are transparent. However, when our AI models make a selection of a complex functional relationship, it is very hard to understand as an end user. Hence the AI models are considered as black box. In this book, we want to make the black box model interpretable so that AI solutions will become increasingly deployable and adaptable.

The day-to-day execution of AI models for decisioning requires transparency, unbiasedness, and ethics. There are various scenarios where it currently lacks explainability:

- Someone applies for a credit card and the AI model rejects the credit card application. It is important to convey why the application was rejected and what corrective actions the applicant may take to amend their behavior.

- In a medical diagnosis based on life style and vital parameters, the AI model predicts whether the person will have diabetes of not. Here, if the AI model predicts that the person might develop diabetes, then it has to also convey why and what the drivers are for getting the disease in future.

- Autonomous vehicles identify objects found on the road and make clear decisions. They also need a clear explanation of why they make these decisions.

There are numerous other use cases where the explanations supporting the output of a model are crucial. It is a human tendency not to adopt something that they cannot interpret or understand. Thereby it reduces their trust factor in believing the predictions of AI model. We are using AI models in order to remove biasness from human decision making; however, the decisions will be dangerous if the outcome is not justifiable, legitimate, and transparent. On the other hand, one may argue that if we cannot interpret and explain the decisions of AI models, then why use them. The reasons are model accuracy and performance. There is always going to be a trade-off between the performance of a model and the explainability of a model. Figure 1-4 explains the trade-off between the two.

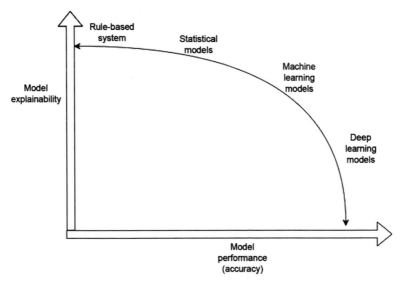

Figure 1-4. *Tradeoff between model explainability and performance (accuracy)*

In Figure 1-4, the horizontal axis explains the performance or accuracy of the models and the vertical axis shows the model interpretation and explanation. A rule-based system is placed at a position where the performance is not optimal; however, the interpretability is good. In contrast, the deep learning-based models provide superior performance and good accuracy at the cost of less interpretability and explainability.

Explainability vs. Interpretability

There is a difference between model interpretation and explainability. Interpretation is about the meaning of the predictions. Explainability is why the model predicted something and why someone should trust the model. To understand the difference better, let's look at a real world example of a sales prediction, where the factors that help in the prediction are advertisement expenses, product quality, sources for making the advertisement, the size of the advertisement, etc. Each factor has a coefficient after the regression modeling is done. The coefficients can be interpreted as the incremental change in sales due to a delta change in one factor such as advertisement expenses. However, if you are predicting that sales next month are going to be $20,000 when the average monthly sales historically have been less than or equal to $15,000, this needs an explanation. As part of model explainability we need the following:

- Model interpretability ensures the decision making is natural and there is no biasness in the prediction.

- Differentiating the false causality from true causality, which helps in making the predictions transparent

- Need to produce explainable models without compromising the high performance of the learning experiences and iterations

- Enable decision makers to trust the AI models.

"XAI applications and products will be a new trend in 2021, as the demand for interpretability, trust, and ethics in AI is loud and clear" – **Pradeepta Mishra** *(Source: Various Research Reports)*

There is a constant research around XAI that makes every attempt in explaining the AI models and their behavior to the end users in order to increase the adoption of AI models. Now the question is, who are the end users of XAI?

- Credit officers who evaluate applications for loans, credit requests, and more. If they understand the decisions, then they can help educate customers in correcting their behavior.

- Data scientists who evaluate their own solutions and ensure improvements are made in the model. Is this the best model that can be made using the present dataset?

- Senior managers who need to meet regulatory and compliance needs at a high level

- Business heads who need to trust the AI black-box decisions and are looking for any historical evidence they can rely upon

- Customer support executives who need to answer complaints and explain decisions

- Internal auditors and regulators who must ensure that a transparent data-driven process is established

The goal of XAI is to achieve the following things:

- **Trust**: The prediction accuracy is a clear function of data quality, true causality, and choice of an appropriate algorithm. However, the models are subject to generating false positives in the prediction process. If the models generate a lot of false positives, then the end user will lose trust in the model. Thus it is important to convey confidence in the model to the end user.

- **Associations**: The ML or DL models learn to make predictions based on associations between various features. The associations can be correlations or mere associations. The correlations that are unexplained are spurious correlations that make the model impossible to interpret. Hence it is important to capture the true correlations.

- **Reliability**: Confidence in the model, the stability of the model in predictions, and the robustness of the model are also very important. This is required in order to have more trustworthiness in AI models and to ensure that the end user has enough confidence in the model predictions. If this is not available, then no user will trust the models.

- **Fairness**: The AI models should be fair and ethically compliant. They should not discriminate among religion, sex, class, and race in generating predictions.

- **Identity**: The AI models should be able to keep privacy considerations intact, without revealing the identity of an individual. Privacy and identity management while generating XAI is very important.

Explainability Types

Machine learning interpretability is an integral part of model explainability. There are various classifications of model interpretations:

- **Intrinsic explanation**: Simple models fall into this category, such as simple linear regression models and decision tree-based models where a simple if/else condition can explain the predictions, which means the XAI is intrinsic in the model itself and there's no need to perform any kind of post analysis.

- **Post-hoc explanation**: Complex models like non-linear models, ensemble tree-based models, stochastic gradient boosted tree-based model, and stacked models where a greater focus needs to be given to create explainability

- **Model specific**: There is a set of explanations that can be drawn from a specific type of model, nothing more than that. For example, a linear regression model does not provide feature importance. However, the coefficients of a linear regression model someone can use as a proxy.

- **Model agnostic**: These explanations some can interpret by looking at the pair of training input data and training output data combinations. In this book, we are going to look at model-agnostic explanations in later chapters.

- **Local interpretation**: This gives an idea about individual predictions, which is the interpretation of a single data point. As an example, if a borrower is predicted by the model as likely to default, why it is so? This is a local interpretation.

- **Global interpretation**: This gives an idea about the global understanding of the predictions for all data points, overall model behavior, and more.

- **Sublocal interpretation**: This explains the local interpretations about a group of data points together rather than all data points. This is different from a local interpretation.

- **Textual explanations**: Text-based explanations include the numeric part as well as language to communicate the meaning of a certain parameters of the model.

- **Visual explanations**: Visual explanations are nice but sometimes they are not intuitive enough to explain the predictions, hence a visual accompanied by textual interpretation is very much needed.

Tools for Model Explainability

There are various tools and frameworks available for generating explainability out of the ML and DL models. The open source Python libraries have some advantages and disadvantages. We are going to use a mix of Python libraries as open source libraries and publicly available datasets from various websites in the examples all through this book. Here are the tools that need to be installed and the environment that needs to be set up.

SHAP

The SHAP (SHapley Additive exPlanations) library is a Python-based unified approach to explain the output of any machine learning model. The SHAP Python library is based on game theory with local explanations. The game theory approach is a way to get predictions if one factor is present vs. when it is absent. If there is a significant change in the expected outcome, then the factor is very important to the target variable. This method unites several previous methods to explain the output generated by the machine learning models. The SHAP framework can be used for different types of models except for time series-based models. See Figure 1-5. The SHAP library can be used to make sense of the models.

In order to install SHAP, the following methods can be used:

- `!Pip install shap` (from Jupyter notebook)

- `conda install -c conda-forge shap` (using terminal)

  `!pip3 install shap`

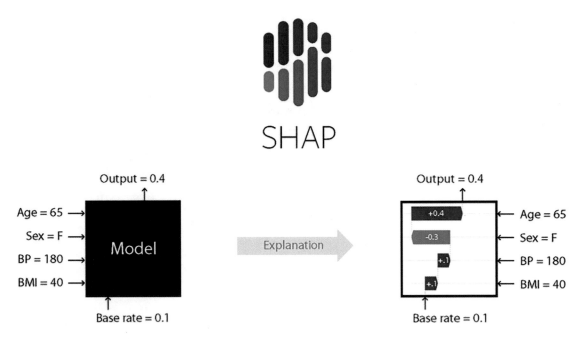

Figure 1-5. *Shapely values and explanation sample image*

LIME

LIME is stands for Local Interpretable Model-Agnostic Explanations. Local refers to the explanation around the locality of the class that was predicted by the model. The behavior of the classifier around the locality gives a good understanding about the predictions. Interpretable means if the prediction cannot be interpreted by a human being, there is no point. Hence the class predictions need to be interpretable. Model agnostic implies instead of understanding a particular model type, the system and method should be able to generate the interpretations.

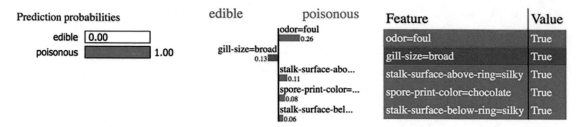

Figure 1-6. *An example of mushroom classification*

A text classification problem such as sentiment analysis or any other text classification is where the input is sentences as documents and the output is a class. See Figure 1-6. When the model predicts a positive sentiment for a sentence, we need to know which words made the model predict the class as positive. These word vectors are sometimes very simple, such as individual words. Sometimes they are complex, such as word embeddings, in which case we need to know how the model interpreted the word embeddings and how it impacts the classification. In those scenarios, LIME is extremely useful in making sense of machine learning and deep learning models. LIME is a Python-based library that can be leveraged to showcase how it works. The following step can be followed to install the library:

```
!pip install lime
```

ELI5

ELI5 is a Python-based library intended to be used for an explainable AI pipeline, which allows us to visualize and debug various machine learning models using a unified API. It has built-in support for several ML frameworks and provides a way to explain black box models. The purpose of the library is to make explanations easy for all kinds of black box models. See Figure 1-7.

Weight	Feature
0.3717	relationship
0.1298	marital_status
0.1247	education_num
0.1108	capital_gain
0.0611	capital_loss
0.0362	age
0.0307	occupation
0.0298	sex
0.0289	hours_per_week
0.0188	workclass
0.0161	native_country
0.0160	race
0.0132	fnlwgt
0.0123	education

Figure 1-7. *Sample image of ELI5*

Figure 1-7 from ELI5 shows the importance of factors in predicting the income class in the income classification use case, which we are going to look at in subsequent chapters. The Python installation of ELI5 can be done using the following syntax:

```
!pip install eli5
```

This requires many Python-based libraries to be updated and you may have to wait for some time for this to happen.

Skater

Skater is an open source unified framework to enable model interpretation for all forms of models to help us build an interpretable machine learning system, which is often needed for real world use-cases. Skater supports algorithms to demystify the learned structures of a black box model both globally (inference on the basis of a complete data set) and locally (inference about an individual prediction).

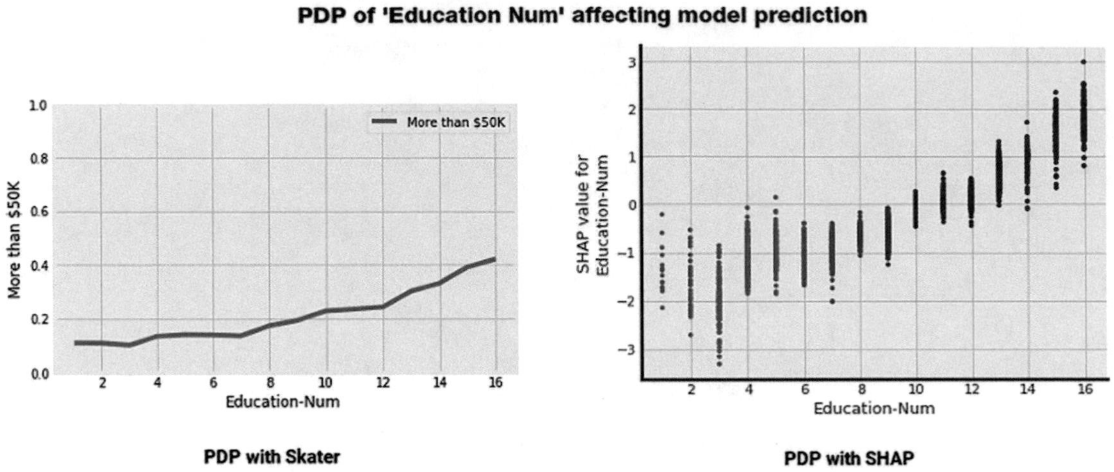

PDP of 'Education Num' affecting model prediction

PDP with Skater   PDP with SHAP

Figure 1-8. *Sample image showing PDP using SHAP and Skater*

Skater enables this vision by providing the ability to infer and debug the model's decision policies as needed, bringing "a human into the loop." See Figure 1-8. To install the Skater library, we can use the following command:

```
!pip install skater
```

Skope_rules

Skope-rules aims at learning logical, interpretable rules for "scoping" a target class (i.e., detecting with high precision instances of this class). Skope-rules is a tradeoff between the interpretability of a decision tree and the modelling power of a random forest. See Figure 1-9.

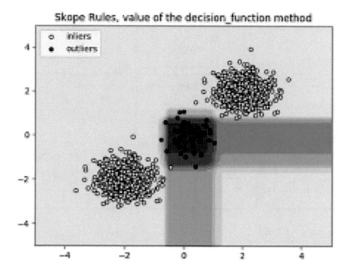

Figure 1-9. *Skope-rules example image*

The above mentioned Python-based libraries are mostly open source and free to use and integrate in any software application. However, there are a bunch of enterprise-based tools and frameworks that are available, such as H2O.ai. The area of XAI is relatively new, as the research is still happening in making model interpretation easy. Tools and frameworks are coming to the forefront to make the process available for the industry to apply in various use cases.

Methods of XAI for ML

The levels of transparency in the machine learning models can be categorized into three groups: transparency of algorithms, decomposition of the parameters and hyper parameters, and reproducibility of the same result in similar situations. Some ML models by design are interpretable and some require a set of other programs to make them explainable. Figure 1-10 explains the methods of model explainability.

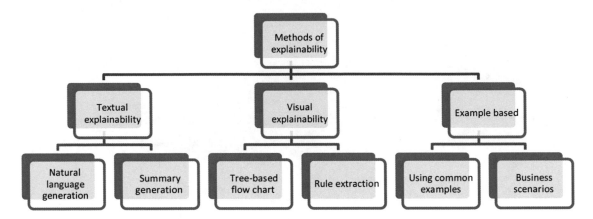

Figure 1-10. *Methods of XAI*

There are three methods of model explainability:

- The textual explanation requires elaborating the meaning of a mathematical formula, an outcome of a model parameter, or metrics defined by the model. The interpretations can be designed based on a predefined template where the story line has to be prepared beforehand and only the parameters need to be populated in the template. There are two different approaches to achieve this: using Natural Language Generation (NLG) methods, which requires gather text and making a sentence that describes the object, and explaining using summary generation.

- The visual explanation can be delivered using custom graphs and charts. Tree-based charts are quite easy and self-explanatory for end users. Each tree based-method is backed by a set of rules. If these rules can be shown to the user in terms of simple if/else statements, it is going to be much more powerful.

- The example-based method ensures that we can take common day-to-day examples to explain the model by drawing parallels. Also, a common business scenario can be used to explain the models.

XAI Compatible Models

Let's have a look at the current state of the models, their built-in nature, how compatible they are for XAI, and whether these models need additional frameworks for explainability.

- **Linear models**: The linear regression models or logistic regression models are easy to interpret by analyzing their coefficient value, which is a number. These values are very easy to interpret. However, if we extend this to regularized regression families, it becomes very difficult to explain. Usually we give more importance to the individual features. We do not incorporate the interaction features. The complexity of the model goes up if we include interactions, such as additive interactions, multiplicative interactions, polynomial of degree two-based interactions, or polynomial of degree three-based interactions. The mathematical result need a simpler way of interpretation. Hence there is a lot more to explain in those complex scenarios.

- **Time series forecasting models**: These are also very simple models which follow a regression kind of scenario that can be explained easily by taking a parametric approach.

- **Tree-based models**: Tree-based models are simpler to analyze and also very intuitive for humans to interpret. However, these models often do not provide better accuracy and performance. They also lack robustness and have inherent problems of biasness and overfitting. Since there are so many drawbacks, the interpretation has no point for the end user.

- **Ensemble-based models**: There are three different types of ensemble models: bagging, boosting, and stacking. All three types lack explainability. A simplified description is required to convey the model results. The feature importance also needs to be simplified.

- **Mathematical models**: Vector mathematics-based support vector machines are used for regression-based tasks and classification-based tasks. These models are quite difficult to explain, hence model simplification is very much needed.

- **Deep learning models**: Deep neural network (DNN) models usually have more than three hidden layers in order to qualify for the definition of deep. Apart from the layers of the deep learning model, there are various model tuning parameters such as weights, regularization types, regularization strength, types of activation functions at different layers, types of loss functions used in the model, and optimization algorithms including the learning rate and momentum parameters. This is very complex in nature and requires a simplified framework for interpretation.

- **Convolutional Neural Network (CNN)**: This is another type of neural network model which is usually applied to object detection and image classification-related tasks. This is considered as a complete black box model. There are convolution layers, max/average pooling layers, and more. If someone asks why the model predicted the cat as a dog, can we explain what went wrong? Currently the answer is no. Extensive work is required in explaining this model to the end user.

- **Recurrent neural networks (RNNs)**: The recurrent neural network-based models are usually applicable in text classification and text prediction. There are variations, such as long short term memory network (LSTM) and bi-directional LSTMs, which are very complex to explain. There is a constant need for better frameworks and methods that can be used to explain such models.

- **Rule-based models**: These are super easy models as we only need the if/else conditions to have these models in place.

XAI Meets Responsible AI

Responsible artificial intelligence is a framework where explainability, transparency, ethics, and accountability are ensured in various software applications, digital solutions, and products. The development of AI is rapidly creating multiple opportunities in different sectors where a common man's life is touched by these technologies, hence AI needs to be responsible and decisions should be explainable.

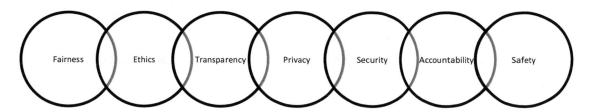

Figure 1-11. *Core pillars of responsible AI*

The seven core pillars of responsible AI are a critical part of explainability (Figure 1-11). Let's have a look at each of the pillars.

- **Fairness**: The predictions generated by AI systems should not lead to discrimination against persons in relation to their cast, creed, religion, gender, political affiliations, ethnicity, and more, hence a greater degree of fairness is required.

- **Ethics**: In the pursuit of building intelligent systems, we should not forget ethics in using data for gathering intelligence.

- **Transparency**: Model predictions and how predictions are generated should be transparent.

- **Privacy**: Personalized data (PII, personalized identifiable information) should be safeguarded when developing AI systems.

- **Security**: Intelligent systems should be secure.

- **Accountability**: In case of an erroneous prediction, the AI model should be able to take accountability in fixing the issue.

- **Safety**: When the AI models make decisions regarding the navigation of self-driving cars, robotic dental surgery, and a data-driven medical diagnosis, any incorrect prediction can lead to dangerous consequences.

Many organizations are in the process of preparing guidelines and standards for using AI in their solutions, in order to avoid unintended negative consequences of AI in future. Let's take organization A. It uses AI to predict the volume of sales. The AI predicts that sales are going to be 30% higher than average and so the business stocks volumes of the product and mobilizes manpower to support sales. But if the actual sales are really at par with the historical sales average, then the stocking of additional volume and manpower was a waste. Here the AI prediction was wrong. With the help of model explainability, this situation could have been analyzed and probably the model can be corrected.

Evaluation of XAI

There is no common standard for the evaluation of different explanations generated by the Python-based libraries over the Internet. The XAI process should follow these steps in evaluating the explanations:

- Each strata should have a separate explanation. If we have a dataset that cannot be used for model training due to high volume, we typically do a sampling of the dataset. If we sample using a stratified sampling approach, then each strata should have a separate explanation.

- **Time constraints**: We know that real-life datasets are quite huge. Even if we are proceeding with distributed computing frameworks, the explanations generated by the XAI libraries typically should not take that much time.

- **Instance invariance**: If the data points are identical based on their attributes, they should be part of same group and hence they should convey similar interpretations.

In various AI projects and initiatives, when we make predictions often a questions arises as to why someone would trust our model. In predictive analytics or machine learning or deep learning, there is a trade-off between what is predicted and why it was predicted. If the prediction is in line with human expectation, then it is good. If it goes beyond human expectation, then we need to know why the model made such a decision. Prediction and expectation deviation are fine if it is a low-risk scenario such as customer targeting, digital marketing, or content recommendation. However, in a high-risk environment such as clinical trials or a drug testing framework, a small deviation in prediction and expectation makes a lot of difference and a lot of questions will arise as to why the model made such a prediction. As human beings, we think ourselves superior to all. There is a curiosity to know how the model arrived at a prediction and why not a human being. An XAI framework is a great tool to identify the inherent biases in the machine learning training process. XAI helps us investigate the reason for bias and find where exactly the bias is appearing.

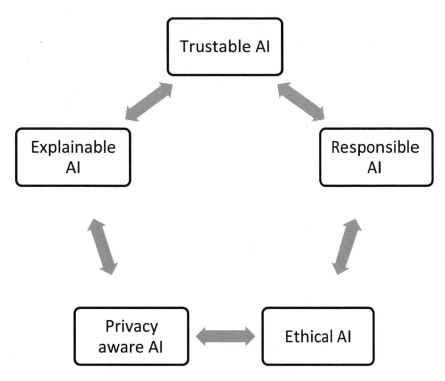

Figure 1-12. *What it takes for AI to increase adoption*

Because many people are not in a comfortable position to explain the outcomes of a machine learning model, they cannot reason out the decisions of a model, so they are not ready to use the AI models (Figure 1-12). This book is an attempt to popularize the concept of XAI frameworks to debug the machine learning and deep learning models in order to increase the AI adoption in the industry. In high-risk environments and use cases, there are regulatory requirements and auditing requirements to reason out the decisions of the model. The book is organized to supply hands-on execution of XAI frameworks for supervised regression, classification, unsupervised learning, clustering, and segmentation-related tasks. In addition, certain time series forecasting models need XAI to describe predictions. Further, XAI frameworks can also be used for unstructured text classification-related problems. A single XAI framework does not suit all kinds of models, so we are going to discuss various types of open source Python libraries and usages in generating XAI-based explanations.

Examining model fairness also requires simulations of what-if scenarios using the prediction outcomes. We are going to cover this too. Then we'll discuss counterfactual and contrastive explanations for AI models. We will cover model explainability for deep learning models, rule-based expert systems, and model-agnostic explanations for prediction invariance and for computer vision tasks using various XAI frameworks.

Model interpretability and explainability are the key focuses of this book. There are mathematical formulas and methods that are typically used to explain decisions made by AI models. Readers are provided with software library methods, classes, frameworks, and functions and how to use them for model explainability, transparency, reliability, ethics, biases, and interpretability. If a human being can understand the reasons behind the decision made by an AI model, it will give much more power to the user to make amendments and recommendations.

Conclusion

Model interpretability and explainability are needs for all of the processes that use AI to predict something, the reason being we need to know the reasons behind the prediction. In this chapter, you learned about the following:

- Model explainability and interpretability basics

- Ethical considerations in AI applications and biases in predictions generated by AI models

- Reliability of the AI models in generating predictions in different use cases

- Methods and systems for interpreting the linear models that are used in AI, non-linear models, and time series models used in AI

- The most complex ensemble models, explainability, and interpretability using frameworks such as Lime, SHAP, Skater, ELI5, and more

- Model explainability for unstructured data and natural language processing-related tasks

CHAPTER 2

AI Ethics, Biasness, and Reliability

This chapter covers different frameworks using Explainable Artificial Intelligence (XAI) Python libraries to control biasness, execute the principles of reliability, and maintain ethics while generating predictions. As digitalization progresses touch different industries, they open up a whole new set of opportunities for the application of artificial intelligence and machine learning-related solutions. The major challenges with the adoption of these AI technologies are ethics, biasness, and the reliability of the system, plus the transparency of the processes. These AI systems raise fundamental questions. Can I trust the predictions made by the AI system? Can I assume that it is unbiased? What kind of risk does it have? Is there any process where I can control the AI systems and their predictions about the future? AI ethics focus more on the legitimate use of AI for human kind and their wellness. AI should not be used for the destruction of human civilization. In this chapter, we are going to discuss various aspects of AI.

AI Ethics Primer

AI is a relatively new field and it is getting streamlined by different governments around the world as they see evidence of inconsistencies. AI is broadly known as the intelligent behavior displayed or demonstrated by computers to reach end goals. The goals are always business defined, such as in a logistics context for arranging a warehouse or defining a robot and its activities to lift and shift packages in a warehouse. Or it can be defined as a robot that can fire a weapon by observing a threat from a human in a self-defense situation. These scenarios are quite different. In the first scenario, the use of AI is permissible. In the second scenario, it is not the best possible use of AI. The AI systems can reason out, think, and perceive actions and reactions and hence can be trained

© Pradeepta Mishra 2022

P. Mishra, *Practical Explainable AI Using Python*, https://doi.org/10.1007/978-1-4842-7158-2_2

to take actions. The central goal of AI is to create machines that can help in sensing, logical reasoning, game playing, decision making by use of modelling techniques, understanding natural language processing, generating text just like human beings, and more.

There is a huge debate on the subject of AI ethics in academics, by politicians in various public speeches, and by practitioners. There is much to say but there is little groundwork to frame certain policies around the ethics of AI. This is not just because of the intent to do so, but because it is difficult to do. AI is evolving and thus a technology policy is difficult to plan and enforce.

It is really difficult to estimate in advance the impact of AI technology on the lives of people, the threat of AI use in the military, and the threat of AI technology in other sectors. Hence policy formulation around the use of AI from an ethical point of view at times is very much iterative in nature. As different organizations use AI for different purposes, there is no consensus among the business power houses on how to use AI and what is right from an ethical point of view. Every government around the world wants to dominate and be powerful with the use of AI technology, hence there is no consensus on building a mutual policy around the ethical use of AI (Figure 2-1). This follows the path of nuclear technology in the past.

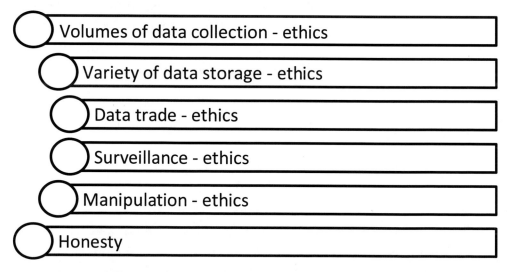

Volumes of data collection - ethics

Variety of data storage - ethics

Data trade - ethics

Surveillance - ethics

Manipulation - ethics

Honesty

Figure 2-1. *Ethics in AI*

- Volume of data (non-anonymous): The data collection process and the storage systems are predominantly cloud specific and completely digital. The data collected from users includes their personalized information as well as their online behavior. This data is no longer anonymous, although companies use this information at an aggregate level, having Personalized Identifiable Information (PIIs) mostly masked. Still the campaigns are at personalized level. Hence the data is no longer anonymous; it can be attributable to individuals. An individual's entire online presence is stored, analyzed, and targeted for any product or service selling activity. Currently many organizations abide by the rules set forth by their clients regarding the usage of data. There is still a need for policies to make the data anonymous.

- Variety of data: Today every activity performed by machines is captured and stored in order to improve the machine performance, optimize maintenance cost, prevent failure in the production process, and more. There is a large amount of data generated by IoT (Internet of Things) applications and systems, such as industrial production systems, telematics data from vehicles on the road, and more.

- Data trade (intended, unintended): Data collected for one purpose from the source systems should not be utilized for another purpose, intended or unintended. The issue of data trade arises when we repurpose data for some other use case. This concern has been taken care of by the GDPR regulation, and similar laws are enforced by different companies and different authorities just to ensure that data trade does not happen. If we create an AI system with traded data, the entire system becomes unethical.

- Surveillance (targeted, non-targeted): AI ethics also applies to blanket surveillance on all populations whether it is targeted or non-targeted, for any purpose. Ethical debates happen over when and how a surveillance system should be enforced. Yes, a biometric-based authentication system without additional safeguards is a cause for concern, which is why there is a constant campaign in favor of halting facial recognition systems around the world.

- Manipulation intervenes rational choice: AI from an ethical point of view should be rational. There has to be a legitimate process, and AI systems should be transparent

- Honesty: It is at the core of defining organizational transparency. From an ethics point of view, it is important for organizations to adhere to explainability and provide technical transparency into core AI products and applications. This applies to the source of the training data, the choice of algorithms, how exactly the system is trained, how the predictions are generated, and more.

Biasness in AI

Many AI systems use ML and DL models to be specific and predictive models in general. Biasness in AI means biasness in predictions. Why do prediction biases arise? How to control biased predictions is a matter of discussion today. The ethical consequences of algorithmic decision making by AI systems is a great concern. The emergence of biases in AI-led decision making has seriously affected the adoption of AI. In order to build an unbiased system, a strong sense of justice needs to be in place to help decision makers act fairly without having any prejudice and favoritism.

Data Bias

The biasness can be categorized as data bias and algorithmic bias. The data bias arises when we consider limited sampling for labeling data from one angle and increase the presence of major group. This leads to a biased dataset. This process can be improved with a connection to the natural source of data collection. This is shown in Figure 2-2. Let's understand the data bias through an example. If we look at the trend of revenue or profit for an ecommerce company over last 15 years, there is definitely an upward trend and every 5 years there is a trend break. The trend break is due to the increase in the unit price of the product. If we want to build a machine learning model to predict the revenue for the next two years, we cannot include the last 15 years of data. If we choose random data points to train the ML model, there is going to be data bias, and this data bias could lead to incorrect predictions.

Algorithmic Bias

Algorithmic bias to some extent is due to data bias, as data bias cannot be completely eradicated by the training process. Hence a wrong model gets trained and this leads to a biased prediction. In order to reduce biasness in the training process and data bias, a proper explanation of the predictions needs to be generated (Figure 2-2). At global level as well as at local level, the predicted model results need to explainable to all stakeholders. Thus there is a constant need for an XAI framework. The explainable AI platform and framework can provide the necessary tools and structure to elaborate the biasness in the algorithm and data, and help educate the decision maker about the existence of biasness.

Artificial intelligence systems display intelligent behavior that can provide significant efficiency in production systems and help create smart applications with smart decision making capability. AI is generally difficult to understand for business stakeholders and users. If the application layer of any software uses an AI model, it becomes difficult to explain the decisions made by the AI system to regulatory authorities, governing law enforcement agencies, and others. The data biasness leads to biasness in the AI decision systems and can land the organization in a loss-of-reputation scenario. Sometimes the AI systems produce results which are not convenient or conducive for the organization. Also, the predictions are outside the control of the organization. In a typical software development scenario, we know under what circumstances the software will work and when it won't work. However, in an AI-driven decisioning system, we are not sure about the conditions under which the AI will not work. It is very hard to predict.

Bias Mitigation Process

To reduce biasness and improve ethical standards, governance plays an important role. AI governance implies adherence to a set of rules, guidelines, standards, practices, and processes through which AI-based decision systems can be controlled and governed. The data bias can be reduced by setting governance standards such as data evaluation, rigorous testing of the application, and so on.

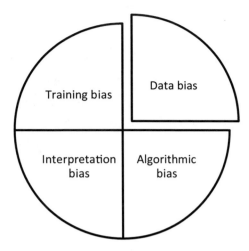

Figure 2-2. *Biasness in an AI-based decision making system*

Interpretation Bias

If the predictions are not generated as per the expected line of thought, then some practitioners use the same metric and math to change the narrative of the model outcome. This is more confusing for the end user or the business user. The interpretation bias is known as bias in usage of predictive models. Suppose we train a ML model using population A and get the required result, but we apply the model on population B, which is in a sense called as transfer learning in machine learning, in order to avoid further training. This is a classic example of interpretation bias. This is because the predictions can be biased because it is trained on a different population, which may have different features or characteristics. Biasness in the algorithmic training process arises due to a constant need for improving the model accuracy. We typically go for smoothing and feature transformation methods such as logarithmic transformation and square transformation. Sometimes to restrict overfitting in the training and testing phase we also go for regularization. This regularization process of trimming the model coefficients and associated steps is also known as algorithmic bias in the model training step.

Training Bias

Training bias in an AI system happens if we either choose an incorrect set of hyper parameters, the wrong selection of model types, or overtrain the model in the pursuit of achieving higher accuracy for the task. In the development of a machine learning model, hyper parameter tuning and cross validation play major roles in the stability of the model. To make an assessment of whether an algorithm is free from biasness or not, we need to look at data collected for the purpose, the model training process, and the assumptions of the modelling process. Let's take an example of willingness to pay for a specific service OTT platform based on people's demographic features and past spend patterns. Can any AI system predict the willingness of people to pay for subscribing to an OTT platform and how much they can pay for a month-long subscription? Is there any biasness in the prediction process or model training process?

Table 2-1. *Difference Between Procedural and Relational Approaches for Bias Measurement*

Procedural	Relational
This is algorithm specific	This is data specific
Focuses more on techniques	Compares different data sets
Types of tasks are known	Tasks are unknown

There are two different approaches for measuring the biasness: the procedural approach and the relational approach. See Table 2-1. If we collect data globally with similar proportions from different groups and different countries and different age, gender, and race in proportional manner, then we can say there is no bias in the collected data for the purpose of prediction. The relational approach helps in finding this bias in the dataset. The procedural approach focuses on the algorithmic training process in making predictions. We may have to train different models in different age group categories as the attributes and relations may not be similar in different age groups.

Table 2-2. *Bias Metrics*

Statistical measures	Homogeneity metrics	Causal reasoning metrics
Metric driven	Look like a metric from a feature set	This is similar to if/else conditions
Sometimes not meaningful	Meaningful to everyone	Extremely useful
Validation not possible	Validation possible	Validation possible

The three most commonly used bias metrics are statistical measures, homogeneity-based measures, and causal reasoning-based metrics (Figures 2-2 and 2-3). Statistical metrics focus on similar predictions for different groups based on their demographic characteristics. If the predicted outcome differs from one group to another and there is a difference in the accuracy for different groups from a similar model, then we can measure this bias in statistical terms. Statistical measures are quite popular. However, they're not sufficient for a certain group of algorithms.

As an alternative process, we can take a look at the similarity measures. If two customers are exactly similar from a features point of view, their predicted result should be similar. If it deviates, then there is bias in the algorithm for a specific customer against the other customer. Here the customer refers to one record from the training data set if we are talking about churn classification, credit scoring, or a loan application type of use case. For this method to be successful, there is a need for similarity metrics to estimate how similar two records are in a training dataset. If they are exactly copied, we can call it perfectly similar. However, if one minor or major feature is different, than what is the similarity percentage? As we extend this to n-features, how this is going to be useful? This method of identifying bias is also not free from limitations. Here the success of the method lies in the similarity measure. The more robust the similarity metric, the better the result.

The third important method of estimating bias is causal reasoning, which can be achieved by creating something like if/else conditions. We understand the if/else condition in a much better way, hence causal reasoning for classifying a record into a binary class would provide an additional insight on the biasness of the algorithm. The if/else/then condition can be applied by taking into consideration all of the features that are present in the training dataset.

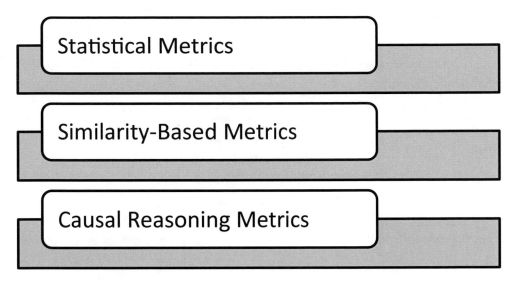

Figure 2-3. *Metrics for measuring bias*

Ethics in AI systems can be addressed by ensuring the quality of the system set by the correctness of the process, the efficiency of the predictions, the robustness of the predictions, the explainability of the decisions at an individual level, ensuring security and privacy considerations, and making a transparent architecture for everyone, so that all the stakeholders are aware of the AI decision making system and its internal processes. A good AI system should be accountable for the decisions that it generates, thus the decisions need to be fair.

The current form of AI governance and the associated policies restrict the reuse of data for other purposes, but not the use of transfer learning in machine learning. The ML and DL models trained in one scenario can be reused in another scenario internally or external to the organization. However, the restrictions do not apply to the models. The models possess critical information about the training data that might be reverse engineered by any developer to gain additional information and reuse it for some other purpose. For example, for a virtual trial of spectacles, we upload an image and the system classifies the face into a specific category which is produced by a trained model, such as oval, square, or round. Accordingly the system displays frames designed for that kind of face classification. This system can be used by another competitor company to generate their own training data and create a parallel system. The General Data Protection Regulation (GDPR) was enacted in 2018 to ensure an individual's right to any AI-driven decisions based on their data. If it is personal data, it is required. However, if it is non-personal data, then the GDPR regulation does not apply.

The high-level bias removal process from the predictive models is shown in Figure 2-4. Prediction 1 and prediction 2 should match. If they do match, then the data point is considered unbiased; otherwise, it is biased. If the data point is biased, then it should be dropped from the model training process in order to get a bias-free model.

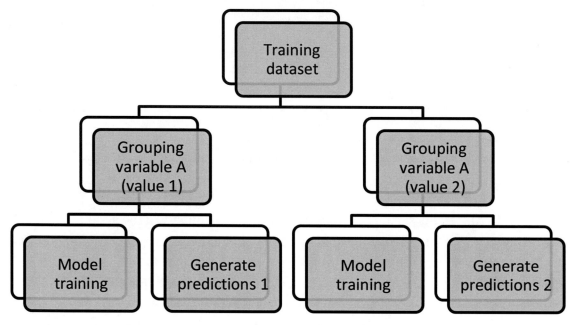

Figure 2-4. *Bias removal process from model training*

To reduce the biasness in an algorithm model, explainability is a must. The machine learning models are generally evaluated before production on the grounds of interpretability, robustness, fairness, security, and privacy, and also whether the trained model has learned the pattern or undertrained or overtrained. ML model fairness should ideally be evaluated for two specific reasons:

- Predictions by the models (that is, the decisions generated by the ML models)

- The role of data biases on the model's fairness

Reliability in AI

The development of AI technology has brought about significant changes in the medical imaging field. 3D printed AR and VR experiences deliver real-life experiences in a software environment. A robust AI system is reliable if it produces ethical insights without any bias and prejudice. There are cases of algorithmic biases that were racial, political, and gender oriented that showed up in predictions. In order to bring reliability to an AI system, we need to bring ML interpretability, design considerations of the ML model, ML model management, and training into the picture. The reliability of an AI system for data-driven automated decision support depends on the unbiasedness of the algorithms.

Algorithmic discrimination is one of the negative consequences of biasness in the decision making process. It leads to unfair treatment of individuals based on their caste, creed, religion, sex, and ethnicity. The reliability of the automated decision support system increases as the solution becomes less biased and has virtually no discrimination. Consider a credit evaluation or assessment system where an AI system makes an evaluation of who should be granted credit and who should not be. The decision made by the algorithm may be rational but sometimes we have to make it very transparent so that certain group of people may not perceive the decision as against their group. Biasness and discrimination in automated decision making systems are two different things.

Discrimination is the unfair and unequal treatment of groups of people or strata based on their demographic features or attributes. This kind of discrimination is found in decision making AI systems when approving loans and credit requests from users. As we move towards more automation and use of AI ML in smart systems, there is a larger risk of finding discrimination in the decision making. Hence the system must be made discrimination-free by explaining the decisions and making the process very transparent. Discrimination is intentional. However, biasness is unintentional and inherent in the model training process. Hence the reliability of the AI systems will only increase and the adoption of AI systems will only go up when we establish a system that is free from both discrimination and biasness.

To increase the trust and reliability of AI models and associated services developed around AI models, it is necessary to explain how the decision is made. Reliability of an AI system should be the joint responsibility of all the stakeholders who are part of developing the AI solution for the client. Typically, the business owner is the client, internal or external to the organization, who provides a high level goal of a system and the features that they want developed.

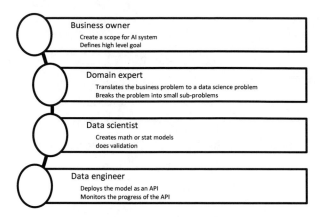

Figure 2-5. *Trust and reliability journey*

It is the role of all the stakeholders to ensure trust and reliability in the creation of AI models and the deployment of AI models in a production system (Figure 2-5). In order to earn trust, proper documentation is required when developing the system. The documentation should address certain questions. What data is being used to train such a system? Can this model be used in some other domain and some other use case? What are the best case scenarios where the model will perform better? Do we know cases where the model performs poorly? If we know the model performs poorly in certain cases, how do we take care of that kind of bias from the system? Is there any mechanism to explain the predictions generated by the AI system? These questions should be documented with examples and names of the domains and case studies.

Conclusion

In this chapter, you learned about ethics in designing AI systems, algorithmic biases, and model reliability. We humans always find ways to make our understanding correct and ways to make it perfect. AI systems are developed and used in an unequal world where disastrous things are quite obvious and happen very frequently. We learn from our mistakes and frame new rules to take care of them in future. From the above three concepts, it is important to bring explainable AI into the fore in order to provide at least interpretability, trust, and reliability regarding the decisions made by the AI system and to maintain an ethical standards set.

CHAPTER 3

Explainability for Linear Models

This chapter explores the use of the SHAP, LIME, SKATER, and ELI5 libraries to explain the decisions made by linear models for supervised learning tasks for structured data. In this chapter, you are going to learn various ways of explaining the linear models and their decisions. In supervised machine learning tasks, there is a target variable, which is also known as a dependent variable, and a set of independent variables. The objective is to predict the dependent variable as a weighted sum of the input variables or independent variables.

Linear Models

Linear models such as linear regression for predicting a real valued output or a logistic regression model for predicting a class and its corresponding probabilities are supervised learning algorithms. These linear models for supervised machine learning tasks are very simple to interpret. They are also easy to explain to business stakeholders. Let's start the explainability for linear models for completeness of the module.

Linear Regression

The use of linear regression is to predict the quantitative outcome of a target variable given a set of predictors. The modelling formula typically looks like

$$y=\beta_0+\beta_1 x_1+\ldots+\beta_p x_p+\epsilon$$

© Pradeepta Mishra 2022
P. Mishra, *Practical Explainable AI Using Python*, https://doi.org/10.1007/978-1-4842-7158-2_3

The beta coefficients are known as parameters, and the epsilon term is known as an error term. The error term can be looked at as a consolidated metric that reflects the inability of a model to predict. We cannot predict with 100% accuracy in the real world as variations in data are a reality. Data keeps on changing. The objective of developing a model is to predict with maximum possible accuracy and stability. The target variable assumes the value of the intercept term when the independent variables assumes zero value. You are going to use a dataset available online, automobile.csv, to create a linear regression model to predict the price of a car, given the attributes of a car.

```
import pandas as pd
import numpy as np
import matplotlib.pyplot as plt
%matplotlib inline
from sklearn.model_selection import cross_val_score, train_test_split
from sklearn.linear_model import LinearRegression

from sklearn import datasets, linear_model
from scipy import linalg

df = pd.read_csv('automobile.csv')

df.info()
df.head()
```

There are 6,019 records and 11 features, which are the base features in this dataset. The data dictionary is shown in Table 3-1.

Table 3-1. *Data Dictionary for the Features*

Sr No	Feature name	Description
0	Price	Price in INR
1	Make	Manufacturer
2	Location	City of car
3	Age	How old the car is
4	Odometer	KM travelled
5	FuelType	Type of fuel
6	Transmission	Transmission type
7	OwnerType	How many owners
8	Mileage	Mileage per litre
9	EngineCC	CC of car
10	PowerBhp	BHP of car

After a data clean-up and feature transformation, which is a basic step before moving to the model development step, the data set will have 11 features with same number of records in the dataset. The following graph shows the correlation between various features. This is important in order to understand the association between various features and the dependent variable. The results are displayed in Figure 3-1 using a paired scatterplot.

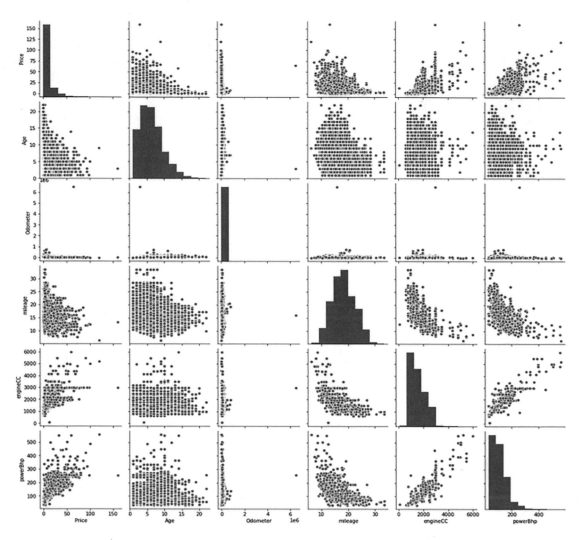

Figure 3-1. *Correlation between dependent and independent variables*

```
import seaborn as sns
sns.pairplot(df[['Price','Age','Odometer','mileage','engineCC','powerBhp']])
```

In order to get the exact correlation between various features, you need to compute the correlations table and the following script shows this. See Table 3-2.

```
corrl = (df[['Price','Age','Odometer','mileage','engineCC','powerBhp']]).corr()
corrl
```

Table 3-2. *Correlation Coefficient Between Variables*

	Price	Age	Odometer	Mileage	EngineCC	PowerBhp
Price	1.000000	-0.305327	-0.011493	-0.334989	0.659230	0.771140
Age	-0.305327	1.000000	0.173048	-0.295045	0.050181	-0.028722
Odometer	-0.011493	0.173048	1.000000	-0.065223	0.090721	0.031543
Mileage	-0.334989	-0.295045	-0.065223	1.000000	-0.641136	-0.545009
EngineCC	0.659230	0.050181	0.090721	-0.641136	1.000000	0.863728
PowerBhp	0.771140	-0.028722	0.031543	-0.545009	0.863728	1.000000

In order to compare the positive and negative correlation on the same table you can use a gradient plot. See Table 3-3.

```
corrl.style.background_gradient(cmap='coolwarm')
```

Table 3-3. *Positive and Negative Correlation Mapping*

	Price	Age	Odometer	Mileage	EngineCC	PowerBhp
Price	1.000000	-0.305327	-0.011493	-0.334989	0.659230	0.771140
Age	-0.305327	1.000000	0.173048	-0.295045	0.050181	-0.028722
Odometer	-0.011493	0.173048	1.000000	-0.065223	0.090721	0.031543
Mileage	-0.334989	-0.295045	-0.065223	1.000000	-0.641136	-0.545009
EngineCC	0.659230	0.050181	0.090721	-0.641136	1.000000	0.863728
PowerBhp	0.771140	-0.028722	0.031543	-0.545009	0.863728	1.000000

Sometimes the correlations table can show spurious correlations as well. In order to verify that, you need to use the statistical significance of each correlation coefficient between various numeric features with the target variable:

```
np.where((df[['Price','Age','Odometer','mileage','engineCC','powerBhp']]).
corr()>0.6,'Yes','No')
array([['Yes', 'No', 'No', 'No', 'Yes', 'Yes'],
       ['No', 'Yes', 'No', 'No', 'No', 'No'],
```

```
        ['No', 'No', 'Yes', 'No', 'No', 'No'],
        ['No', 'No', 'No', 'Yes', 'No', 'No'],
        ['Yes', 'No', 'No', 'No', 'Yes', 'Yes'],
        ['Yes', 'No', 'No', 'No', 'Yes', 'Yes']], dtype='<U3')
```

What you can see from the table is that PowerBhp is highly positively correlated with Price, and EngineCC is also highly correlated with Price. There are four categorical variables for which you need to introduce dummy variables in order to perform matrix multiplication. You cannot use the string as it is in the calculation process. In machine learning, it's called *one hot encoder* that needs to be applied on categorical columns in order to generate flags corresponding to each category, so that we can introduce the information to the model. In a statistical modelling framework, the same technique is called *dummy variable creation*. The variables for which you create dummy variables are Location, FuelType, Transmission, and OwnerType. The following program does that dummy variable calculation:

```
Location_dummy = pd.get_dummies(df.Location,prefix='Location',drop_first=True)

FuelType_dummy = pd.get_dummies(df.FuelType,prefix='FuelType',drop_first=True)

Transmission_dummy = pd.get_dummies(df.Transmission,prefix='Transmission',
drop_first=True)

OwnerType_dummy = pd.get_dummies(df.OwnerType,prefix='OwnerType',
drop_first=True)

combine_all_dummy = pd.concat([df,Location_dummy,FuelType_dummy,
Transmission_dummy,OwnerType_dummy],axis=1)

combine_all_dummy.head()
combine_all_dummy.columns
Index(['Price', 'Make', 'Location', 'Age', 'Odometer', 'FuelType',
       'Transmission', 'OwnerType', 'Mileage', 'EngineCC', 'PowerBhp',
       'mileage', 'engineCC', 'powerBhp', 'Location_Bangalore',
       'Location_Chennai', 'Location_Coimbatore', 'Location_Delhi',
       'Location_Hyderabad', 'Location_Jaipur', 'Location_Kochi',
       'Location_Kolkata', 'Location_Mumbai', 'Location_Pune',
       'FuelType_Diesel', 'FuelType_Electric', 'FuelType_LPG',
```

```
        'FuelType_Petrol', 'Transmission_Manual',
        'OwnerType_Fourth +ACY- Above', 'OwnerType_Second', 'OwnerType_Third'],
      dtype='object')
clean_df = combine_all_dummy.drop(columns=['Make','Location','FuelType',
                                           'Transmission','OwnerType',
                                           'Mileage', 'EngineCC',
                                           'PowerBhp'])
clean_df.columns
Index(['Price', 'Age', 'Odometer', 'mileage', 'engineCC', 'powerBhp',
       'Location_Bangalore', 'Location_Chennai', 'Location_Coimbatore',
       'Location_Delhi', 'Location_Hyderabad', 'Location_Jaipur',
       'Location_Kochi', 'Location_Kolkata', 'Location_Mumbai',
       'Location_Pune', 'FuelType_Diesel', 'FuelType_Electric', 'FuelType_LPG',
       'FuelType_Petrol', 'Transmission_Manual',
       'OwnerType_Fourth +ACY- Above', 'OwnerType_Second', 'OwnerType_Third'],
      dtype='object')
```

Before creating a linear regression model you need to check the assumptions of the model, which are given in the script notebook. After the necessary feature transformation, such as normalization of the columns and outlier management, you come up with the following dataset: you split the dataset into 75% for training purposes and 25% for the testing or validation of the model. You use the sklearn Python API, which is a machine learning API.

```
#split the dataset into training and testig
data_train, data_test = train_test_split(clean_df,test_size=0.25,
random_state=1234)

data_train.shape,data_test.shape

XTrain = np.array(data_train.iloc[:,0:(clean_df.shape[1]-1)])
YTrain = np.array(data_train['Price'])

XTest = np.array(data_test.iloc[:,0:(clean_df.shape[1]-1)])
YTest = np.array(data_test['Price'])

XTrain.shape, XTest.shape
```

After the end of the model training, you extract the training accuracy and testing accuracy. Both are 100% accuracy. When you look at the coefficients, you find all coefficients are 0 and the intercept term is 1. Something went wrong. Here comes the role of explainable AI in making clear what happened.

```
#multiple linear regression model
reg = linear_model.LinearRegression()
reg

reg.fit(XTrain,YTrain) #training the model

print('Coefficients: \n', np.round(reg.coef_,4))

print('Intercept: \n', np.round(reg.intercept_,0))

reg.score(XTrain,YTrain) # R-square value from the trained model

reg.score(XTest,YTest) # R-square value from the test set
```

To verify the results, you can also use the statistical API from the stat models to understand if there is any difference in the output. Table 3-4 shows the results of the stat models API.

```
from scipy import stats

# Using Statistical API

import statsmodels.api as sm

y = np.array(clean_df['Price'])
xx = np.array(clean_df[['Price', 'Age', 'Odometer', 'mileage', 'engineCC',
'powerBhp',
        'Location_Bangalore', 'Location_Chennai', 'Location_Coimbatore',
        'Location_Delhi', 'Location_Hyderabad', 'Location_Jaipur',
        'Location_Kochi', 'Location_Kolkata', 'Location_Mumbai',
        'Location_Pune', 'FuelType_Diesel', 'FuelType_Electric', 'FuelType_LPG',
        'FuelType_Petrol', 'Transmission_Manual',
        'OwnerType_Fourth +ACY- Above', 'OwnerType_Second', 'OwnerType_Third']])
```

```
y
mod = sm.OLS(y, xx)

results = mod.fit()
print(results.summary())
```

From the OLS regression results table it is clear and confirmed that the result is same. There is no difference. See Table 3-4.

Table 3-4. *OLS Regression Results*

```
                           OLS Regression Results
==============================================================================
Dep. Variable:                      y   R-squared (uncentered):              1.000
Model:                            OLS   Adj. R-squared (uncentered):         1.000
Method:                 Least Squares   F-statistic:                     4.310e+28
Date:                Sat, 19 Dec 2020   Prob (F-statistic):                   0.00
Time:                        23:01:57   Log-Likelihood:                  1.5711e+05
No. Observations:                6019   AIC:                             -3.142e+05
Df Residuals:                    5995   BIC:                             -3.140e+05
Df Model:                          24
Covariance Type:            nonrobust
```

The summary of the regression result shows an error in the model creation process. This could be due to strong multicollinearity. The R square value shows 1.0, which means 100% of the variance of the dependent variable can be explained by the independent variables. There is no error in this model, which is quite impossible to believe. The high degree of multicollinearity between various variables can be explained by the VIF (variance inflation factor). The VIF for any predictor should be less than 10. In any situation it cannot be more than 10.

```
# This might indicate that there are strong multicollinearity

print('Parameters: ', results.params)
print('R2: ', results.rsquared)

print('Parameters: ', results.params)
print('Standard errors: ', results.bse)
print('Predicted values: ', results.predict())
```

The following script shows how to calculate the VIF for all variables, sort them out, and show the top five variables with a high VIF value:

```
infl = results.get_influence()
print(infl.summary_frame().filter(regex="dfb"))
from statsmodels.stats.outliers_influence import variance_inflation_factor

def calc_vif(X):

    # Calculating VIF
    vif = pd.DataFrame()
    vif["variables"] = X.columns
    vif["VIF"] = [variance_inflation_factor(X.values, i) for i in
    range(X.shape[1])]

    return(vif)
X = clean_df.drop('Price',axis=1)
vif_df = calc_vif(X)
vif_df.sort_values(by='VIF', ascending=False).head()
X = clean_df.drop(['Price','engineCC'],axis=1)

vif_df = calc_vif(X)

vif_df.sort_values(by='VIF', ascending=False).head()

X = clean_df.drop(['Price','engineCC','FuelType_Diesel'],axis=1)

vif_df = calc_vif(X)

vif_df.sort_values(by='VIF', ascending=False).head()

X = clean_df.drop(['Price','engineCC','FuelType_Diesel','mileage'],axis=1)

vif_df = calc_vif(X)

vif_df.sort_values(by='VIF', ascending=False).head()

# VIF less than 10 is acceptable
# the more your VIF increases, the less reliable your regression results
  are going to be.
# In general, a VIF above 10 indicates high correlation and is cause for
  concern.
X = clean_df.drop(['Price','engineCC','mileage'],axis=1)

vif_df = calc_vif(X)
```

```
vif_df.sort_values(by='VIF', ascending=False).head()

X = clean_df.drop(['Price','engineCC','FuelType_Diesel','mileage'],axis=1)

vif_df = calc_vif(X)

vif_df.sort_values(by='VIF', ascending=False).head()
X = clean_df.drop(['Price','engineCC','FuelType_Diesel','mileage',
'powerBhp'],axis=1)

vif_df = calc_vif(X)

vif_df.sort_values(by='VIF', ascending=False).head()
```

	Variables	VIF
0	Age	6.322638
15	Transmission_Manual	3.482934
14	FuelType_Petrol	1.997771
6	Location_Hyderabad	1.838072
11	Location_Pune	1.760061

VIF and the Problems It Can Generate

VIF is the variance inflation factor. This metric quantifies the extent of multicollinearity that exists in a model. Multicollinearity can be defined as the existence of high correlation between more than two independent variables. It is a standard industry practice to follow the VIF < = 10 rule to detect multicollinearity in the model. The problem that it can generate can be explained by an example. Let's take two features, X1 and X2. Both can be used to predict a dependent variable Y. The coefficient of X1 is 0.20 and it can be defined as *if X1 changes by one unit, the dependent variable is predicted to change by 0.20 times*, keeping all other variables in the model constant. When X1 and X2 both are highly correlated, the assumption of keeping all other variables constant is violated. Hence multicollinearity should be removed from the model in order to generate the right interpretation of the coefficient value corresponding to each predictor variable.

A VIF of less than 10 is acceptable. The more your VIF increases, the less reliable your regression results are going to be. In general, a VIF above 10 indicates high correlation and is cause for concern. The following script shows the VIF after the deletion of the multicollinear variables. The model is retrained on the refined set of variables. The training score is now 70% and the test score is now 69%, hence this is a good model. Once the model is finalized as a good model, you can use explainable AI Python packages to explain the components of the model.

```
y = clean_df['Price']
x = clean_df.drop(['Price','engineCC','FuelType_Diesel','mileage'],axis=1)
xtrain,xtest,ytrain,ytest = train_test_split(x,y,test_size=0.25,
random_state=1234)

xtrain.shape,ytrain.shape,xtest.shape,ytest.shape

new_model = LinearRegression()

new_model.fit(xtrain,ytrain)

print(new_model.score(xtrain,ytrain))

print(new_model.score(xtest,ytest))

0.7000714797069869
0.6902967954209108
```

The coefficients table shows the variable names, their coefficient values, and their sequence in the dataset.

```
resultsDF = pd.DataFrame()
resultsDF['Variables'] = pd.Series(xtrain.columns)
resultsDF['coefficients'] = pd.Series(np.round(new_model.coef_,2))
resultsDF.sort_values(by='coefficients',ascending=False)
```

Variables	Coefficients	
13	FuelType_Electric	9.02
17	OwnerType_Fourth +ACY- Above	4.70
5	Location_Coimbatore	2.35
3	Location_Bangalore	1.96
7	Location_Hyderabad	1.92
19	OwnerType_Third	1.66
14	FuelType_LPG	1.50
4	Location_Chennai	1.05
8	Location_Jaipur	0.65
12	Location_Pune	0.21
2	powerBhp	0.14
1	Odometer	0.00
9	Location_Kochi	-0.06
6	Location_Delhi	-0.12
18	OwnerType_Second	-0.53
11	Location_Mumbai	-0.60
0	Age	-0.93
10	Location_Kolkata	-0.97
15	FuelType_Petrol	-1.31
16	Transmission_Manual	-2.68

The goodness of the fit of a regression model is known from the adjusted R square value. The R square value may be high due to the addition of any redundant variables in the dataset/training process. However, the adjusted R square value takes care of the impact of additional variables in the model training process.

```
#adjusted R square
def AdjustedRSquare(model,X,Y):
    YHat = model.predict(X)
    n,k = X.shape
```

```
    sse = np.sum(np.square(YHat-Y),axis=0) #sum of suare error
    sst = np.sum(np.square(Y-np.mean(Y)),axis=0) # sum of square total
    R2 = 1- sse/sst #explained sum of squares
    adjR2 = R2-(1-R2)*(float(k)/(n-k-1))
    return adjR2, R2

from scipy import stats

def ReturnPValue(model,X,Y):
    YHat = model.predict(X)
    n,k = X.shape
    sse = np.sum(np.square(YHat-Y),axis=0)
    x = np.hstack((np.ones((n,1)),np.matrix(X)))
    df = float(n-k-1)
    sampleVar = sse/df
    sampleVarianceX = x.T*x
    covarianceMatrix = linalg.sqrtm(sampleVar*sampleVarianceX.I)
    se = covarianceMatrix.diagonal()[1:]
    betasTstat = np.zeros(len(se))
    for i in range(len(se)):
        betasTstat[i] = model.coef_[i]/se[i]
    betasPvalue = 1- stats.t.cdf(abs(betasTstat),df)
    return betasPvalue

resultsDF['p_value'] = pd.Series(np.round(ReturnPValue(new_model,xtrain,
ytrain),2))
resultsDF.sort_values(by='coefficients',ascending=False)
```

Variables	Coefficients	p_value	
13	FuelType_Electric	9.02	0.02
17	OwnerType_Fourth +ACY- Above	4.70	0.03
5	Location_Coimbatore	2.35	0.00
3	Location_Bangalore	1.96	0.00
7	Location_Hyderabad	1.92	0.00
19	OwnerType_Third	1.66	0.01
14	FuelType_LPG	1.50	0.29
4	Location_Chennai	1.05	0.01
8	Location_Jaipur	0.65	0.08
12	Location_Pune	0.21	0.31
2	powerBhp	0.14	0.00
1	Odometer	0.00	0.04
9	Location_Kochi	-0.06	0.44
6	Location_Delhi	-0.12	0.38
18	OwnerType_Second	-0.53	0.02
11	Location_Mumbai	-0.60	0.06
0	Age	-0.93	0.00
10	Location_Kolkata	-0.97	0.01
15	FuelType_Petrol	-1.31	0.00
16	Transmission_Manual	-2.68	0.00

```
reg.adjR2, reg.R2 = AdjustedRSquare(new_model,xtrain,ytrain)
print (reg.adjR2, reg.R2)
```

0.6987363872507527 0.7000714797069869

```
def ErrorMetric(model,X,Y):
    Yhat = model.predict(X)
    MAPE = np.mean(abs(Y-Yhat)/Y)*100
    MSSE = np.mean(np.square(Y-Yhat))
```

```
    Error = sns.distplot(Y-Yhat)
    return MAPE, MSSE, Error
```

```
resultsDF.sort_values(by='p_value',ascending=False)
```

The p-value of the probability value of a beta coefficient shows the statistical significance of the predictors in a linear regression scenario. The p-value threshold is considered as 0.05, keeping a 5% level of significance for the statistical test. If for any predictor the p-value is less than 0.05, then the predictor is significant; otherwise, it is not. If the p-value is greater than 0.05, the beta coefficient value would be closer to zero. There are five variables in this model that have a p-value greater than 0.05. Figure 3-2 shows the correlation between actual Y variable or target variable and the predicted target variable. You can see a good correlation between the actual and predicted Y variables, which is 0.83, which implies this is a good model. You can then look at the coefficients table with the respective p-values sorted in descending order. Any predictor with greater than 0.05 p-value can be removed from the model in an iterative manner.

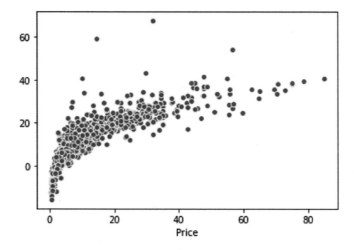

Figure 3-2. *Correlation between actual Y and predicted Y*

Final Model

After removing highly multicollinear variables and redundant variables having statistical insignificance, the model accuracy still remains close to 70% on the training set and 69% on the test set.

```
y = clean_df['Price']
x = clean_df.drop(['Price','engineCC','FuelType_Diesel','mileage',
'Location_Kochi'],axis=1)
xtrain,xtest,ytrain,ytest = train_test_split(x,y,test_size=0.25,
random_state=1234)

xtrain.shape,ytrain.shape,xtest.shape,ytest.shape

new_model = LinearRegression()

new_model.fit(xtrain,ytrain)

print(new_model.score(xtrain,ytrain))

print(new_model.score(xtest,ytest))
```

Model Explainability

Model interpretation can be done by looking at the beta coefficients of the model. The biggest advantages of a linear regression model are simplicity and linearity, which makes the model interpretation easy. Linear regression also forces the prediction to be a linear combination of the features. The confidence interval is the range of values within which the true prediction value will fall. A 95% confidence interval means 95% of the times the true value of prediction will fall within the range. In the current example, you are looking at a 95% confidence interval. The level of significance means in a two tailed test of hypothesis scenario, which is a 5% level of significance, the interpretation can be explained in Table 3-5. The intercept value has no significance in a modelling scenario from interpretation point of view. If all the numerical features in the training data are zero and all the binary features are at their reference category, then the prediction generated by the model would be equivalent to the intercept term. This is a very exceptional scenario, but in a case where all the numerical features are there in the training dataset and they are standardized with mean zero and standard deviation 1, then the intercept term reflects the predicted outcome of the instance, where all features are at their mean value.

```
resultsDF = pd.DataFrame()
resultsDF['Variables'] = pd.Series(xtrain.columns)
resultsDF['coefficients'] = pd.Series(np.round(new_model.coef_,2))
```

```
resultsDF['p_value'] = pd.Series(np.round(ReturnPValue(new_model,xtrain,
ytrain),2))
resultsDF.sort_values(by='p_value',ascending=False)
```

Table 3-5. *Interpretation of Model Parameters in a Linear Model*

Interpretation of the regression coefficients	The target column is the price of the automobiles, which is a function of various variables, numeric as well as categorical.
Age = -0.911	An increase in the age of the automobile by one year leads to an estimated reduction in the prices of automobiles by 0.911 units. Assuming the price is in 000s, the reduction in the price of the car would be $911.00 with each runtime year, keeping all other features constant.
PowerBhp = 0.141	An increase in PowerBph of the automobile by one unit leads to an estimated increase in prices of automobiles by 0.141 units. The higher the BHP, the higher the price of the car, assuming all other features are the same.
Location_Jaipur = 0.663	The estimated prices of a car would increase by $663 if the base location of the car is from Jaipur vs. from somewhere else, assuming all other features are constant.
FuelType_ Electric = 8.972	The estimated price of a car would increase by $8972 if the car is an electric car vs. any other fuel type, assuming no change in the other features of the model.
OwnerType_Second = -0.54	The base price of the car would decrease by $540 if the ownership is second hand vs. any other number of ownership, assuming no change in the other features.
Transmission_manual = -2.671	The price of the car would decrease by $2671 if the transmission type is manual vs. all other types, keeping all other factors constant.

Trust in ML Model: SHAP

In order to trust the linear regression-based machine learning model, you need to understand the R square value derived from the model. The R square value indicates the goodness of the fit of a regression model, which means the proportion of the explained variance in the target variable by all the features together. The R square value ranges from 0.0-1.0. If the R square value is zero, then the model shows there is no correlation between the dependent and independent variables. If it is 1, then it shows the features are very highly correlated. It should be 0.80 or more in order to qualify as a good model on whose predictions you can trust. In the above automobile example, the R square value is 0.70, which is very close to a standard model you can trust. Instead of R square, it is the adjusted R square value that is most referred to as it takes into account the number of features used in the model. The R square and adjusted R square relationship is shown below using the formula. In the following formula, N means the total number of training examples and p means the total number of features:

$$Adjusted \ R^2 = 1 - \frac{\left(1 - R^2\right)\left(N - 1\right)}{N - p - 1}$$

The R square value may increase as you add redundant variables into the model, but the adjusted R square will remain unchanged. The adjusted R square will only increase if the feature has any contribution to the overall model explainability.

In order to generate additional explainability and gain deeper understanding into how the model works, you can get help from additional Python-based libraries. Shapley values are a widely used approach from cooperative game theory that come with desirable properties. You understand from the model coefficients how the outcome variable is predicted or estimated to change as you change the input parameters. However, it does not tell you which features are important. The value of each coefficient is dependent on the scale of the input features. As an example, the car age can scale between 0-15 years. However, the BHP can range from a 34.20-560.00 in the above dataset. Hence the magnitude of the model coefficient is not necessarily a good measure of feature importance in a linear regression model.

Some data scientists use the absolute value of t-statistics as a measure of importance of features in a linear regression model.

$$t_{\hat{\beta}_j} = \frac{\hat{\beta}_j}{SE\left(\hat{\beta}_j\right)}$$

One of the ways to understand feature importance is to look at the partial dependency plot of the feature against the model output.

```
!pip install shap
```

Once SHAP is successfully installed, you can use the library to generate the partial dependency plot shown in Figure 3-3.

```
import shap
shap.plots.partial_dependence("Age", new_model.predict,xtrain, ice=False,
model_expected_value=True, feature_expected_value=True)
```

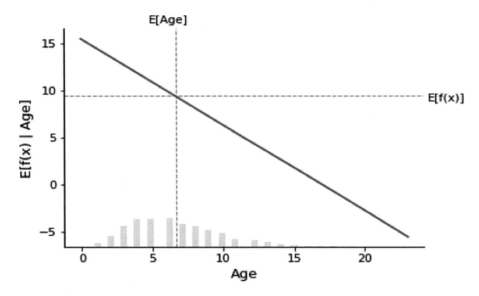

Figure 3-3. *Partial dependency plot*

The dotted horizontal line shows the expected value of the model output when applied to the dataset, the vertical dotted line shows the average age value feature, and the blue partial dependence plot line, which the is average value of the model output when you fix the age feature to a given value, on the graph always passes through the intersection of the two gray expected value lines. This intersection point can be considered as the "center" of the partial dependence plot with respect to the data distribution. The vertical grey boxes on the horizontal axis line show that the age distribution is slightly skewed towards the right.

The main idea behind the Shapley value established model explanations is to use an impartial distribution of results from cooperative game theory to allocate credit for a model's output (x) among its input features. In order connect game theory with machine learning models, it is necessary to both match a model's input features with players in a game and also to match the model function with the rules of the game. In game theory, a player has the option to join or not join a game, similar to the way a feature can "join" or "not join" a model.

What is a SHAP value and how it is computed? This provides a fair idea about the interpretation and meaning of a SHAP value. The Shapely value for each feature value is computed by the following formula:

$$\phi_i = \sum_{S \subseteq F \setminus \{i\}} \frac{|S|!(|F|-|S|-1)!}{|F|!} \left[f_{S \cup \{i\}}\left(x_{S \cup \{i\}}\right) - f_S(x_S) \right]$$

The following points clarify how it works:

- To compute each feature's contribution, SHAP requires retraining the model on all feature subsets S.

- In the above formula, i is the individual feature.

- F is the set of all features.

- S is the subset of features from the set F.

- For any feature I, two models are created: model 1 with the feature i and model 2 without feature i. Then the difference between the predictions computed.

- The effect of one feature on the model depends on how the other features in the model behave.

- The differences in prediction are computed for all possible subsets of S and their average values are taken.

- The weighted average value of all possible differences is used to populate feature importance.

The most common way to define what it means for a feature to "join" a model is to say that a feature has "joined a model" when we know the value of that feature, and it has not joined a model when we don't know the value of that feature. This happens when the weight/coefficient of a feature in a model assumes 0.000, then we consider that feature has not joined the game. If the coefficient of a feature is not equal to 0.000, then we consider that feature as part of the game. Let's look at the SHAP values for the linear regression model.

```
# compute the SHAP values for the linear model
background = shap.maskers.Independent(xtrain, max_samples=2000)
background
xtrain.shape
```

This `shap.maskers.Independent` function masks out tabular features by integrating over the given background dataset. Here the background dataset has 4,500 records from the training dataset, which is the maximum number of samples to use from the passed background data. If data has more than `max_samples`, then `shap.utils.sample` is used to subsample the dataset. The number of samples coming out of the masker (to be integrated over) matches the number of samples in the background dataset. This means a larger background dataset causes longer runtimes. Normally about 1, 10, 100, or 1000 background samples are reasonable choices.

```
explainer = shap.Explainer(new_model, background)
explainer

shap_values = explainer(xtrain)

shap_values
```

The above script shows the output of SHAP values, background data samples, and the base values from the model. The following script shows the standard partial dependency plot, taking into account the age feature and the model predict function, for sample record number 23 from the dataset. The SHAP value for a specific feature i is just the difference between the expected model output and the partial dependence plot at the feature's value xi, the additive nature of Shapley values. One the fundamental properties of Shapley values is that they always sum up the difference between the game outcome when all players are present and the game outcome when no players are present. For machine learning models, this means that SHAP values of all input features will always sum up to the difference between the baseline (expected) model output and the current model output for the prediction being explained. The easiest way to see this is through a waterfall plot that starts your background prior expectation for a home price [(*X*)] and then adds features one at a time until you reach the current model output (*x*). Corresponding to the age feature of 10 years, the vertical difference between the blue line and grey dotted line is the SHA value for the feature.

Local Explanation and Individual Predictions in a ML Model

The SHAP partial dependency plot (Figure 3-4) is a good way to explain the individual predictions, get additional insight for the individual predictions, and explain what features matter for that particular individual prediction.

```
# make a standard partial dependence plot
sample_ind = 23
fig,ax = shap.partial_dependence_plot(
    "Age", new_model.predict, xtrain, model_expected_value=True,
    feature_expected_value=True, show=False, ice=False,
    shap_values=shap_values[sample_ind:sample_ind+1,:],
    shap_value_features=X.iloc[sample_ind:sample_ind+1,:]
)
```

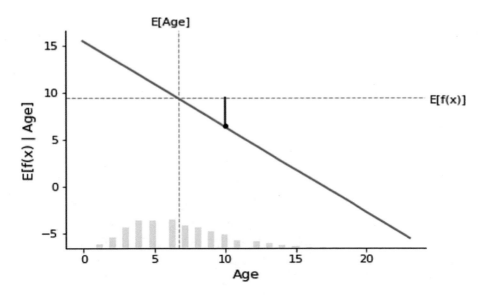

Figure 3-4. *Partial dependence plot of age and expected value of prediction*

Figure 3-5 explains the correlation in terms of a scatter plot between the age feature and the SHAP value of an age feature.

```
shap.plots.scatter(shap_values[:,"Age"])
```

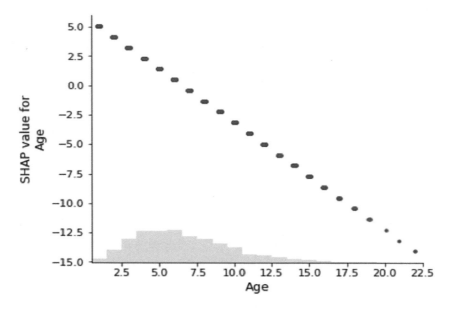

Figure 3-5. *SHAP value of age and age association*

Getting the SHAP values for a sample row from the dataset can be explained through a waterfall chart (Figure 3-6). This is part of the local explanation. Waterfall plots are designed to display explanations for individual predictions, so they expect a single row of an explanation object as input. The bottom of a waterfall plot starts as the expected value of the model output, and then each row shows how the positive (red) or negative (blue) contribution of each feature moves the value from the expected model output over the background dataset to the model output for this prediction.

Let's take an example to understand the SHAP values: record number 60 from the training dataset, which is the 2966th row in the overall dataset. Use it as a new data point and make a prediction using the trained model. The predicted value is 4.7656. However, the actual price value for the same record is 4.85. The waterfall plot from the SHAP library shows how the predicted value of 4.766 is reached from the SHAP base values from the function to the predicted value.

```
xtrain[60:61]
```

```
new_model.predict(xtrain[60:61])
```

```
ytrain[60:61]
```

```
# the waterfall_plot shows how we get from shap_values.base_values to
model.predict(X)[sample_ind]
shap.plots.waterfall(shap_values[60])
```

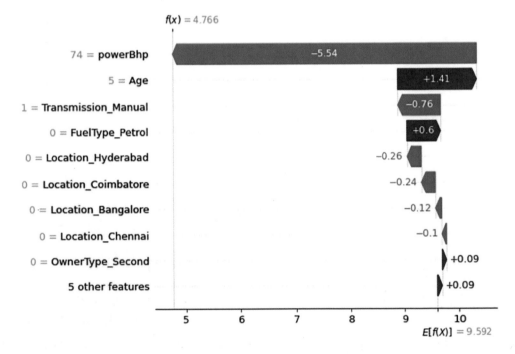

Figure 3-6. *Waterfall chart showing positive and negative SHAP values*

From the above waterfall chart, it is clear that for record number 60, the most impactful predictors are power BHP, age, petrol fuel type, and manual transmission. There are five least important features that are collapsed together and their joint contribution towards the prediction is +0.09. If you remove that restriction of collapsing into a single feature, you can expand by changing the max display option. The following script shows a modified version of the waterfall chart from the SHAP values for local interpretation of the prediction (Figure 3-7):

```
shap.plots.waterfall(shap_values[60],max_display=30)
```

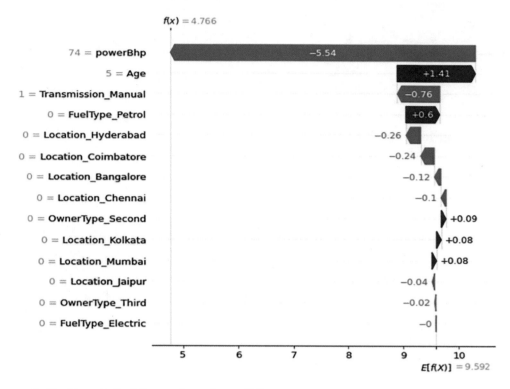

Figure 3-7. *Expanded form showing all features*

Global Explanation and Overall Predictions in ML Model

The beeswarm plot is a visualization designed to display an information-dense summary of how the top features in a dataset impact the model's output. Each instance of the given explanation is represented by a single dot on each feature row. The center position of the dot is determined by the SHAP value of that feature, and the dots "pile up" along each feature row to show density. Color is used to display the original value of a feature. In the plot in Figure 3-8, you can see that age and power BHP are the most important features on average.

- The higher the power BHP, the higher the impact on the model output, as you know that with higher power BHP comes a higher car price.

- Similarly, the age of the car is negatively associated with the predicted price of the car. Hence, the younger the car, the more impact it will have on the model output, as displayed on the graph below.

- By default, the beeswarm plot shows 10 features. You can change that parameter by changing the max display option. By default, the features are ordered based on the mean absolute value of the SHAP values.

- By default, the features are ordered using shap_values.abs.mean(0), which is the mean absolute value of the SHAP values for each feature. This order, however, places more emphasis on a broad average impact and less on rare but high magnitude impacts.

- If you want to find features with high impacts for individual people, you can instead sort by the max absolute value.

```
# the waterfall_plot shows how we get from shap_values.base_values to
model.predict(X)[sample_ind]
shap.plots.beeswarm(shap_values)
```

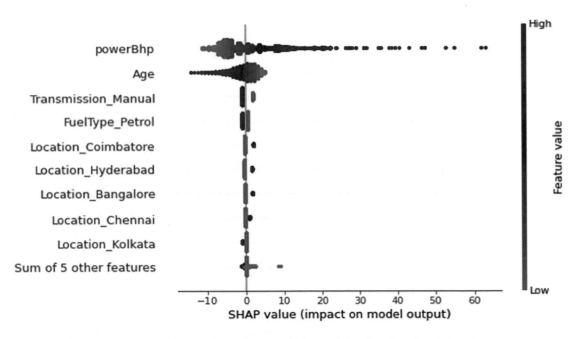

Figure 3-8. Beeswarm chart showing positive and negative SHAP value

By default, the beeswarm plot uses a color palate of red and blue. You can customize and change the colors as well (Figure 3-9).

```
import matplotlib.pyplot as plt
shap.plots.beeswarm(shap_values, color=plt.get_cmap("cool"))
```

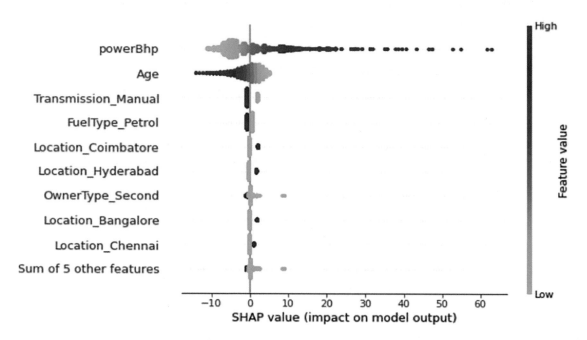

Figure 3-9. *Beeswarm plot using a different color palate*

There is one option to show the SHAP values using the bar plot, where the mean absolute average of the SHAP values are taken into consideration. The horizontal axis in Figure 3-10 shows the mean absolute SHAP value and the vertical axis shows the features. The five least important features are clubbed together. Also, there is an option to see the maximum absolute value of all features with respect to the features. The max absolute SHAP values indicate influential observations in the training data set that swayed the predictions. Passing a matrix of SHAP values to the heatmap plot function creates a plot with the instances on the x-axis, the model inputs on the y-axis, and the SHAP values encoded on a color scale. By default, the samples are ordered using shap. order.hclust, which orders the samples based on a hierarchical clustering by their explanation similarity. See Figures 3-11 and 3-12 as well.

```
shap.plots.bar(shap_values)
```

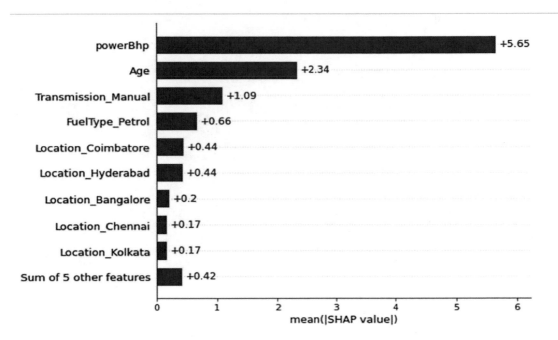

Figure 3-10. *Mean absolute values of SHAP values*

```
shap.plots.bar(shap_values.abs.max(0))
```

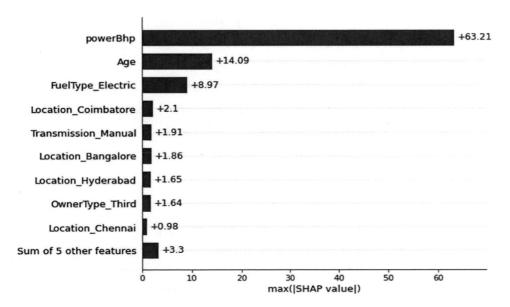

Figure 3-11. *Maximum absolute SHAP values*

```
shap.plots.heatmap(shap_values[:1000])
```

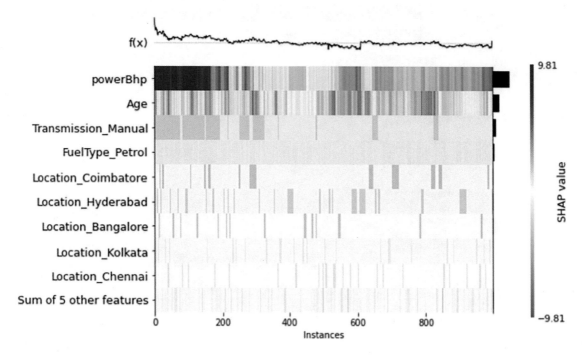

Figure 3-12. *Feature instance with SHAP association*

This results in samples that have the same model output for the same reason getting grouped together (such as people with a high impact from power BHP and age). The output of the model is shown above the heatmap matrix in Figure 3-12 (centered around the explanation's .base_value), and the global importance of each model's input is shown as a bar plot on the right-hand side of the plot (by default, this is the shap.order.abs.mean measure of the overall importance).

LIME Explanation and ML Model

LIME, or Local Interpretable Model-Agnostic Explanations, is an algorithm that can explain the predictions of any classifier or regressor in a faithful way by approximating it locally with an interpretable model. It modifies a single data sample by tweaking the feature values and observes the resulting impact on the output. It performs the role of an "explainer" to explain predictions from each data sample. The output of LIME is a set of explanations representing the contribution of each feature to a prediction for a single sample, which is a form of local interpretability. Interpretable models in LIME can be, for instance, linear regression or decision trees, which are trained on small perturbations (e.g. adding noise, removing words, or hiding parts of the image) of the original model to provide a good local approximation. LIME can be installed using the pip command.

You can take up the model training dataset with the target column and train a regression model afresh, instead of the previous model object new_model, because LIME is a model-agnostic technique and it retrains the models while generating the explainer. LIME localizes a problem and explains the model at local level rather than global explanations.

```
!pip install lime
```

```
import lime
import lime.lime_tabular
```

```
explainer = lime.lime_tabular.LimeTabularExplainer(np.array(xtrain),
                                        mode='regression',
                                        feature_names=xtrain.columns,
                                        class_names=['price'],
                                        verbose=True)
```

The LIME tabular explainer requires a numpy array as an input, hence the training data format changes. The mode is selected as regression after perturbation and the target column is price. Once the explainer has been developed, detailed local explanations can be further generated. The feature frequencies option provides the distribution of features and how many times it has been part of the perturbation process.

```
explainer.feature_selection
explainer.feature_frequencies
```

If you want to use the previously trained model object, then you can use the explain instance option. This requires a test dataset, model object, and number of features that can be used. Let's take the same 60th record from the test dataset. You will get the result as an intercept term, a local prediction value, and right, which is global prediction value. For the 60th record from the test dataset, if you use a predict function, you get a predicted value of 27.5854, which is equal to the right value from the explain instance. The local mode of prediction is 28.54, which is closer to the actual predicted value of 35.0.

```
# asking for explanation for LIME model
i = 60
exp = explainer.explain_instance(np.array(xtest)[i],
                                 new_model.predict,
                                 num_features=14
                                 )
```

```
new_model.predict(xtest)[60]
```

```
ytest[60:61]
```

```
Intercept 18.186435664326485
Prediction_local [28.15539047]
Right: 27.58547373488966
exp.show_in_notebook(show_table=True)
exp.as_list()
```

You can show the explainer in a tabular format with the predicted value, positive and negative feature values, and overall features and their value in the table. The predicted value is 46.62. In the second chart, the positive feature and negative feature values are displayed for the same instance, number 60. The horizontal bars in the second chart indicate the feature importance for the record. The third table shows the LIME value corresponding to each feature. The methodology and the local explanations are quite intuitive. This can be explained to any business user. The sample locality of the 60th record selects the single data point uniformly and at random, creating perturbed data points and a corresponding predicted value from the model. By default, the feature selection method is auto. LIME focuses on fitting the interpretable model on the shuffled dataset (perturbed) using the sample weights and provides local explanations using the newly trained model. See Figure 3-13.

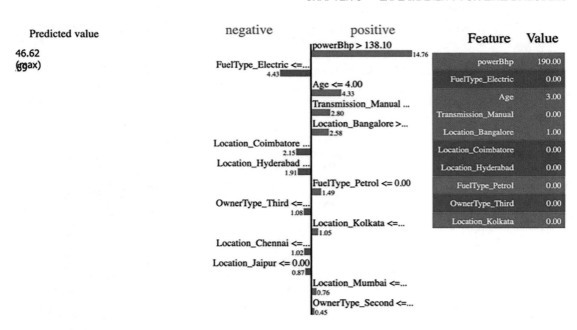

Figure 3-13. *Contributions of positive and negative values from different features towards the predicted value*

The explainer for the 60th record can also be displayed as a list as above. There is another class function called a sub modular pick for generating a global decision boundary.

```
# Code for SP-LIME
import warnings
from lime import submodular_pick

# Remember to convert the dataframe to matrix values
# SP-LIME returns exaplanations on a sample set to provide a non redundant
global decision boundary of original model
sp_obj = submodular_pick.SubmodularPick(explainer, np.array(xtrain),
                                new_model.predict,
                                num_features=14,
                                num_exps_desired=10)

[exp.show_in_notebook() for exp in sp_obj.sp_explanations ]
```

Here the number of features used for generating a global decision boundary is 14, and the number of experiments desired is 10. This part of the script will take some time to complete since you are generating multiple iterations. See Figure 3-14.

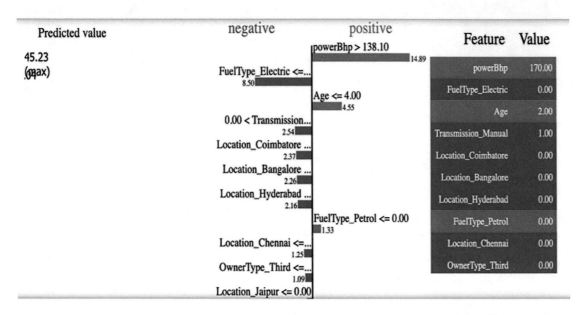

Figure 3-14. *Sub-modular pick explanations*

LIME tries to trade off between fidelity and interpretability. Fidelity means the model should be able to replicate the model behavior in the locality of the instance used in prediction. Interpretability you already know is clarity so humans can understand the model output. The following equation shows the relationship between the two:

$$\xi(x) = \operatorname*{argmin}_{g \in G} \quad L(f, g, \pi_x) + \Omega(g)$$

Let's understand each of the symbols used in the above formula:

- F is the original predictor.

- g is the model explanation.

- The original features are x.

- The pi of x is a proximity measure defining the locality around xx.

- The omega of x is a measure of model complexity for explanation.

One of the limitations of LIME is the inaccurate definition of neighborhood and proximity. While sampling the records in the locality, it uses a Gaussian distribution, which does not take into consideration the relationship between various features. If the relationship between the dependent and independent variables is non-linear, then the explanations will not be accurate. Another limitation is the sub-modular pick, which is a set of n-samples from the dataset that best explains the model. The sub-modular pick generates a lot of output, which is at times difficult to interpret. Despite the limitations of the module, LIME is mostly used for generating model-agnostic local interpretations of individual predictions. It is quite popular because of the simplicity of its output and how easy it is to explain.

Skater Explanation and ML Model

Skater is an open source unified framework to enable model interpretation for all forms of models to help us build an interpretable machine learning system often needed for real world use-cases. Skater supports algorithms to demystify the learned structures of a black box model both globally (inference on the basis of a complete data set) and locally (inference about an individual prediction). The package was originally developed by Aaron Kramer, Pramit Choudhary, and the rest of the DataScience.com team to help data scientists and data enthusiasts gain better model insight. Skater enables this vision by providing the ability to infer and debug the model's decision policies as needed, bringing "a human into the loop."

The Skater library can be installed by using the pip or conda install scripts. It's also easy to install in a Jupyter environment. The model object can be implemented by two classes: an in-memory model and a deployed model. Models that are callable functions can be consumed via the in-memory model; models that are deployed and callable via Rest APIs are exposed via the deployed model object.

```
!pip install skater
import skater
from skater import Interpretation
# An Interpretation consumes a dataset, and optionally some meta data like
  feature names and row ids

interpreter = Interpretation(xtrain, feature_names=xtrain.columns)
interpreter
```

```
from skater.model import InMemoryModel

model = InMemoryModel(new_model.predict, examples = xtrain[:10])
model
```

The interpretation module consumes a dataset. From the interpreter you can extract the feature importance of a regression object. The in-memory model requires a predict function and a sample of data for which the prediction need to be explained.

```
interpreter.feature_importance.feature_importance(model)
#Computes feature importance of all features related to a model instance.
#Supports regression.
```

From the feature importance table above, the two important features are power BHP and age; they cumulatively contribute 75% of the importance. The other 12 features contribute 25% of the importance. The model report function shows the details metadata such as model type trained, output variable type, output shape, input shape, and probability status about the model.

```
model.model_report(examples=xtrain)
```

To generate a partial dependency plot or two-way partial dependency plot, the interpreter requires you to load the training dataset again, and the feature names also need to be provided.

```
# Skater is intutively designed to support
# - InMemoryModel : A model which is currently being built and estimator
instance is still in the scope
# - DeployedModel: A model which is operationalized, or a third party
deployed model
interpreter.load_data(xtrain, feature_names=xtrain.columns)
```

```
print("2-way partial dependence plots")
# Features can passed as a tuple for 2-way partial plot
pdp_features = [('Age', 'powerBhp')]
interpreter.partial_dependence.plot_partial_dependence(
    pdp_features, model, grid_resolution=10
)
```

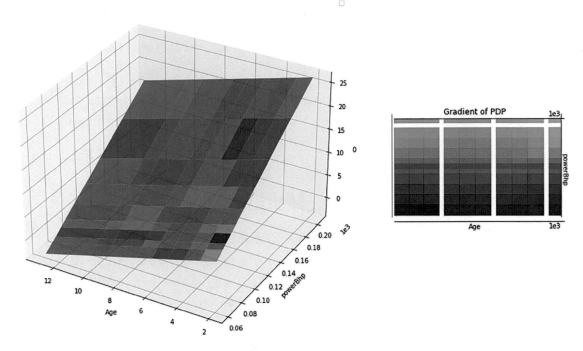

Figure 3-15. *Two-way partial dependency plot*

Using two powerful features with the dependent variable, the above two partial dependency plot shown in Figure 3-15 is generated. The colors on the plot show mere associations and should not be interpreted as causality. From the second gradient graph from Figure 3-15, the higher contribution towards predicted value is shown using green and the lower contribution to the predicted value by those two features, age and power BHP jointly, is shown by the deep blue color. The light green color shows the higher predicted value and the blue color shows the lower predicted value. Similarly, a one-way partial dependency plot can be generated. The PDP plot with the confidence interval can be populated on the same one-way PDP graph.

```
print("1-way partial dependence plots")
# or as independent features for 1-way partial plots
pdp_features = ['powerBhp', 'Age']
interpreter.partial_dependence.plot_partial_dependence(
    pdp_features, model, grid_resolution=30
)
```

```
# Partial Plot with variance effect
interpreter.partial_dependence.plot_partial_dependence(
    pdp_features, model, grid_resolution=30, with_variance=True
)
```

The two graphs each from the two plots are not printed here as at this time they will not add much value. You can plot as many PDP charts from the dataset as you want. The relevant ones provide important insights about the features.

ELI5 Explanation and ML Model

ELI5 is a Python package that helps debug machine learning classifiers and explain their predictions. It provides support for the following machine learning framework and package: scikit-learn. Currently ELI5 can explain weights and predictions of the scikit-learn linear classifiers and regressors, print decision trees as text or as SVG, show feature importance, and explain predictions of decision trees and tree-based ensembles. ELI5 understands text processing utilities from scikit-learn and can highlight text data accordingly. It also allows you to debug scikit-learn pipelines which contain HashingVectorizer by undoing hashing.

The weights of features have a bias feature also. This is nothing but the intercept term for a linear regression model. The features are listed based on descending order of their weight. ELI5 means *explain like I am five*. It supports all of the scikit-learn algorithms. It also has global interpretation using the show_weights() function. It also has local interpretation using the show_prediction() function. In the ELI5 library there is a permutation model. It only works for global interpretation. Here is how it works:

- First, it takes the baseline model from the training dataset and computes the error.

- It shuffles the values of the features, retrains the model, and computes the error.

- It compares the decrease in error after shuffling and before shuffling.

A feature is considered important if post shuffling the error delta becomes very high, and a feature is considered unimportant if post shuffling the error rate remain unchanged. The result displays the average importance and standard deviation of the features with multiple shuffle steps. It is not a way to look at which feature impacts the model performance. It only tells us the magnitude of changes in feature weights, so we cannot really consider the weights as feature important at a scale. The above process is demonstrated using the following script:

```
!pip install eli5
import eli5
eli5.show_weights(new_model,
                  feature_names=list(xtrain.columns))
eli5.explain_weights(new_model, feature_names=list(xtrain.columns))
eli5.explain_prediction(new_model,xtrain.iloc[60])
from eli5.sklearn import PermutationImportance
perm = PermutationImportance(new_model)
perm.fit(xtest, ytest)
eli5.show_weights(perm,feature_names=list(xtrain.columns))
```

The explain individual prediction provides a local interpretation of a record. Also it tells you the top three features that have higher weights in making the prediction. From the permutation importance plot, it is clear that power BHP and age are the most important features. This is in line with similar exercises from the other XAI Python libraries you implemented so far by taking into consideration the automobile.csv.

Now as a next step, let's look at a linear classification model, which is also known as a logistic regression model, to understand various aspects of XAI from a logistic regression model. A partial dependency plot depicts the relationship between the target feature or dependent variable and a feature known as an independent variable. The relationship can be linear, non-linear, curvilinear, or more complex like a circular or cyclical monotonic relationship.

Logistic Regression

The linear regression model is applicable when the target feature is continuous, but when the target feature is binary such as 0 or 1, true or false, accept or reject, the linear regression model is not applicable. This is because the predicted value for the target feature may exceed the range of 0 and 1, but the expectation is to limit the output into two classes since you need to predict the two classes separately. This is why you need a logistic regression model, which takes the binary values to compute the log odds, known as the odds ratio. The odds ratio is linearly related to the features. This is why the logistic regression model is known as the linear model.

Logistic regression is typically used when you need to model the probabilities when the outcome is binary or multinomial in nature. You cannot apply a linear regression model there, because in a logistic regression scenario the outcome variable is either 0 or 1 (or at times it can be multinomial as well, where more than two outcomes are also possible). If you apply a linear regression there, the prediction range could exceed the range of 0 and 1. It won't provide the probabilities for any of the classes. In a multinomial class classification model, class separation would be a big challenge. A linear regression model based on an ordinary least square method assumes that the relationship between the dependent variable and the independent variables is linear; however, the logistic regression model assumes the relationship to be logarithmic.

There are many real-life scenarios where the variable of interest is categorical in nature, like buying a product or not, approving a credit card or not, or a tumor is cancerous or not. Logistic regression not only predicts a dependent variable class but it predicts the probability of a case belonging to a level in the dependent variable. The independent variables need not be normally distributed and need not have equal variance. Logistic regression belongs to the family of non-linear regression. If the dependent variable has two levels, logistic regression can be applied, but if it has more than two levels, such as high, medium, and low, then multinomial regression model can be applied. The independent variables can be continuous, categorical, or nominal.

The logistic regression model can be explained using the following equation:

$$Sigmoid\ (t) = \frac{1}{1 + exp(-t)}$$

The above function is also known as a sigmoid function.

$$Ln\left(\frac{P}{1-P}\right) = \beta_0 + \beta_1 X_1 + \beta_2 X_2 + \ldots + \beta_k X_k$$

Ln (P/1-P) is the log odds of the outcome. The beta coefficients mentioned in the above equation explain how the odds of the outcome variable increase or decrease for every one unit increased or decreased in the explanatory variable. Figure 3-16 shows the shape of the sigmoid function. It looks like an s-shaped curve. The interpretation of a logistic regression model is quite different from a linear regression model. The weighted sum from the equation on the right-hand side is converted/transformed into a probability value. The left-hand side of the equation is called the log odds, as it is the ratio of the probability of an event happening to the probability of the event not happening. More interpretations about the log odds can be understood by taking into account an example which we are going to discuss further.

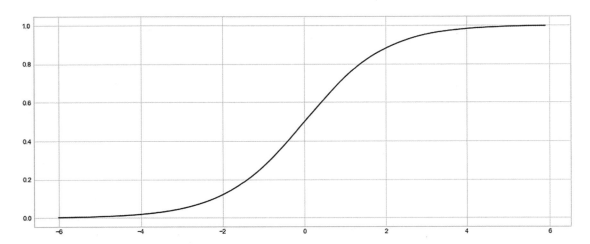

Figure 3-16. *Logistic/sigmoid function, x-axis shows features, y-axis shows probabilities*

To explain the logistic regression model and how the decision making happens, you need to understand the probabilities and odds ratio as well. You are going to use churndata.csv, which belongs to the telecom domain and has close to 3,333 records and 18 features in it. You are going to predict whether the customer is likely to churn or not churn given the feature values.

```
import pandas as pd
import numpy as np
import matplotlib.pyplot as plt
%matplotlib inline

from sklearn.linear_model import LogisticRegression, LogisticRegressionCV

from sklearn.metrics import confusion_matrix, classification_report

df_train = pd.read_csv('ChurnData.csv')
```

As a first step, you get the data, transform certain features that are already in a string format, and apply a label encoder to do the transformation. Post transformation, you do a split of 80% for training purposes and 20% for testing purposes. When creating the train/test split, you maintain the proportion of churn cases and no-churn cases in order to maintain the balance between the classes. Then you train the model and apply the trained model on the test data and compare the accuracy of the train and test datasets.

```
del df_train['Unnamed: 0']

df_train.shape
df_train.head()

from sklearn.preprocessing import LabelEncoder

tras = LabelEncoder()

df_train['area_code_tr'] = tras.fit_transform(df_train['area_code'])

df_train.columns

del df_train['area_code']

df_train.columns

df_train['target_churn_dum'] = pd.get_dummies(df_train.
churn,prefix='churn',drop_first=True)
df_train.columns
del df_train['international_plan']
del df_train['voice_mail_plan']
del df_train['churn']
df_train.info()

df_train.columns

from sklearn.model_selection import train_test_split

df_train.columns

X = df_train[['account_length', 'number_vmail_messages', 'total_day_minutes',
        'total_day_calls', 'total_day_charge', 'total_eve_minutes',
        'total_eve_calls', 'total_eve_charge', 'total_night_minutes',
        'total_night_calls', 'total_night_charge', 'total_intl_minutes',
```

```
        'total_intl_calls', 'total_intl_charge',
        'number_customer_service_calls', 'area_code_tr']]
Y = df_train['target_churn_dum']
```

Only the area code variable is transformed. The rest of the features are either integers or floats, which is fine to go ahead with training a model.

Now you can look at the distribution of probabilities, log odds and odds ratios, and model parameters from the model in order to understand how the decisioning around a prediction is made. If you take a reference of SHAP values to explain the probability of a logistic regression model, you can see strong interaction effects. This is due to the non-additive behavior of the logistic regression model in the probability space. If you use the log odds of the model as output, you can see a strong correlation or perfect linear relationship between the model's input and output.

```
xtrain,xtest,ytrain,ytest=train_test_split(X,Y,test_size=0.20,stratify=Y)
log_model = LogisticRegression()

log_model.fit(xtrain,ytrain)

print("training accuracy:", log_model.score(xtrain,ytrain)) #training accuracy

print("test accuracy:",log_model.score(xtest,ytest)) # test accuracy
```

By looking at the accuracy, you can conclude that it is a good model and possibly there is no overfitting issue, since there is no deviation in train and test accuracy.

```
np.round(log_model.coef_,2)

log_model.intercept_

X.columns
```

There are two utility functions you created to produce the required output, which can further be utilized in a graphical representation of SHAP values.

```
# Provide Probability as Output
def model_churn_proba(x):
    return log_model.predict_proba(x)[:,1]

# Provide Log Odds as Output
def model_churn_log_odds(x):
    p = log_model.predict_log_proba(x)
    return p[:,1] - p[:,0]
```

Since you already covered the interpretation of a dependency plot in the regression section of this chapter, a similar interpretation can be done for a logistic regression model as well. The partial dependency plot takes a record from the dataset as an example as it is a local explanation.

```
# make a standard partial dependence plot
sample_ind = 25
fig,ax = shap.partial_dependence_plot(
    "total_day_minutes", model_churn_proba, X, model_expected_value=True,
    feature_expected_value=True, show=False, ice=False
)
```

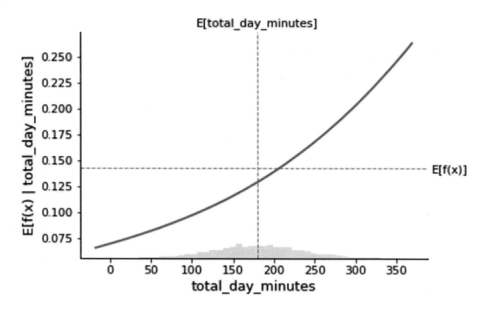

Figure 3-17. *Partial dependency plot of total day minutes with churn probability*

For record number 25, the partial dependency plot in Figure 3-17 for the feature total day in minutes shows the relationship between the probability value or expected value of the function with the feature is positive but seems not linear.

```
# compute the SHAP values for the linear model
background_churn = shap.maskers.Independent(X, max_samples=1000)
explainer = shap.Explainer(log_model, background_churn,
feature_names=list(X.columns))
```

```
shap_values_churn = explainer(X)
shap_values = pd.DataFrame(shap_values_churn.values)
shap_values.columns = list(X.columns)
shap_values
```

The SHAP.Explainer module has the important parameters listed in Table 3-6.

Table 3-6. *Explainer Parameters from the SHAP Library*

Parameter	Description
Model	Model object name
Masker	This is a function to mask out hidden features
Link	The function is used to map between the output units of the model and the SHAP value units
Algorithm	It's used to estimate Shapely values named auto, permutation, partition, tree, kernel, sampling, linear, deep, and gradient. The default is auto.

When you look at the scatterplot of the account length vs. the SHAP values of the account length (Figure 3-18), there is a strong, perfect linear relationship.

```
shap.plots.scatter(shap_values_churn[:,'account_length'])
```

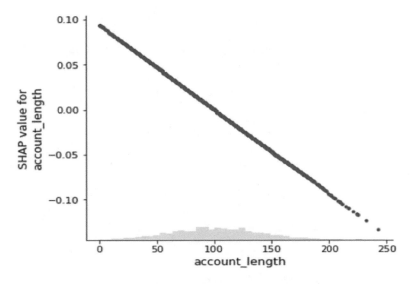

Figure 3-18. *Relationship between account length feature and the SHAP values*

The SHAP values and the average absolute values for the respective features are represented in the following graph. This displays which feature has the higher weight in the classification problem. The number of customer service calls is a good driver for churn as people with more complaints are more likely to call customer service and hence are fence sitters; they can churn at any time. The second most important factor is total day in minutes and the third is number of voice email messages. Towards the end you can see the seven least important features are clubbed together. There is another way of representation for the SHAP values. The maximum absolute SHAP value for each feature is represented, but there is no major difference between the two graphs. There is another view called a beeswarm plot, which shows the SHAP value and its impact on model output. The heatmap view of the SHAP values for thousands of records shows the density of the SHAP value against the features of the model. A high SHAP value is seen for the best feature and gradually the feature importance reduces and also the SHAP value decreases. See Figures 3-19 through 3-22.

```
# make a standard partial dependence plot
sample_ind = 25
fig,ax = shap.partial_dependence_plot(
    "number_vmail_messages", model_churn_proba, X, model_expected_value=True,
    feature_expected_value=True, show=False, ice=False
)
shap_values_churn.feature_names

# compute the SHAP values for the linear model
explainer_log_odds = shap.Explainer(log_model, background_churn,
feature_names=list(X.columns))
shap_values_churn_log_odds = explainer_log_odds(X)
shap_values_churn_log_odds
shap.plots.bar(shap_values_churn_log_odds)
```

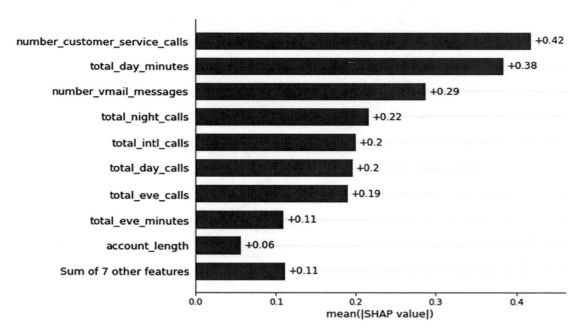

Figure 3-19. *Mean absolute SHAP values contributed by each feature*

```
shap.plots.bar(shap_values_churn_log_odds.abs.max(0))
```

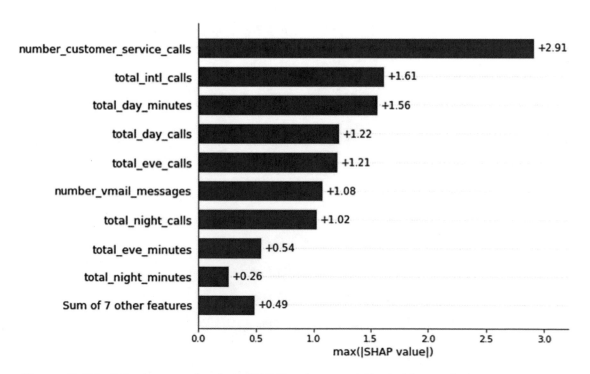

Figure 3-20. *Maximum absolute SHAP value contributed by each feature*

```
shap.plots.beeswarm(shap_values_churn_log_odds)
```

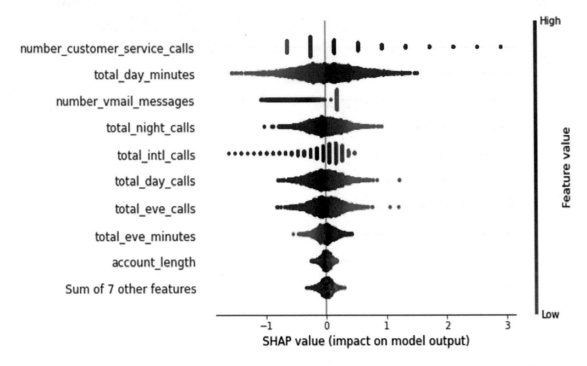

Figure 3-21. *Positive and negative contributions of features towards the SHAP value*

```
shap.plots.heatmap(shap_values_churn_log_odds[:1000])
```

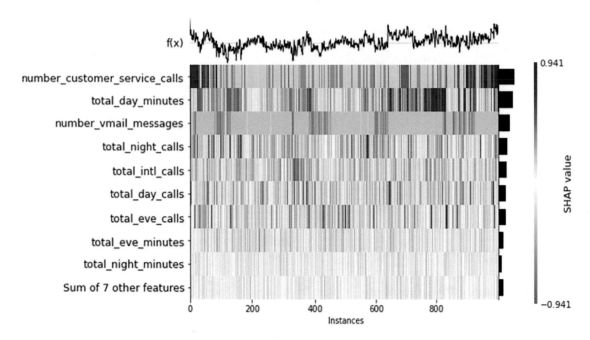

Figure 3-22. *Incidence of SHAP values contributed by each feature for instances used in the training process*

```
temp_df = pd.DataFrame()
temp_df['Feature Name'] = pd.Series(X.columns)
temp_df['Coefficients'] = pd.Series(log_model.coef_.flatten())
temp_df.sort_values(by='Coefficients',ascending=False)
```

Feature Name	Coefficients	
14	number_customer_service_calls	0.383573
2	total_day_minutes	0.008251
4	total_day_charge	0.001378
5	total_eve_minutes	0.000947
7	total_eve_charge	0.000098
10	total_night_charge	-0.000048
13	total_intl_charge	-0.000196
11	total_intl_minutes	-0.000464
0	account_length	-0.000573

8	total_night_minutes	-0.001730
3	total_day_calls	-0.009254
9	total_night_calls	-0.010050
6	total_eve_calls	-0.012706
1	number_vmail_messages	-0.019944
15	area_code_tr	-0.033119
12	total_intl_calls	-0.097870

Interpretation

When you increase the value of one feature by one unit, the model equation will produce two odds: one is the base and the other is an incremental value of a feature. The objective here is to look at the ratio of odds with every increase or decrease in the value of a feature. A change in a feature by one unit leads to changes in the odds ratio by a factor of exponential corresponding beta coefficients. This can be further explained using the following equation where beta 0 is the intercept term, beta 1 up to beta k are the parameters of the models, and x1 up to xk are the independent predictors for the model:

$$\frac{P(y=1)}{1-P(y=1)} = odds = exp\left(\beta_0 + \beta_1 x_1 + \ldots + \beta_p x_p\right)$$

Let's call the right-hand side of the equation as exp(a), where a is the equation representing the linear regression concept. If you increase any parameter of the model, then the equation will change by one unit, hence let's call it b, so the RHS becomes exp(b). The odds ratio with respect to the change in one unit value of a predictor will be odds_new/odd_old = exp(a-b). You can interpret all numeric features in this format. This can be followed for all categorical features or binary features as well.

LIME Inference

In order to explain the logistic regression model, you can use the SHAP values. However, the complexity is time. If you have a million records and you take a fairly large sample to generate all permutations and combinations to arrive at a global level to explain the local accuracy, you need more time. To avoid this bottleneck in processing large datasets, LIME offers speed in terms of generating explanations. In order to explain the tabular matrix data which is the structured data, you have to use Lime Tabular Explainer. For numerical features, perturb them by sampling from a Normal(0,1) and doing the inverse operation of mean-centering and scaling, according to the means and standard deviations in the training data. For categorical features, perturb by sampling according to the training distribution, and making a binary feature that is 1 when the value is the same as the instance being explained.

When generating a LIME explainer, you need to pass the data as an array, provide the list of column names, provide the target column name, and make the mode as regression and the classification based on the machine learning task that you are planning to use. The verbose option is to enable predictions from the model.

```
import lime
import lime.lime_tabular

explainer = lime.lime_tabular.LimeTabularExplainer(np.array(xtrain),
          feature_names=list(xtrain.columns),
          class_names=['target_churn_dum'],
          verbose=True, mode='classification')
# this record is a no churn scenario
exp = explainer.explain_instance(xtest.iloc[0], log_model.predict_proba,
num_features=16)
exp.as_list()
```

Once the explainer model object is generated, you can check for individual predictions and global predictions for generating explanations. In a classification where you have two classes or multi-classes, you can generate separate feature importances for each class with respect to the features column. In this instance, you consider two records: record 1 where the model predicts the outcome correctly and record 20 where the model incorrectly makes prediction. You will explain for both scenarios why this decision was made by the model. Features that have a positive relationship with the target class are a positive number and the class with a negative relationship has a negative sign. You can show the results in a tabular notebook kind of view. You can also restrict the view by taking into consideration the most important features in it.

```
pd.DataFrame(exp.as_list())
```

The weights of the features in a DataFrame view are shown in Table 3-7.

Table 3-7. *Features with a Threshold and Their Weights to Prediction Value*

0	1	
0	number_customer_service_calls <= 1.00	-0.106490
1	total_day_minutes <= 143.70	-0.082492
2	number_vmail_messages <= 0.00	0.063827
3	total_eve_calls > 114.00	-0.046997
4	101.00 < total_night_calls <= 114.00	-0.014762
5	total_eve_minutes > 235.07	0.009634
6	account_length > 126.00	-0.007626
7	1.00 < area_code_tr <= 2.00	-0.007580
8	2.27 < total_intl_charge <= 2.75	0.006753
9	87.00 < total_day_calls <= 101.00	0.006710
10	166.93 < total_night_minutes <= 200.40	0.005046
11	total_day_charge <= 24.43	-0.004913
12	3.00 < total_intl_calls <= 4.00	0.004285
13	7.51 < total_night_charge <= 9.02	-0.001845
14	total_eve_charge > 19.98	-0.001836
15	8.40 < total_intl_minutes <= 10.20	-0.000155

Corresponding to record number 1, the following table can be generated. The intercept term is 0.126, the local predicted probability of churn by LIME is 0.18, and the predicted probability of churn by the logistic regression model is 0.15. Basically it is the intercept term plus all the weights from the different features. Since the probability of churn is less, it is classified as a no-churn scenario. Hence the blue color bar in Figure 3-23 shows the probability of no churn as 0.84 and the probability of churn as 0.16. The overall importance of features by their weights is mentioned on the right-hand side of the table. The middle table shows the weights by feature value.

```
exp.show_in_notebook(show_table=True)
```

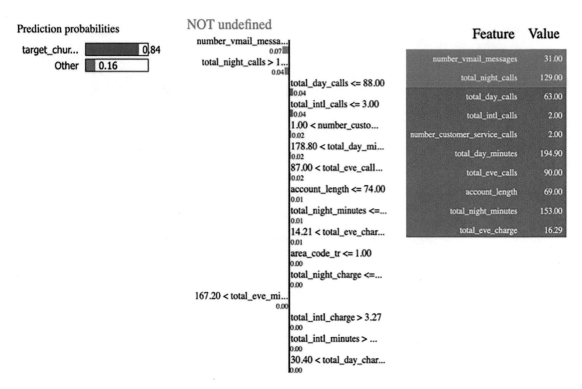

Figure 3-23. *Summary for record 1 from the test set and local interpretation for the same*

For record 20 from the test set, the model predicts a different result and the actual test has a different result. This is a scenario where the model prediction differs from the ground truth, hence the model needs to explain why this happened. You can get a better view using the LIME local instance.

```
# This is s churn scenario
exp = explainer.explain_instance(xtest.iloc[20], log_model.predict_proba,
num_features=16)
exp.as_list()

exp.show_in_notebook(show_table=True)
xtest.iloc[20]
```

In Figure 3-24, the prediction probabilities has two bars: the blue one shows the probability of no churn and the orange bar shows the probability of churn. If you look at the adjacent table, it clearly shows the features and their weights in contributing to the overall orange bar.

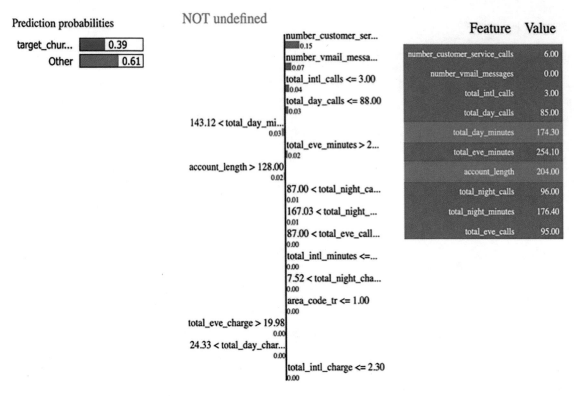

Figure 3-24. *Local interpretation for record 20 from the test set*

Except for two features, total day minutes and account length, all other features contribute to the churn probability, hence the model correctly predicts the outcome and the prediction is explained. The threshold values for each of the features are given along with their weights. This gives a better picture for business people to understand the behavior of the predictive model.

```
explainer = lime.lime_tabular.LimeTabularExplainer(np.array(xtrain),
        feature_names=list(xtrain.columns),
        class_names=['target_churn_dum'],
        verbose=True, mode='classification')
# Code for SP-LIME
import warnings
from lime import submodular_pick
# SP-LIME returns exaplanations on a sample set to provide a non redundant
global decision boundary of original model
```

```
sp_obj = submodular_pick.SubmodularPick(explainer, np.array(xtrain),
                                        log_model.predict_proba,
                                        num_features=14,
                                        num_exps_desired=10)
```

The sub-modular pick option provides a global decision boundary of the original model. You can use the explainer object, training dataset, and extracted probabilities from the trained model, and then specify the number of features that should be present in the description and number of expressions desired. See Figures 3-25 through 3-28.

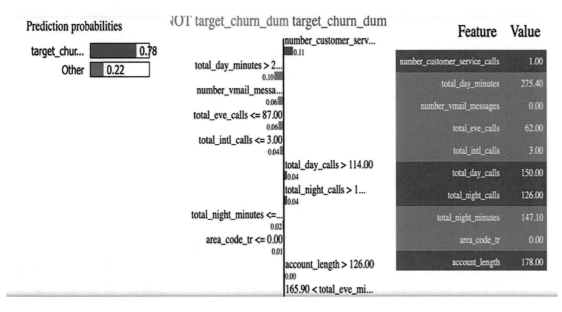

Figure 3-25. *Local interpretation for the first record of of 10 records*

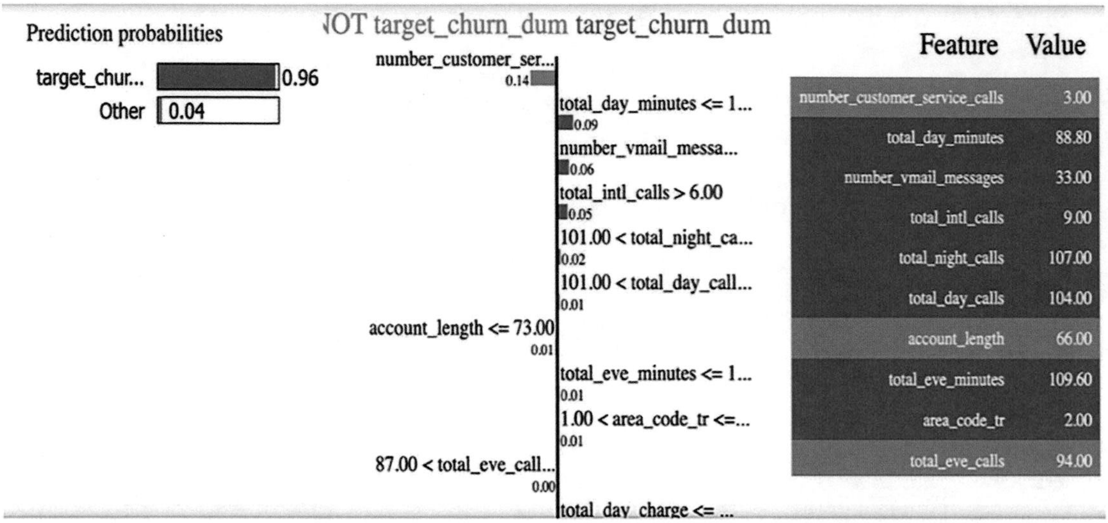

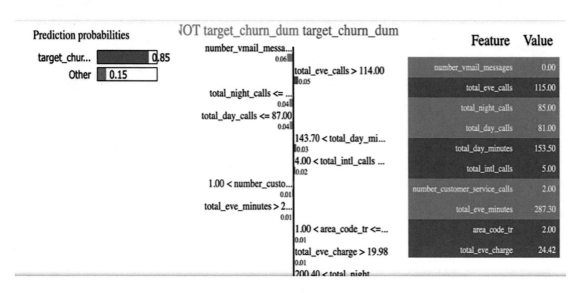

Figure 3-26. *Local interpretation for the second record of 10 records*

Figure 3-27. *Local interpretation for the third record of 10 records*

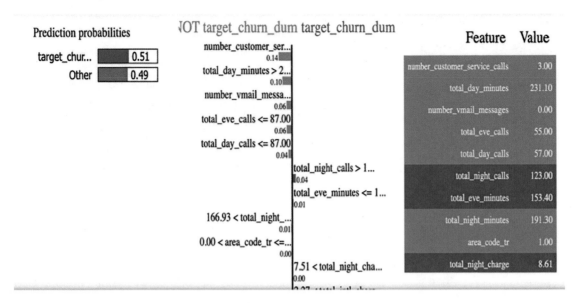

Figure 3-28. *Local interpretation for the fourth record of 10 records*

Skater generates similar results as the LIME library, hence the descriptions are not elaborated on since we covered them using the LIME library. ELI5 is mostly used for text classification use cases, thus ELI5 is not applicable for explaining linear or logistic regression models. See Table 3-8 for more information.

Table 3-8. *When to Use Which Library Summary View*

Library name	Definition	When to use	Advantages	Limitations
SHAP	Uses Shapley values to explain any machine learning model	Tabular data, image data	Better explanation with more metrics and statistics	Not evident
LIME	Local Interpretable Model Explanation (LIME)	For local interpretation, tabular data	Good for individual instance explainability	Global explanation not intuitive. Not for image data.

(*continued*)

Table 3-8. (*continued*)

Library name	Definition	When to use	Advantages	Limitations
Skater	The general workflow within the Skater package is to create an interpretation, create a model, and run interpretation algorithms.	Tabular data, available in two modules: in-memory and deployed model	Model training and interpretation need to be run once. No need to run as a separate process.	Only a few models are supported. Not exhaustive in covering all types of models
ELI5	A Python package that helps debug machine learning classifiers and explain their predictions	Scikit-learn models, text classification, Keras model explanation	Good for text classification	Not a mature library for all other tasks. Explanations are very basic.

Conclusion

In this chapter, you learned how to interpret linear models, linear regression models for predictions, and logistic regressions for binary classification. In a similar fashion the logistic regression model can also be extended to multinomial classification. The linear models are simpler ones to interpret and everyone understands really well how these models work. Therefore, there is always high degree of trust for linear models. Yet, in this chapter you looked at various angles of creating views for linear models using explainable AI libraries such as LIME and SHAP. In the next chapter, you will learn about model explainability for non-linear models.

## CHAPTER 4

Explainability for Non-Linear Models

This chapter explores the use of LIME, SHAP, and Skope-rules explainable AI-based Python libraries to explain the decisions made by non-linear models for supervised learning tasks with structured data. In this chapter, you are going learn various ways of explaining non-linear and tree-based models and their decisions in predicting the dependent variable. In a supervised machine learning task, there is a target variable, which is also known as a dependent variable, and a set of independent variables. The objective is to predict the dependent variable as a weighted sum of input variables or independent variables, where there is high degree of feature interaction and non-linear complex relationship exists.

Non-Linear Models

A decision tree is a non-linear model which maps the independent variable to the dependent variable. At a local level this may be considered as a piece-wise linear regression, but at a global level this is a non-linear model, as there is no one-to-one mapping between the dependent and independent variables. Unlike a linear regression model, there is no mathematical equation to show the relationship between the input and output variables. If we keep the maximum tree depth parameter to an infinite level, then the decision tree might fit the data perfectly, which is a classic scenario of model overfit. Whether the training dataset is linearly separable or not, decision trees are prone to overfitting. This needs to be addressed. People usually go for tree pruning in order to get a best fit decision tree model. One can view the decision tree as a series of conditional statements that results in a value or a class in the output column. As an example, if a person is 45 years old and works in the private sector and has a PhD degree, then they are definitely earning more than $50K a year. Decision trees are a supervised

© Pradeepta Mishra 2022
P. Mishra, *Practical Explainable AI Using Python*, https://doi.org/10.1007/978-1-4842-7158-2_4

learning algorithm that is applicable when there are infinite possible combinations of features that could impact the target column. In a decision tree, we split the population into two or more subpopulations based on the most significant splitter or differentiator in input variables.

Primarily the decision tree algorithm follows the ID3 (iterative dichotomiser 3) algorithm, although there are other algorithms such as C4.5, CART, MARS, and CHAID. It is based on the following things:

- Identification of the best attribute or feature based on information gain (having a high predictive value) from the dataset and placing that at the root of the tree

- Splitting the training dataset into subsets in such a way that each subset has the same value for an attribute

- Repeating the above two steps until all of the classes are separated into one node, or a minimum number of samples required in the node are satisfied

In decision tree models, to predict a class label for a record, we start from the root of the tree. We compare the root attributes and use the best attribute at the beginning and subsequently keep on developing the decision tree. When we look at model explainability, the ability of a decision tree to explain the predictions is quite good. In simpler terms, a decision tree provides rules that can be directly consumed by any application. The rules are mostly a bunch of if/else statements. In situations where there is a relationship between features, such as an interaction between features, square or cubic values of features are related to the dependent variable, etc. In such situations, the linear regression and the logistic regression are bound to fail. This is because the number of feature interactions could be many. The tree-based models take into account the feature values, decide a threshold value, and break the feature into two parts and keep growing the branches of the tree. The process of splitting the data into multiple subgroups helps in capturing the nonlinearity existing in the dataset. In a similar fashion, the square and cubic features also follow the if/else rules as outlined by the model.

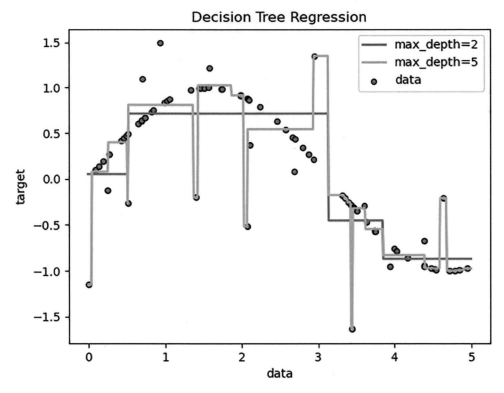

Figure 4-1. *Decision tree regression captures non-linearity*

As shown in Figure 4-1 (source: `https://scikit-learn.org/`), the relationship between the data and target is nonlinear. The non-linearity is approximated by a decision tree model by increasing the maximum depth parameter. As the maximum depth parameter increases from 2 to 5, all the points off the curve also become part of the model, hence they appear in the rule set generated by the decision tree model.

Decision Tree Explanation

Figure 4-2 depicts the start of the tree. It happens using a root feature. The branching logic is based on the best possible feature that creates a split.

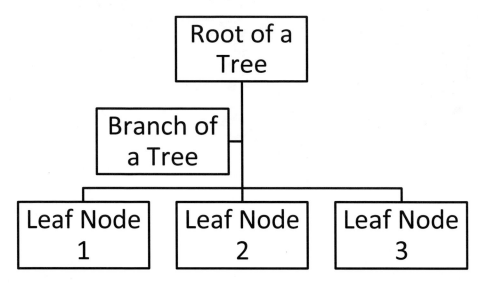

Figure 4-2. *The anatomy of a decision tree*

The terminal nodes are the ending nodes where the tree construction stops. To predict the outcome of a particular record, the average outcome of the overall data is used.

As shown in Figure 4-3, the model explainability can be achieved in two ways: the XAI library and the base ML library.

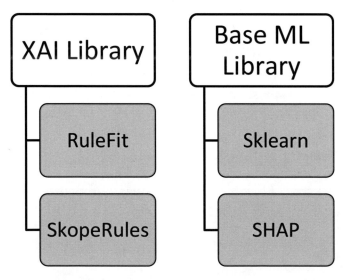

Figure 4-3. *Two ways to explain tree-based models*

The difference is that if we are using the parent ML library, we can use the already trained model. Otherwise, we may have to train the ML model again if we are using the XAI library. Now coming back to explaining the model results or outcome, if we retrain the model, it is an overhead as model retraining. Hyperparameter tuning and best model selection are different processes and take a lot of time.

However, if we have a readily available model and we can just generate the model explanations, it's beneficial for the end user. The following code shows the necessary libraries required for creating the decision tree model. You are going to use the telecom churn data you used in Chapter 3. This dataset has 20 features and 3,333 records in the dataset. For certain categorical variables such as area code you need to transform the variable and perform label encoder.

Data Preparation for the Decision Tree Model

The following script shows the necessary libraries for preparing a decision tree model. You're also importing the required data to develop the model as a CSV format.

```
import pandas as pd
import numpy as np
import matplotlib.pyplot as plt
%matplotlib inline

import numpy as np, pandas as pd, matplotlib.pyplot as plt
from sklearn import tree, metrics, model_selection, preprocessing
from IPython.display import Image, display
from sklearn.metrics import confusion_matrix, classification_report

df_train = pd.read_csv('ChurnData.csv')
del df_train['Unnamed: 0']
df_train.shape
df_train.head()
```

The additional column present in the data is deleted. The shape function provides an idea about the number of rows and columns present in the dataset. Also, the head function provides the first five records from the data frame.

```
from sklearn.preprocessing import LabelEncoder

tras = LabelEncoder()

df_train['area_code_tr'] = tras.fit_transform(df_train['area_code'])

df_train.columns

del df_train['area_code']

df_train.columns
```

There are some string columns present in the data, such as area code. This data needs to be converted to numbers by using a label encoder. This is required for model training, as you cannot use the string variables as they are.

```
df_train['target_churn_dum'] = pd.get_dummies(df_train.
churn,prefix='churn',drop_first=True)
df_train.columns
del df_train['international_plan']
del df_train['voice_mail_plan']
del df_train['churn']
df_train.info()
df_train.columns
```

As a next step, you are going to split the dataset into train and test datasets. The train set is to develop a model and the test set is to generate inferences or predictions.

```
from sklearn.model_selection import train_test_split

df_train.columns

X = df_train[['account_length', 'number_vmail_messages', 'total_day_
minutes',
        'total_day_calls', 'total_day_charge', 'total_eve_minutes',
        'total_eve_calls', 'total_eve_charge', 'total_night_minutes',
        'total_night_calls', 'total_night_charge', 'total_intl_minutes',
        'total_intl_calls', 'total_intl_charge',
        'number_customer_service_calls', 'area_code_tr']]
Y = df_train['target_churn_dum']
```

```
xtrain,xtest,ytrain,ytest=train_test_split(X,Y,test_size=0.20,stratify=Y)

tree.DecisionTreeClassifier() # plain tree model

# default hyper-parameters for a decision tree classifier
class_weight=None,
criterion='gini',
max_depth=None,
max_features=None,
max_leaf_nodes=None,
min_impurity_decrease=0.0,
min_impurity_split=None,
min_samples_leaf=1,
min_samples_split=2,
min_weight_fraction_leaf=0.0,
presort=False,
random_state=None,
splitter='best'

dt1 = tree.DecisionTreeClassifier()
dt1.fit(xtrain,ytrain)
print(dt1.score(xtrain,ytrain))
print(dt1.score(xtest,ytest))
```

Table 4-1. *Hyper Parameter Explanation for Decision Tree*

Parameters	Explanation
Class_weight	Weights associated with classes
Criterion	The function to measure the quality of a split, gini, and entropy
max_depth	The maximum depth of the tree
max_features	The number of features to consider when looking for the best split
max_leaf_nodes	Grow a tree with max_leaf_nodes in best-first fashion
min_samples_leaf	The minimum number of samples required to be at a leaf node
min_samples_split	The minimum number of samples required to split an internal node

There are many other hyper parameters in the decision tree model, but the important ones are mentioned in Table 4-1. Some hyper parameters are used to control the overfitting of the model and some hyper parameters are used to increase the accuracy of the model.

Creating the Model

The next step is to create the model and verify the accuracy between the train and test accuracy. There are two models, dt1 and dt2: one has a restricted maximum depth and the other has no limit to the maximum depth. The difference is that dt1 is an overfitted model and dt2 is a model where tree pruning happened and there is no overfit of the model.

```
dt1 = tree.DecisionTreeClassifier()
dt1.fit(xtrain,ytrain)
print(dt1.score(xtrain,ytrain))
print(dt1.score(xtest,ytest))

1.0
0.8590704647676162

dt2 = tree.DecisionTreeClassifier(max_depth=3)
dt2.fit(xtrain,ytrain)
print(dt2.score(xtrain,ytrain))
print(dt2.score(xtest,ytest))

0.9021005251312828
0.8875562218890555
```

The limitation of an unrestricted overfitted model is that it will produce a large decision tree and the rules to arrive at a prediction will be many. Thus all the rules may not be important because as the tree grows, some redundant rules may take part in the tree construction process.

```
!pip install pydotplus
!pip install graphviz
import pydotplus
```

```
dot_data = tree.export_graphviz(dt1, out_file=None, filled=True, rounded=True,
                                feature_names=list(xtrain.columns),
                                class_names=['yes','no'])
graph = pydotplus.graph_from_dot_data(dot_data)
display(Image(graph.create_png()))
```

Figure 4-4. *Decision tree visualization with default model using GraphViz*

The decision tree trained with all the default hyper parameters will produce a large tree and will also lead to the generation of multiple rules, which is not only difficult to interpret but is also hard to implement in a real-life project scenario. The largest possible decision tree as shown in Figure 4-4 is a result of setting the maximum depth of tree parameters to None, which means you ask the decision tree to keep growing branches.

```
dot_data = tree.export_graphviz(dt2, out_file=None, filled=True, rounded=True,
                                feature_names=list(xtrain.columns),
                                class_names=['yes','no'])
graph = pydotplus.graph_from_dot_data(dot_data)
display(Image(graph.create_png()))
```

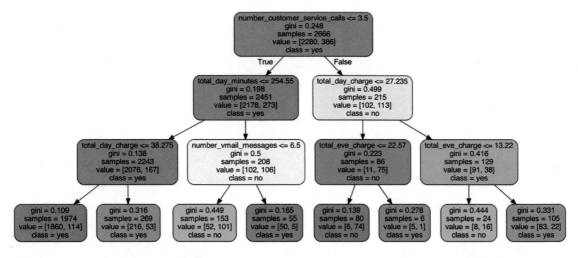

Figure 4-5. *A pruned version of same decision tree model*

```
tree.plot_tree(dt1)
tree.plot_tree(dt2)
```

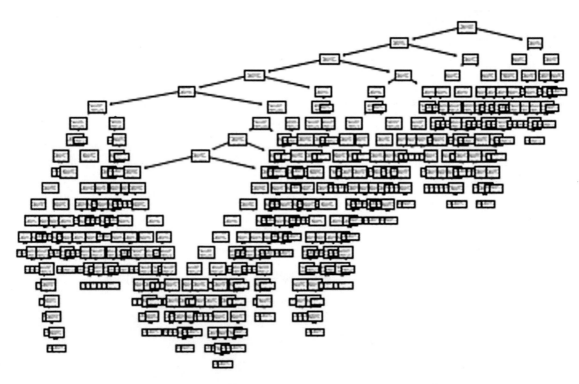

Figure 4-6. *Decision tree visualization using the plot_tree method*

The same model shown in Figure 4-4 is reproduced in Figure 4-5 and 4-6. The latter figure is reproduced with another option using the sklearn Python library's built-in function plot_tree. There is no difference; it is just a matter of two libraries. If there is an issue with the GraphViz library installation or the Pydotplus library installation in a production environment, you can switch to the plot tree function.

The tree from the dt1 model is so big that it becomes difficult for anyone to navigate and interpret the results. After applying the tree pruning method of restricting the maximum depth parameter to 3, you can see a much smaller tree with only relevant features taking part in the tree construction (Figure 4-7).

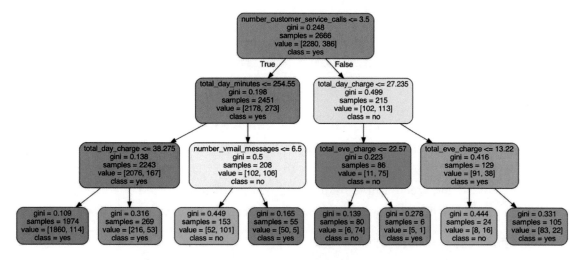

Figure 4-7. *A pruned version of the decision tree model shown in Figure 4-5*

The pruned version of the decision tree model object dt2 uses a maximum depth parameter of 3, which means after the third layer of branching, the tree should stop further expansion. This version of the model produces a smaller tree with robust rules as an if/else conditions to be used. This is a most conservative approach of modelling a decision tree free from overfitting.

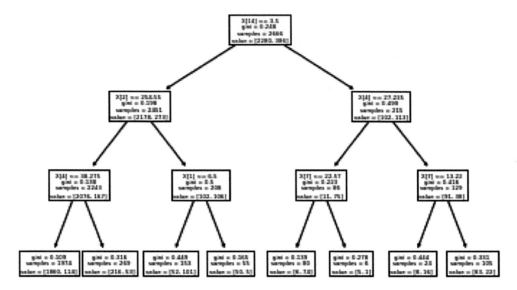

Figure 4-8. *A pruned tree visual using the plot tree function*

The version of the decision tree shown in Figure 4-8 uses fewer rules, which makes it easier to understand how a decision is made and easier to integrate into any production system.

If you want to interpret or implement or embed the rules generated by the decision tree model into some other external application, you can do that by exporting the rule text.

```
from sklearn.tree import export_text
r = export_text(dt1,feature_names=list(xtrain.columns))
print(r)
```

From the dt1 model many rules are generated, which are difficult to interpret. Let's have a look at the dt2 model generated rule. Class 0 is a no-churn scenario and class 1 is an indicator for a possible churn customer. The rule text shows that if the total day charge is less than or equal to 44.96, the number of customer service calls is less than or equal to 3.5, and the total day minutes is less than or equal to 223.25, then it is a no-churn case. Similarly, the reverse scenario can be interpreted as a churn scenario. You can print and look at all the rules below.

```
from sklearn.tree import export_text
r = export_text(dt2,feature_names=list(xtrain.columns))
print(r)
```

```
|--- number_customer_service_calls <= 3.50
|    |--- total_day_minutes <= 254.55
|    |    |--- total_day_charge <= 38.27
|    |    |    |--- class: 0
|    |    |--- total_day_charge >  38.27
|    |    |    |--- class: 0
|    |--- total_day_minutes >  254.55
|    |    |--- number_vmail_messages <= 6.50
|    |    |    |--- class: 1
|    |    |--- number_vmail_messages >  6.50
|    |    |    |--- class: 0
|--- number_customer_service_calls >  3.50
|    |--- total_day_charge <= 27.24
|    |    |--- total_eve_charge <= 22.57
|    |    |    |--- class: 1
|    |    |--- total_eve_charge >  22.57
|    |    |    |--- class: 0
|    |--- total_day_charge >  27.24
|    |    |--- total_eve_charge <= 13.22
|    |    |    |--- class: 1
|    |    |--- total_eve_charge >  13.22
|    |    |    |--- class: 0
```

The feature importance from the dt1 model is shown below.

```
list(zip(dt1.feature_importances_,xtrain.columns))
```

```
[(0.04051943775304626, 'account_length'),
 (0.08298083105277364, 'number_vmail_messages'),
 (0.0644144400251063, 'total_day_minutes'),
 (0.028172622004021135, 'total_day_calls'),
 (0.20486110565087778, 'total_day_charge'),
 (0.10259170929879882, 'total_eve_minutes'),
 (0.03586253729017199, 'total_eve_calls'),
 (0.0673761405897894, 'total_eve_charge'),
 (0.0613662104733965, 'total_night_minutes'),
 (0.05654698887273517, 'total_night_calls'),
```

```
 (0.03894924950827072, 'total_night_charge'),
 (0.01615654226052593, 'total_intl_minutes'),
 (0.039418913794511345, 'total_intl_calls'),
 (0.02842685405881307, 'total_intl_charge'),
 (0.11203068621155501, 'number_customer_service_calls'),
 (0.020325731155606916, 'area_code_tr')]
# extract the arrays that define the tree
children_left = dt2.tree_.children_left
children_right = dt2.tree_.children_right
children_default = children_right.copy() # because sklearn does not use
                                                    missing values
features = dt2.tree_.feature
thresholds = dt2.tree_.threshold
values = dt2.tree_.value.reshape(dt2.tree_.value.shape[0], 2)
node_sample_weight = dt2.tree_.weighted_n_node_samples

print("      children_left", children_left)
# note that negative children values mean this is a leaf node
print("     children_right", children_right)
print("   children_default", children_default)
print("            features", features)
print("          thresholds", thresholds.round(3))
print("              values", values.round(3))
print("node_sample_weight", node_sample_weight)
```

The decision tree classifier model has an attribute called tree_, which allows you to get a detailed explanation about the model object. It stores the entire binary tree structure in the form of parallel arrays. Node 0 is the root node and the rest of the parameters are explained in Table 4-2. The ID of the left child or right child whenever it assumes a negative value such as -1 implies that it is a leaf node, where the decision tree terminates.

Table 4-2. *Low-Level Attribute Extraction for a Decision Tree*

Parameters	Explanation
dt2.tree_.node_count	Total number of nodes in the tree
tree_.children_left[i]	Id of the left child of node i
tree_.children_right[i]	Id of the right child of node i
tree_. feature[i]	Feature used for splitting node i
tree_.threshold[i]	Threshold value at node i
tree_.n_node_samples[i]	The number of training samples reaching node i
tree_. impurity[i]	The impurity at node i
tree_.weighted_n_node_samples	n_node_samples is the count of actual dataset samples in each node. weighted_n_node_samples is the same, weighted by the class_weight and/or sample_weight.

```
# define a custom tree model
tree_dict = {
    "children_left": children_left,
    "children_right": children_right,
    "children_default": children_default,
    "features": features,
    "thresholds": thresholds,
    "values": values,
    "node_sample_weight": node_sample_weight
}
model = {
    "trees": [tree_dict]
}

import shap
explainer = shap.TreeExplainer(model)

# Provide Probability as Output
def model_churn_proba(x):
    return dt2.predict_proba(x)[:,1]
```

```
# Provide Log Odds as Output
def model_churn_log_odds(x):
    p = dt2.predict_log_proba(x)
    return p[:,1] - p[:,0]

# make a standard partial dependence plot
sample_ind = 25
fig,ax = shap.partial_dependence_plot(
    "total_day_minutes", model_churn_proba, X, model_expected_value=True,
    feature_expected_value=True, show=False, ice=False
)
```

Decision Tree – SHAP

The SHAP Python library can be used to explain a decision tree. The SHAP library has useful functions that provide additional insights into model explainability.

```
import shap
explainer = shap.TreeExplainer(model)
# Provide Probability as Output
def model_churn_proba(x):
    return dt2.predict_proba(x)[:,1]

# Provide Log Odds as Output
def model_churn_log_odds(x):
    p = dt2.predict_log_proba(x)
    return p[:,1] - p[:,0]
# make a standard partial dependence plot
sample_ind = 25
fig,ax = shap.partial_dependence_plot(
    "total_day_minutes", model_churn_proba, X, model_expected_value=True,
    feature_expected_value=True, show=False, ice=False
)
```

Partial Dependency Plot

A partial dependency plot (PDP) is used to visualize the interaction between the feature and target columns or the response column. The target column has two labels: 0 for no-churn cases and 1 for churn cases. When you use the predict probability function you can generate the probability for class 0 and class 1.

```
pd.DataFrame(dt2.predict_proba(X)) # 0 - No Churn, 1- Churn
model_churn_proba(X).max()
model_churn_proba(X).mean()
model_churn_proba(X).min()
```

In the above script is a function to select column 1, which is the probability of churn. As an example, the first record shows a probability of 0.090909, which means the chance of churn is less than 10%. You can conclude that it is a no-churn sample. In the following script, model_churn_proba only shows the second column probability of churn.

Before plotting the probability of churn against the feature of total day minutes, which is shown in the PDP plot in Figure 4-10, you should take a look at the distribution of probability of churn using a distribution plot. This will help you get an idea about interpreting the partial dependency plot. The probability distribution is shown in Figure 4-9.

```
import seaborn as sns
sns.distplot(model_churn_proba(X))
pd.DataFrame(model_churn_proba(X))
from sklearn.inspection import plot_partial_dependence
xtrain.columns
plot_partial_dependence(dt2, X, ['account_length', 'number_vmail_messages',
'total_day_minutes'])
plot_partial_dependence(dt2, X, [
      'total_day_calls', 'total_day_charge', 'total_eve_minutes',
  ])
plot_partial_dependence(dt2, X, [
      'total_eve_calls', 'total_eve_charge', 'total_night_minutes'])
```

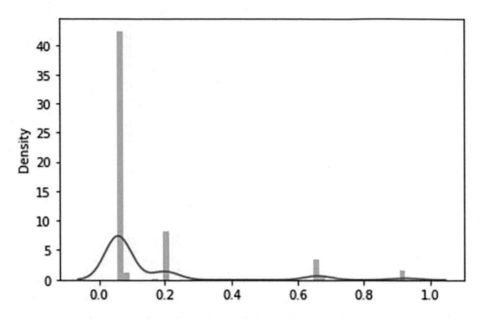

Figure 4-9. *Distribution of probability of churn from a decision tree model*

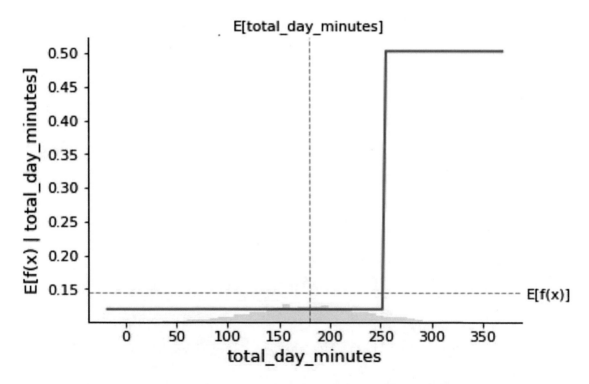

Figure 4-10. *Total day minutes and the probability of churn PDP*

The expected value of total day minutes and total day minutes represented on the graph in Figure 4-10 is piecewise linear, but when you look at the entire blue line it is not linear. This is a local interpretation for sample number 25. Total day minutes is a numeric and is considered as a continuous column in the training dataset. For the same sample observation 25, the number of voice mail message also impacts the marginal contribution of this feature to the churn prediction. In Figure 4-10, if the user spends up to 225 total day minutes, then the probability of churn is going to be less than or equal to the average probability of churn, which is 14.25. Even in cases where the total day minutes are greater than 225 minutes, still the probability of churn is less than 25%.

```
# make a standard partial dependence plot
sample_ind = 25
fig,ax = shap.partial_dependence_plot(
    "number_vmail_messages", model_churn_proba, X, model_expected_value=True,
    feature_expected_value=True, show=False, ice=False
)
```

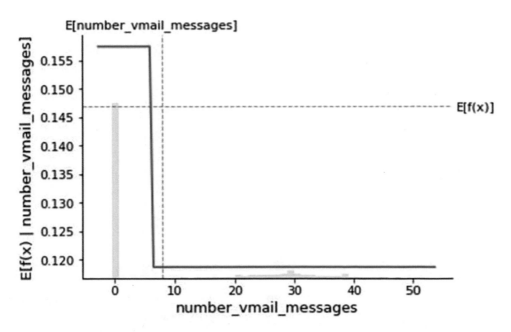

Figure 4-11. *PDP for number of voice mail messages with probability of churn*

When you look at the relationship between the marginal contribution of account length to the churn prediction and account length, you can see a blue parallel line (Figure 4-11). It indicates that irrespective of the account length the marginal contribution stays constant, which indicates that this feature has no predictive value, it is not important, and it does not play a role in the churn prediction model.

```
# make a standard partial dependence plot
sample_ind = 25
fig,ax = shap.partial_dependence_plot(
    "account_length", model_churn_proba, X, model_expected_value=True,
    feature_expected_value=True, show=False, ice=False
)
```

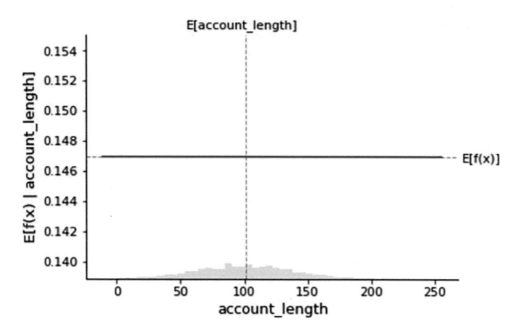

Figure 4-12. *PDP for account length feature*

The PDP for account length has no impact on the probability of churn, which is clearly evident from the blue straight line in Figure 4-12. The blue line follows the average probability of the churn value.

```
# make a standard partial dependence plot
sample_ind = 25
fig,ax = shap.partial_dependence_plot(
    "number_customer_service_calls", model_churn_proba, X, model_expected_
    value=True,
    feature_expected_value=True, show=False, ice=False
)
```

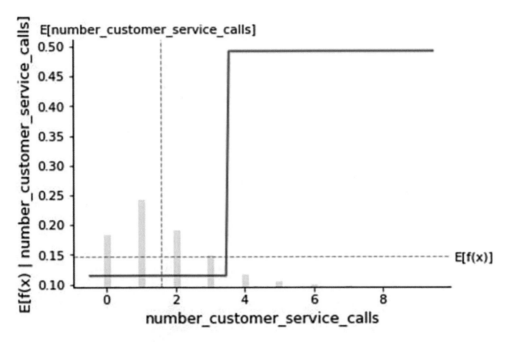

Figure 4-13. *PDP for number of customer service calls*

It is important to note that the higher the number of customer service calls, the higher the probability of churn. This is because someone is facing issues, which is why the number of customer service calls goes up. You can see the same pattern in Figure 4-13: more than four calls increases the probability of churn.

```
# make a standard partial dependence plot
sample_ind = 25
fig,ax = shap.partial_dependence_plot(
    "total_day_charge", model_churn_proba, X, model_expected_value=True,
    feature_expected_value=True, show=False, ice=False
)
```

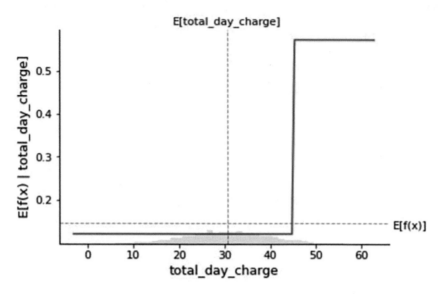

Figure 4-14. *PDP for total day charges*

If the total day charges exceeds $45, then the probability of churn will be higher (Figure 4-14). This is due to higher charges; the user would be forced to opt for alternate providers.

```
# make a standard partial dependence plot
sample_ind = 25
fig,ax = shap.partial_dependence_plot(
    "total_eve_minutes", model_churn_proba, X, model_expected_value=True,
    feature_expected_value=True, show=False, ice=False
)
```

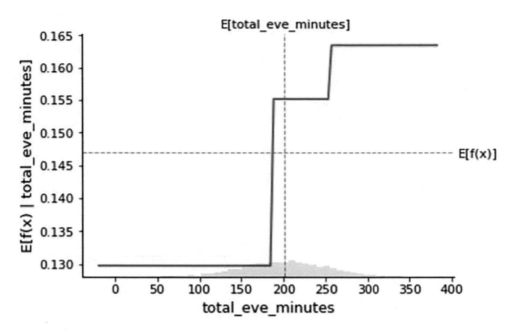

Figure 4-15. *PDP for total evening minutes*

The total evening minutes shows some impact on the probability of churn, but it doesn't change a user from a no-churn case to a churn case (Figure 4-15). The probability of churn remains very low and constant for up to 180 total evening minutes, which is 13%. The probability of churn increases slightly to 15.5% at more than 180 minutes. The probability increases to 16.5% at 250 minutes and after 250 total evening minutes, which is comparatively very low.

```
# make a standard partial dependence plot
sample_ind = 25
fig,ax = shap.partial_dependence_plot(
    "total_eve_calls", model_churn_proba, X, model_expected_value=True,
    feature_expected_value=True, show=False, ice=False
)
```

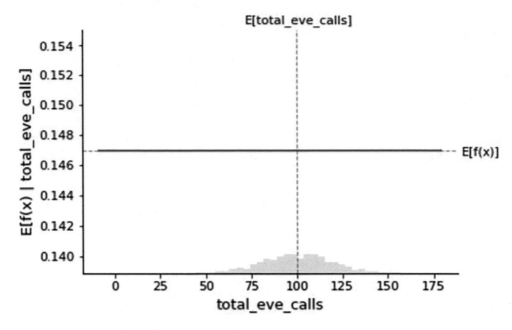

Figure 4-16. *PDP of total evening calls*

The total evening calls has no impact on the probability of churn, as the probability remains unchanged at the average probability value, irrespective of the increase in total evening calls (Figure 4-16). Table 4-3 shows the feature importance score for each feature.

```
shap_values_churn.feature_names
temp_df = pd.DataFrame()
temp_df['Feature Name'] = pd.Series(X.columns)
temp_df['Score'] = pd.Series(dt2.feature_importances_.flatten())
temp_df.sort_values(by='Score',ascending=False)
```

Table 4-3. *Feature Importance Score for Each Feature*

Feature name		Score
4	total_day_charge	0.306375
14	number_customer_service_calls	0.282235
2	total_day_minutes	0.223336
1	number_vmail_messages	0.105760
5	total_eve_minutes	0.082294
0	account_length	0.000000
3	total_day_calls	0.000000
6	total_eve_calls	0.000000
7	total_eve_charge	0.000000
8	total_night_minutes	0.000000
9	total_night_calls	0.000000
10	total_night_charge	0.000000
11	total_intl_minutes	0.000000
12	total_intl_calls	0.000000
13	total_intl_charge	0.000000
15	area_code_tr	0.000000

In the above figures, you saw SHAP library-based partial dependency plot graphs. The same can be generated using the scikit-learn library inspection module.

PDP Using Scikit-Learn

There is a new module in the scikit-learn suite of modules that can help you generate partial dependency plots. You can use the inspection module from the scikit-learn library. See Figures 4-17 through 4-22.

```
from sklearn.inspection import plot_partial_dependence
xtrain.columns
plot_partial_dependence(dt2, X, ['account_length', 'number_vmail_messages',
'total_day_minutes'])
```

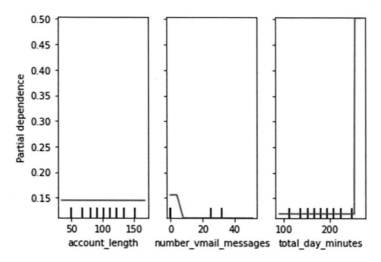

Figure 4-17. *PDP for three variables together*

```
plot_partial_dependence(dt2, X, [
       'total_day_calls', 'total_day_charge', 'total_eve_minutes',
  ])
```

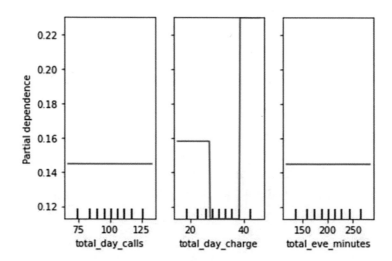

Figure 4-18. *PDP for the next set of three features*

```
plot_partial_dependence(dt2, X, [
      'total_eve_calls', 'total_eve_charge', 'total_night_minutes'])
```

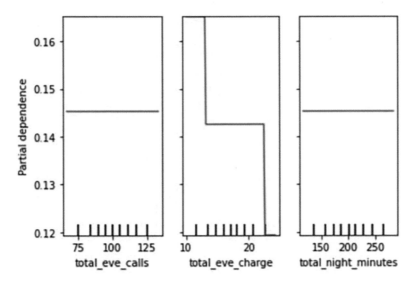

Figure 4-19. *PDP for another three variables*

```
plot_partial_dependence(dt2, X, [
      'total_night_calls', 'total_night_charge', 'total_intl_minutes'])
```

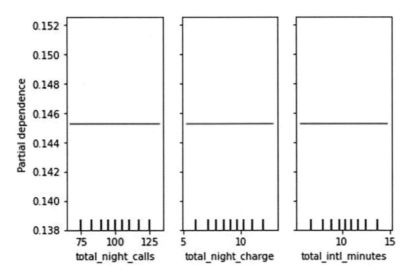

Figure 4-20. *PDP of three features that do not impact the probability of churn*

```
plot_partial_dependence(dt2, X, [
        'total_intl_calls', 'total_intl_charge'])
```

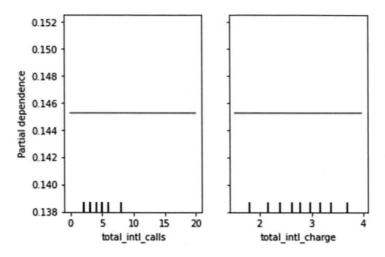

Figure 4-21. *PDP of total international calls and total international charges*

```
plot_partial_dependence(dt2,X, [
        'number_customer_service_calls', 'area_code_tr'])
```

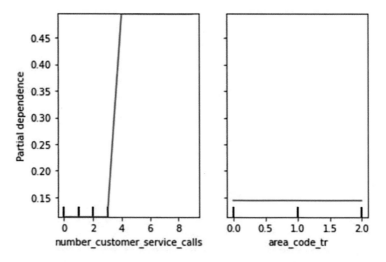

Figure 4-22. *PDP for number of customer service calls and area code*

Figures 4-17 through 4-22 are generated through a function that is part of the scikit-learn library, which produces an explanation similar to the SHAP library. The interpretations also can be derived in a similar fashion.

Non-Linear Model Explanation – LIME

The top important features that play a role in the churn prediction process are total day charge, number of customer service calls, total day minutes, number of voice mail messages, and total evening minutes. The other features have no role to play, so the partial dependency plots for the unrelated features are parallel lines.

You can also leverage some functions from the LIME Python library to explain the decisions made by the decision tree model.

```
import lime
import lime.lime_tabular

explainer = lime.lime_tabular.LimeTabularExplainer(np.array(xtrain),
                    feature_names=list(xtrain.columns),
                    class_names=['target_churn_dum'],
                    verbose=True, mode='classification')
# this record is a no churn scenario
exp = explainer.explain_instance(xtest.iloc[0], dt2.predict_proba,
                                num_features=16)
exp.as_list()
pd.DataFrame(exp.as_list())
exp.show_in_notebook(show_table=True)
```

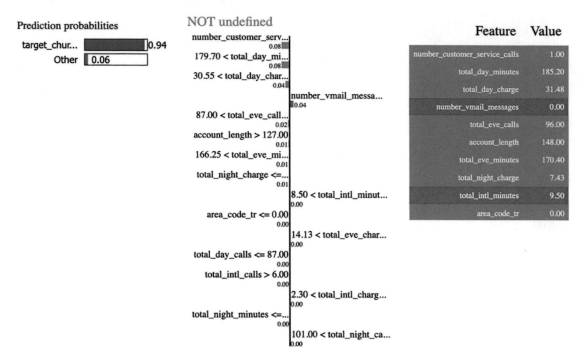

Figure 4-23. *Feature importance and positive and negative contribution towards prediction probabilities of record 0*

Figure 4-23 shows the local interpretation model explanation for the first record from test set xtest[0] The middle chart in Figure 4-23 shows two colors. The blue color shows the contribution to the target churn prediction probability and the orange color shows the contribution towards the other class, which is the no-churn scenario. The decision tree produces features as a range of values such as total day minutes between 179.90 and 216.20 as a feature contributes to churn probability by 0.08 (8%). If you remove two features from the model number of customer service calls <= 1.00 and total day minutes > 179.90 and <= 216.20, then the target churn prediction probability will reduce by 0.16 (16%), that is (0.94 – 0.08 -0.08) which is 0.78 (78%). On the other hand, if you remove the number of voice mail messages <=0.00, then the target churn probability increases by 4% (0.04). The third table in Figure 4-23 shows the contribution value of each feature towards the prediction. A similar kind of analysis and interpretation can be done for few more records, as shown in Figures 4-24 through 4-26.

```
# This is s churn scenario
exp = explainer.explain_instance(xtest.iloc[20], dt2.predict_proba,
num_features=16)
```

```
exp.as_list()
exp.show_in_notebook(show_table=True)
```

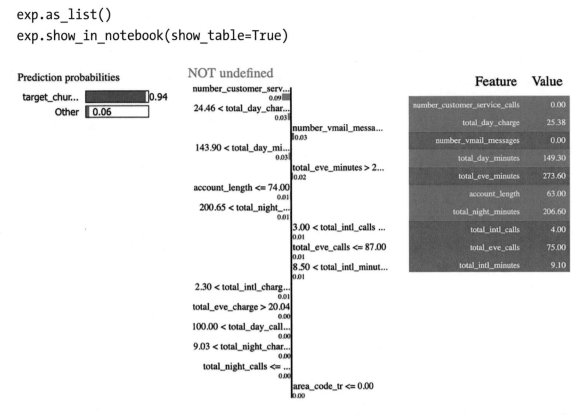

Figure 4-24. *Feature importance and positive and negative contributions towards prediction probabilities for record number 20*

```
xtest.iloc[20]
ytest.iloc[20]
dt2.predict(xtest)[20]
explainer = lime.lime_tabular.LimeTabularExplainer(np.array(xtrain),
                feature_names=list(xtrain.columns),
                class_names=['target_churn_dum'],
                verbose=True, mode='classification')
# Code for SP-LIME
import warnings
from lime import submodular_pick
```

```
# SP-LIME returns exaplanations on a sample set to provide a non redundant
global decision boundary of original model
```

```
sp_obj = submodular_pick.SubmodularPick(explainer, np.array(xtrain),
                                        dt2.predict_proba,
                                        num_features=14,
                                        num_exps_desired=10)
```

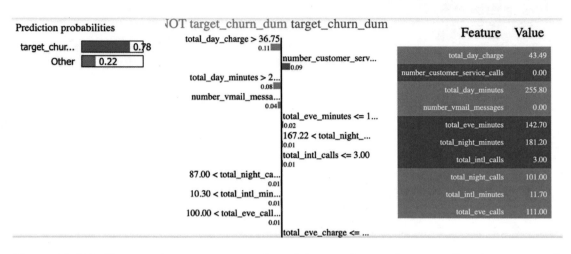

Figure 4-25. *Feature importance and positive and negative contributions towards prediction probabilities for all records*

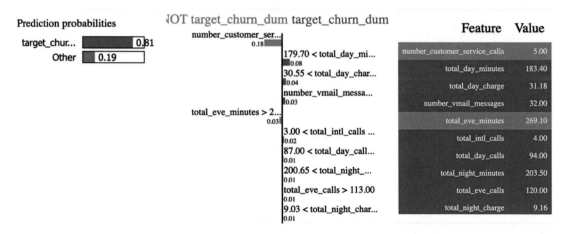

Figure 4-26. *Feature importance and positive and negative contributions towards prediction probabilities of all records*

Non-Linear Explanation – Skope-Rules

There is another explainability library named Skope-rules that can be used to generate rules from the training model, and the rules can be used to make predictions on any new dataset.

The following code can be used to install the Python-based library. See Table 4-4 for the parameters.

```
!pip install skope-rules
import six
import sys
sys.modules['sklearn.externals.six'] = six
import skrules
from skrules import SkopeRules
clf = SkopeRules(max_depth_duplication=2,
                 n_estimators=30,
                 precision_min=0.3,
                 recall_min=0.1,
                 feature_names=list(xtrain.columns))
clf
clf.fit(xtrain,ytrain)
print('The 5 most precise rules are the following:')
for rule in clf.rules_[:5]:
    print(rule[0])
```

Table 4-4. *Explaining the Skope-Rules Parameters*

Parameters	Explanation
feature_names	The name of each feature to be used for returning rules in a string format
precision_min	The minimal precision of a rule to be selected
recall_min	The minimal recall of a rule to be selected
n_estimators	The number of base estimators (rules) to use for a prediction
max_depth_duplication	The maximum depth of the decision tree for rule deduplication
max_depth	The maximum depth of the decision trees
max_samples	The number of samples to draw from X to train each decision tree, from which rules are generated and selected

Using the clf.fit() method the decision tree model can be trained and the following rules can be drawn. The rules can be filtered or curated using precision and recall parameters. The threshold value if reduced to a lower level means a lot of rules will be generated, which is of no use to the user as false positive rules will enter the business application. A higher threshold will reduce the number of rules and only the most relevant rules will be used in the business applications.

The five most precise rules are the following:

```
number_vmail_messages <= 5.5 and number_customer_service_calls <= 3.5 and
total_day_minutes > 249.70000457763672

number_vmail_messages <= 6.5 and total_day_charge > 44.989999771118164 and
total_eve_minutes > 145.39999389648438

number_customer_service_calls > 3.5 and total_day_minutes <=
263.5500030517578 and total_day_charge <= 29.514999389648438

number_customer_service_calls <= 3.5 and total_day_minutes >
245.0999984741211 and total_eve_minutes > 204.20000457763672

number_customer_service_calls > 3.5 and total_day_charge <=
30.65999984741211
```

```
clf.predict(xtest)
clf.predict_top_rules(xtest,5)
clf.score_top_rules(xtest)
```

The predict function uses all rules to predict the target churn class: 0 is no churn and 1 is churn.

The predict_top_rules function is used to leverage the five rules to predict the outcome. Five is the number of rules used for the prediction. If one of the n_rules most performing rules is activated, the prediction is equal to 1. For each observation, the function tells whether or not (1 or 0) it should be considered as an outlier according to the selected rules.

```
clf.decision_function(xtrain)
clf.decision_function(xtest)
```

Score top rules, representing an ordering between the base classifiers (rules). The score is high when the instance is detected by a performing rule. Positive scores represent outliers and null scores represent inliers.

The decision function is the anomaly score of an input sample and is computed as the weighted sum of the binary rules outputs, the weight being the respective precision of each rule. For the anomaly score of the input samples, the higher it is, the more abnormal it is. Positive scores represent outliers and null scores represent inliers.

Conclusion

In this chapter, you learned how to interpret non-linear models, specifically decision tree models, instead of logistic regression for binary classification. In a similar fashion, the decision tree model can be used for a regression model and can also be extended to multinomial classification. The non-linear models are simpler ones to interpret and everyone understands how these models work using simple if/then else rules. Therefore there is a high degree of trust in the tree-based non-linear models. In this chapter, you looked various angles for creating views for non-linear models using the explainable AI libraries such as LIME, SHAP, and Skope-rules. In the next chapter, you are going to learn about model explainability for ensemble models.

## CHAPTER 5

Explainability for Ensemble Models

Ensemble models are a group of models where the predictions are aggregated using some metric in order to generate a final prediction. As an example, a group of tree-based models can be developed to predict a real valued output, like a regression model. The predictions from all of the trees are averaged and taken for the final output. In a similar way, classification models generate individual class predictions and then take a voting rule. The class with the highest number is taken as final output. The ensemble models are not only difficult to interpret but also difficult to explain to the end user. Consider a scenario where four trees predict Yes, and six trees predict No; we will consider No as the final answer based on the majority rule of 6/4. Here it is hard to explain to the end user why some models predicted yes. Hence it is very important to explain the ensemble models. In this chapter, you are going to use SHAP predominantly to explain ensemble model predictions.

Ensemble Models

Ensemble models are the most complex set of models that need detailed explanation as the output is a combined result of multiple predictions. *Ensemble* simply implies *grouping*. What is important in the case of ensemble models is how to explain the predictions, which model variant actually produced the prediction, and how to read the marginal contribution of the features in the final prediction process.

The advantage of the decision tree model is that it takes into consideration the potential non-linearity existing in the dataset. The variable interactions come into play while generating model predictions. However, the limitation of decision tree model is that it is prone to bias, as the powerful or stronger features take part in the

© Pradeepta Mishra 2022
P. Mishra, *Practical Explainable AI Using Python*, https://doi.org/10.1007/978-1-4842-7158-2_5

tree construction process and weak features are not able to enter the tree branching process as they lack predictive power. Hence the model becomes biased towards a few selective and stronger features from the dataset. This also sometimes leads to model overfitting. To balance out the impact of strong features, it is important to regulate the entry of features into the tree-based models. If you keep the strong features out of the model creation step and only include the weak features in the tree creation, you will still be able to generate predictions, but this will again be a biased model. Hence treating the model bias and at the same time controlling the overfitting can only be done when you use a combination of strong and weak features in the tree construction process. The combination can be done purely based on a bootstrap method, and number of trees can be increased sufficiently to average out the predictions.

Types of Ensemble Models

The ensemble models are of three types: bagging models (also known as bootstrap aggregation models), boosting models, and stacking models (Figure 5-1). The stacking models can be of two types: same group stacking and different variant model stacking. The same group stacking involves homogenous model types such as only including tree-based models and putting each model outcome against the other models. The heterogeneous stacking model means putting tree-based and non-tree-based models against each other and combining their predictions. Model explainability for stacking models is not difficult at all as we can identify the particular model and explain the predictions and parameters; however, explaining the bagging and boosting models are little tricky. The random forest model is an example of a bagging model, where many trees are grown and finally the predictions are combined to arrive at final result. Boosting models take a base model and learn from the results of the base model and try to improve the model in an iterative manner.

Bagging   Boosting   Stacking

Figure 5-1. *Three types of ensemble models*

Why Ensemble Models?

When the total number of features in a dataset increases, say to over 50, it cannot be accommodated in a single decision tree due to the following reasons:

- The features that are powerful will occupy the branch creation step in the decision tree construction; hence the weak features will not take part in the tree formation.

- The models in a single decision tree scenario become more biased because a few powerful features govern the prediction.

- Hyper parameter choices are limited due to a few powerful features.

- This problem even gets bigger when you think that of 100 plus features, 20% of the powerful features drive the prediction. The remaining 80% of the weak features are unutilized.

- Due to a single tree, not all features get a fair chance in the prediction.

- Bias mitigation in a single decision tree scenario is mostly done by pruning.

In order to address the above limitations of a single decision tree model, there is a need to have a group of trees, hence the name *tree ensembles*. Bagging, boosting, and stacking models can be applied to regression-based problems as well as classification based-problems. Figure 5-2 offers a pictorial view of differentiating the three types of ensemble models.

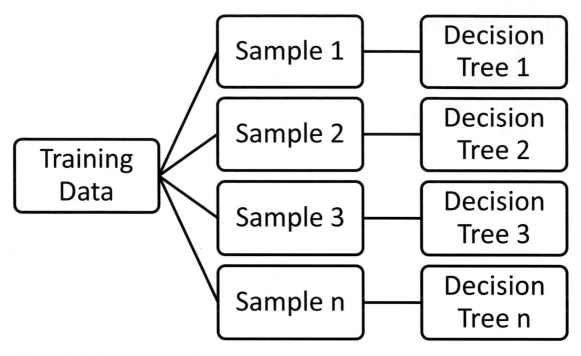

Figure 5-2. Bagging model

Bagging (also known as bootstrap aggregation) takes different samples of features and records from the training dataset and tries to train a decision tree. In Figure 5-2, you can develop n trees where n can be 100, 500, or 1000. As you increase the number of trees, the accuracy of the model goes up when you have more features in a training dataset. If you have less features and samples, and if you increase the number of trees, then you will be able to get more accuracy, but in the process you will generate a lot of duplicate trees. They are duplicate trees because the same set of features appears in each tree. Bagging is parallel in nature, as you can train multiple trees in parallel for both classification and regression-based tasks. Hence it is recommended to use ensemble when you have more than 50 features and more than 50,000 records in the training dataset, as per industry practice.

Boosting, on the other hand, is a sequential process where a base classifier is trained to classify or predict the target column. Then correctly predicted cases are separated in the classification scenario and the error distribution is picked up in a regression-based scenario in order to retrain the model on the same configuration or setting. This process is repeated multiple times, until there is no possibility of improving the accuracy further. This is sequential in nature because the second model works on the results of the first model. This is a powerful technique to get the ensemble models. The process is explained in Figure 5-3.

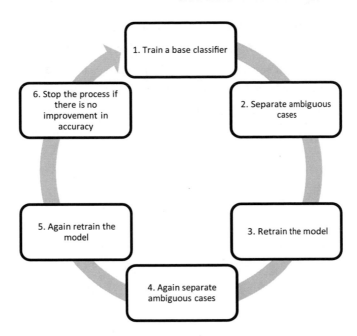

Figure 5-3. *Boosting model training process*

The third variant of the ensemble model is stacking. There two ways to stack model predictions: homogenous group stacking and heterogeneous group stacking. See Table 5-1.

Table 5-1. *Regression Problem Homogenous Group Stacking*

	Models					
Test data	**DT**	**RF**	**Adaptive boosting**	**Gradient boosting**	**XGBoost**	**Prediction**
1	25.3	25.2	24.3	26.1	24.5	25.08
2	12.5	13.21	14.1	11.9	12.2	12.782
3	17.8	15.3	16.3	16.7	17.1	16.64

The last column, Prediction, is the average of the values predicted by different models. You considered only three records from the test dataset. Now see Table 5-2.

Table 5-2. *Classification Problem Homogenous Group Stacking*

	Models					
Data	**DT**	**RF**	**Adaptive boosting**	**Gradient boosting**	**XGBoost**	**Prediction**
1	Yes	No	Yes	Yes	Yes	Yes
2	No	No	No	Yes	No	No
3	Yes	Yes	No	No	No	No

In the first row there are four Yes answers and one No, hence the final prediction is Yes. Likewise, in the second and third rows, the final prediction is guided by majority voting. In a heterogeneous stacking scenario, not only the tree-based models but other models can take part, such as logistic regression models, support vector machine models, etc. In Table 5-3, you can see the regression model heterogeneous group stacking and in Table 5-4, you can see the classification model with heterogeneous group stacking.

Table 5-3. *Regression Problem Heterogenous Group Stacking*

Data	DT	RF	Models					Prediction
			Adaptive boosting	Gradient boosting	XGBoost	SVM	LR	
1	25.3	25.2	24.3	26.1	24.5	24.9	24.6	24.98571429
2	12.5	13.21	14.1	11.9	12.2	12.6	11.9	12.63
3	17.8	15.3	16.3	16.7	17.1	16.8	17.1	16.72857143

Table 5-4. *Classification Problem Heterogenous Stacking*

Data	DT	RF	Models					Prediction
			Adaptive boosting	Gradient boosting	XGBoost	SVM	LR	
1	Yes	No	Yes	Yes	Yes	No	No	Yes
2	No	No	No	Yes	No	Yes	Yes	No
3	Yes	Yes	No	No	No	No	Yes	No

Using SHAP for Ensemble Models

You will take into consideration two different datasets. You will use the popular Boston housing prices dataset to explain the model predictions in a regression use case scenario and the adult dataset to explain the classification scenario. The following are the variables from the Boston housing prices dataset:

- CRIM: Per capita crime rate by town

- ZN: Proportion of residential land zoned for lots over 25,000 sq.ft.

- INDUS: Proportion of non-retail business acres per town

- CHAS: Charles River dummy variable (1 if tract bounds river; 0 otherwise)

- NOX: Nitric oxide concentration (parts per 10 million)

- RM: Average number of rooms per dwelling

- AGE: Proportion of owner-occupied units built prior to 1940

- DIS: Weighted distances to five Boston employment centers

- RAD: Index of accessibility to radial highways

- TAX: Full value property tax rate per $10,000

- PTRATIO: Pupil-teacher ratio by town

- B: 1000(Bk - 0.63)^2 where Bk is the proportion of blacks by town

- LSTAT: % lower status of the population

- MEDV: Median value of owner-occupied homes in $1000s

```
import pandas as pd
import shap
import sklearn

# boston Housing price prediction
X,y = shap.datasets.boston()
X100 = shap.utils.sample(X, 1000) # 1000 instances for use as the
background distribution

# a simple linear model
model = sklearn.linear_model.LinearRegression()
model.fit(X, y)
```

The Boston housing prices dataset is now part of the SHAP library. The base model calculation happens using the linear regression model so that you can perform the ensemble model on this dataset and compare the results.

```
print("Model coefficients:\n")
for i in range(X.shape[1]):
    print(X.columns[i], "=", model.coef_[i].round(4))
```

Table 5-5. *Model Coefficients from the Linear Regression Model*

Model coefficients:
CRIM = -0.108
ZN = 0.0464
INDUS = 0.0206
CHAS = 2.6867
NOX = -17.7666
RM = 3.8099
AGE = 0.0007
DIS = -1.4756
RAD = 0.306
TAX = -0.0123
PTRATIO = -0.9527
B = 0.0093
LSTAT = -0.5248

The coefficients from a base model are the starting point (Table 5-5). Subsequently you will look at the complex ensemble models and compare the coefficients with the base linear model. Also, you can compare the explanations. The better the prediction, the better the explainability.

```
shap.plots.partial_dependence(
    "RM", model.predict, X100, ice=False,
    model_expected_value=True, feature_expected_value=True
)
```

The horizontal dotted line E[f(x)] shown in Figure 5-4 is nothing but the predicted median value of the housing price average.

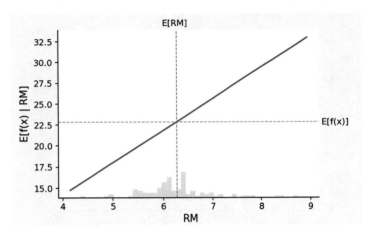

Figure 5-4. *PDP for RM and predicted housing price using the X100 subset sample*

If you take the average of the predicted outcome, it is 22.84. There is a linear relationship between the RM feature and the predicted outcome from the model, as shown in Figure 5-4.

```
# compute the SHAP values for the linear model
explainer = shap.Explainer(model.predict, X100)
shap_values = explainer(X)

# make a standard partial dependence plot
sample_ind = 18
shap.partial_dependence_plot(
    "RM", model.predict, X100, model_expected_value=True,
    feature_expected_value=True, ice=False,
    shap_values=shap_values[sample_ind:sample_ind+1,:]
)
```

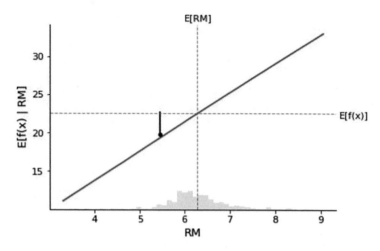

Figure 5-5. *Row number 18 from the dataset is superimposed on the PDP plot*

Figure 5-5 shows that the marginal contribution of the RM feature towards the predicted value of the target column is a linear relationship, as shown by the upward-rising straight line. The red line shows the difference between the predicted value and the average predicted value. The SHAP value is equivalent to the predicted value.

```
X100 = shap.utils.sample(X,100)
model.predict(X100).mean()
model.predict(X100).min()
model.predict(X100).max()
shap_values[18:19,:]
X[18:19]
model.predict(X[18:19])
shap_values[18:19,:].values.sum() + shap_values[18:19,:].base_values
```

So the predicted outcome for record no 18 is 16.178 and the sum of the SHAP values from different features plus the base value, which is the average prediction value, is equivalent to the predicted value, which is 16.178.

```
shap.plots.scatter(shap_values[:,"RM"])
```

In Figure 5-6, the relationship is linear because the SHAP values are generated using the linear model as an explainer. If you switch to a non-linear model, you can expect the line to be non-linear.

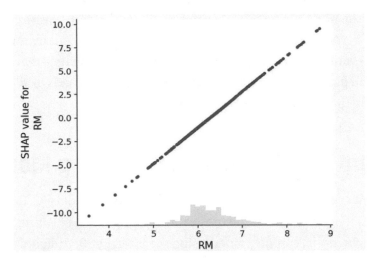

Figure 5-6. *Linear relationship between the RM and SHAP values for RM*

```
# the waterfall_plot shows how we get from shap_values.base_values to
model.predict(X)[sample_ind]
shap.plots.waterfall(shap_values[sample_ind], max_display=14)
```

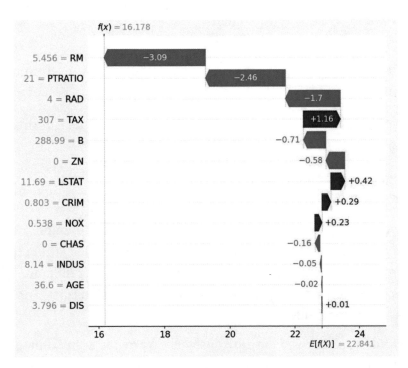

Figure 5-7. *Relationship between predicted result and SHAP values*

In Figure 5-7, the horizontal axis shows the predicted outcome average value, which is 22.841, and the vertical axis shows the SHAP values from different features. Each feature's assumed values from the dataset are shown in grey, the negative SHAP values are in blue, and the positive SHAP values are in red. The vertical axis also displays the predicted outcome for the 18th record, which is 16.178.

Using the Interpret Explaining Boosting Model

In this section, you are going to use the generalized additive models (GAM) to predict the housing prices. You can explain the model fitted using the SHAP library. The generalized additive model can be trained using the interpret Python library, and then the trained model object can be passed through the SHAP model to generate explanations for the boosting models.

The interpret library can be installed three ways:

```
!pip install interpret-core
```

This is without any dependency using the pip install process.

```
conda install -c interpretml interpret-core
```

This is using an anaconda distribution. You can install using the terminal from the conda environment.

```
git clone https://github.com/interpretml/interpret.git && cd interpret/
scripts && make install-core
```

This is straight from the source using GitHub.

The interpret Python library supports two kinds of algorithms:

- **Glassbox models**: These are designed to be more interpretable, using the scikit-learn framework, maintaining the same level of accuracy as the state-of-the-art sklearn library. They support four different kinds of models: linear models, decision trees, decision rules, and boosting-based models.

- **Blackbox explainers**: These are designed to provide approximate explanations on how the model behaves and the model predictions. These variants of algorithms will be useful when none of the components of the machine learning model are interpretable. They support Shapely explanations, LIME explanations, partial dependency plots, and Morris sensitivity analysis.

```
# fit a GAM model to the data
import interpret.glassbox
model_ebm = interpret.glassbox.ExplainableBoostingRegressor()
model_ebm.fit(X, y)
```

First, you must import the glassbox module from interpret, initialize the explainable boosting regressor, and fit the model. The model object is model_ebm.

```
# explain the GAM model with SHAP
explainer_ebm = shap.Explainer(model_ebm.predict, X100)
shap_values_ebm = explainer_ebm(X)
```

You will sample the training dataset and take 100 samples to create a background for generating explanations using the SHAP library. In the SHAP explainer you use model_ebm.predict and you take 100 samples to generate the explanations.

```
# make a standard partial dependence plot with a single SHAP value overlaid
fig,ax = shap.partial_dependence_plot(
    "RM", model_ebm.predict, X, model_expected_value=True,
    feature_expected_value=True, show=False, ice=False,
    shap_values=shap_values_ebm[sample_ind:sample_ind+1,:]
)
```

Figure 5-8 shows the boosting-based model. You can see a stage-wise break non-linear curve and the non-linear relationship between the RM values and the predicted target column, which is the average value of housing prices. Again you are explaining the same 18th record here, as shown by the red straight line.

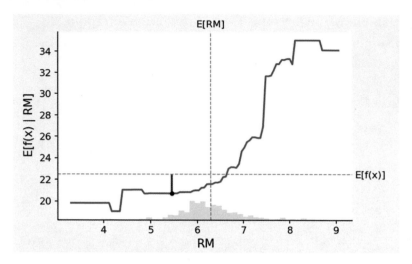

Figure 5-8. *Boosting model PDP plot for RM feature*

```
shap.plots.scatter(shap_values_ebm[:,"RM"])
```

In Figure 5-9 the relationship shows as a non-linear curve. In the initial stages, as the RM increases, the predicted value does not increase much, but after a certain stage as the RM value increases, the SHAP value for RM also increases exponentially. See also Figure 5-10.

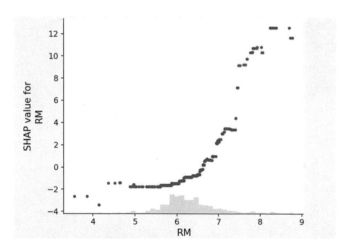

Figure 5-9. *The RM and SHAP for RM*

```
# the waterfall_plot shows how we get from explainer.expected_value to
model.predict(X)[sample_ind]
shap.plots.waterfall(shap_values_ebm[sample_ind], max_display=14)
```

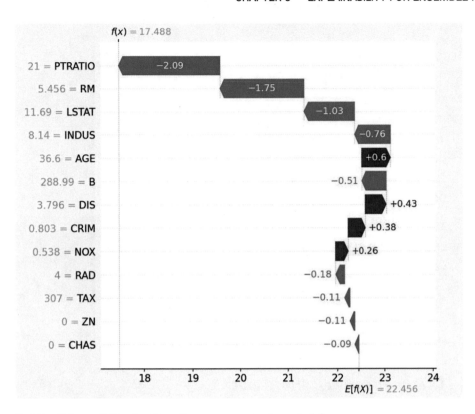

Figure 5-10. *Waterfall plot for the same set of variables*

```
# the waterfall_plot shows how we get from explainer.expected_value to
model.predict(X)[sample_ind]
shap.plots.beeswarm(shap_values_ebm, max_display=14)
```

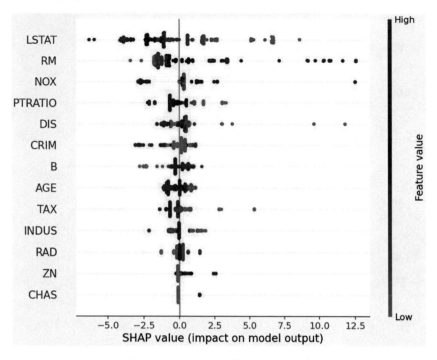

Figure 5-11. *Feature value vs. SHAP value*

Figure 5-11 is another visualization of the SHAP value and the feature value.

```
# train XGBoost model
import xgboost
model_xgb = xgboost.XGBRegressor(n_estimators=100, max_depth=2).fit(X, y)

# explain the GAM model with SHAP
explainer_xgb = shap.Explainer(model_xgb, X100)
shap_values_xgb = explainer_xgb(X)

# make a standard partial dependence plot with a single SHAP value overlaid
fig,ax = shap.partial_dependence_plot(
    "RM", model_xgb.predict, X, model_expected_value=True,
    feature_expected_value=True, show=False, ice=False,
    shap_values=shap_values_ebm[sample_ind:sample_ind+1,:]
)
```

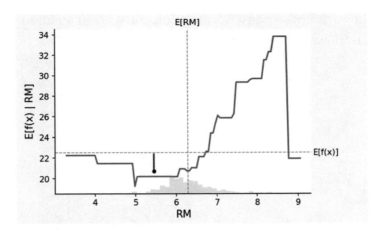

Figure 5-12. *PDP plot for RM and SHAP values extracted*

In Figure 5-12, the extreme gradient boosting regression model is used to explain the ensemble models and here also you can see there is a non-linear relationship.

```
shap.plots.scatter(shap_values_xgb[:,"RM"])
```

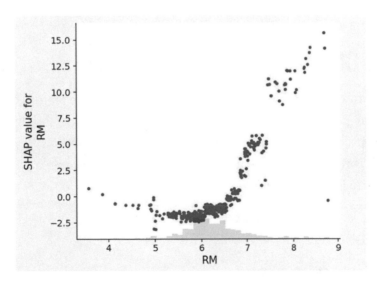

Figure 5-13. *RM and SHAP values of the RM scatterplot*

In Figure 5-13, there is a curve that shows a non-linear association between RM and the SHAP value of RM.

```
shap.plots.scatter(shap_values_xgb[:,"RM"], color=shap_values)
```

Figure 5-14 shows the same non-linear relationship with an additional overlay of the TAX feature, which shows the higher the RM value, the higher the TAX component and vice versa.

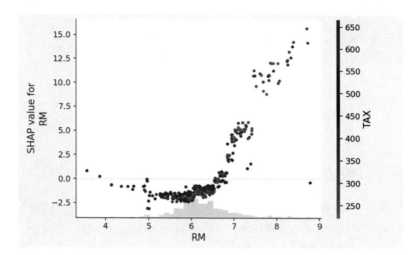

Figure 5-14. *RM and the SHAP of RM can be shown by a third dimension, which is color*

Ensemble Classification Model: SHAP

For a regression model you have seen the SHAP features and the feature importance, both including the partial dependency plot for a few features. Now let's look at the common and popular income census classification dataset (popularly known as the adult dataset). It is popular because it is easy to understand and relatable and appears in almost all machine learning example code.

```
# a classic adult census dataset price dataset
X_adult,y_adult = shap.datasets.adult()

# a simple linear logistic model
model_adult = sklearn.linear_model.LogisticRegression(max_iter=10000)
model_adult.fit(X_adult, y_adult)
```

In the above script, the census income dataset, which is already part of the SHAP library, is loaded. A logistic regression model is trained as this is a binary classification problem. Finally, a model fit process creates a trained model.

```
def model_adult_proba(x):
    return model_adult.predict_proba(x)[:,1]
def model_adult_log_odds(x):
    p = model_adult.predict_log_proba(x)
    return p[:,1] - p[:,0]
```

For a classification example using the census income dataset, the target column has two labels: people who make more than $50K per annum and people who make less than $50K per annum. It is a binary classification model and as a baseline you can use a logistic regression model to showcase the PDP as a linear function of SHAP values. Then you can use an ensemble model to compare the PDP and show how the function becomes non-linear. The non-linear and complex relationship is captured by the ensemble model. The two functions named model proba and model log odds provide the probability value of the two classes and the log odds ratio, respectively.

```
# make a standard partial dependence plot
sample_ind = 18
fig,ax = shap.partial_dependence_plot(
    "Capital Gain", model_adult_proba, X_adult, model_expected_value=True,
    feature_expected_value=True, show=False, ice=False
)
```

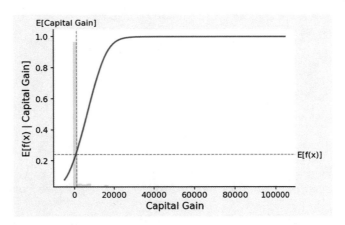

Figure 5-15. *PDP between capital gain and the probability of making less than $50K*

The x-axis in Figure 5-15 shows the capital gain variable and the y-axis shows the predicted probabilities of making less than $50K. The probability value ranges from 0.05 to 0.99, and after that it becomes flat closer to 100% but not exactly 100%. The explanation here is that as the capital gains amount exceeds $20K, it has no impact on the predicted probability value. Up to $20K, as the capital gain increases, the predicted probability also increases.

```
# compute the SHAP values for the linear model
background_adult = shap.maskers.Independent(X_adult, max_samples=100)
explainer = shap.Explainer(model_adult_proba, background_adult)
shap_values_adult = explainer(X_adult[:1000])

shap.plots.scatter(shap_values_adult[:,"Age"])
```

Figure 5-16 shows the linear relationship but there is a variation in the scatterness of the data points, which shows a possibly that non-linearity exists and that it cannot be captured correctly using a linear model. Hence there is a need for the ensemble model.

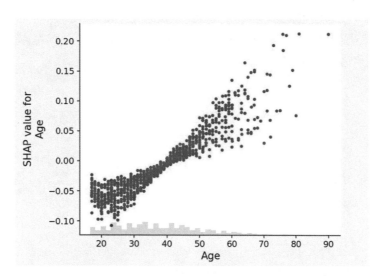

Figure 5-16. *Scatterplot between age and SHAP value for age for a linear model*

```
# compute the SHAP values for the linear model
explainer_log_odds = shap.Explainer(model_adult_log_odds, background_adult)
shap_values_adult_log_odds = explainer_log_odds(X_adult[:1000])

shap.plots.scatter(shap_values_adult_log_odds[:,"Age"])
```

```
# make a standard partial dependence plot
sample_ind = 18
fig,ax = shap.partial_dependence_plot(
    "Age", model_adult_log_odds, X_adult, model_expected_value=True,
    feature_expected_value=True, show=False, ice=False
)
```

```
# train XGBoost model
model = xgboost.XGBClassifier(n_estimators=100, max_depth=2).fit(X_adult,
y_adult)
```

```
# compute SHAP values
explainer = shap.Explainer(model, background_adult)
shap_values = explainer(X_adult)
```

```
# set a display version of the data to use for plotting (has string values)
shap_values.display_data = shap.datasets.adult(display=True)[0].values
```

Now let's see the extreme gradient boosting classifier model. As a boosting model, it improves the accuracy of the classifier and at the same time it provides explanations of the predicted outcomes.

```
shap.plots.bar(shap_values)
```

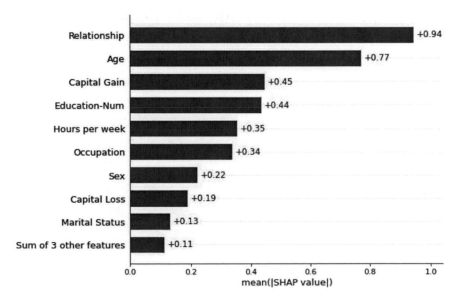

Figure 5-17. *Average absolute SHAP values to rank the features*

In Figure 5-17, the relationship variable shows the highest average absolute SHAP value, which is a reflection that this variable is important in predicting the class of the target column. The second most important variable is age, then capital gain, and so on.

```
shap.plots.bar(shap_values.abs.max(0))
```

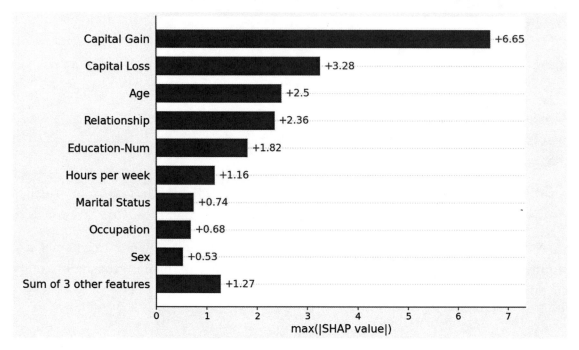

Figure 5-18. *Maximum of absolute SHAP value by different features*

In Figure 5-18, the capital gain feature has the highest SHAP value so this could be one of the outliers. Similarly, the capital loss is also possibly an outlier. This will get clarified by Figure 5-19.

In Figure 5-19, the SHAP values show how the feature values impact the model output. The blue points indicate low feature values and the red points indicate high feature values.

```
shap.plots.beeswarm(shap_values)
```

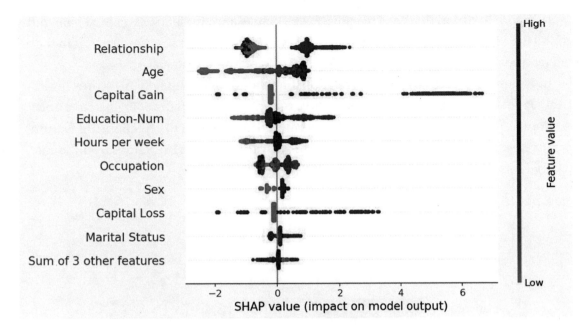

Figure 5-19. *SHAP values plotted against feature values*

```
shap.plots.beeswarm(shap_values.abs, color="shap_red")
```

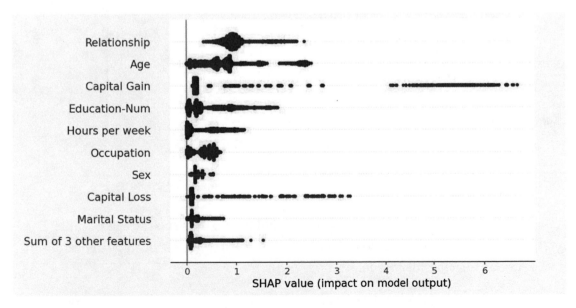

Figure 5-20. *Absolute value of SHAP*

In Figure 5-20 you don't see negative SHAP values and two features, capital gain and capital loss, indicate a lot of variation in SHAP values, which means the variation in these two features' actual values could produce inconsistent predictions.

In Figure 5-21, let's consider the relationship feature. It has high SHAP scores until the 430th instance. After that the SHAP values turn negative until the 580th instance and continue until the 610th instance. Afterwards all the instances of the relationship feature produce negative SHAP values. This graph shows variation in SHAP values by different instances as present in the training dataset.

```
shap.plots.heatmap(shap_values[:1000])
```

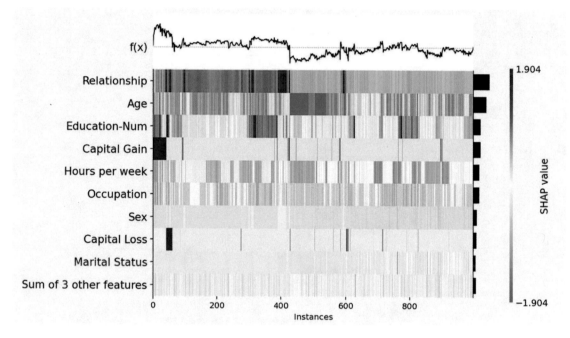

Figure 5-21. *Feature value variation by instance and SHAP values*

Figure 5-22 explains the strict non-linear relationship between the age variable and the SHAP scores of the age variable. This non-linearity is produced by the extreme gradient boosting classifier model.

```
shap.plots.scatter(shap_values[:,"Age"])
```

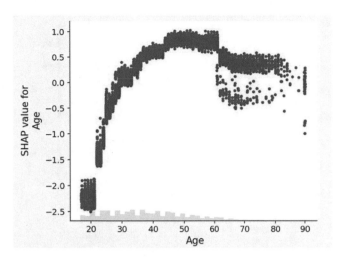

Figure 5-22. *Age and SHAP value of age*

```
shap.plots.scatter(shap_values[:,"Age"], color=shap_values)
```

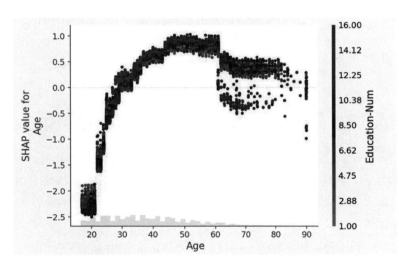

Figure 5-23. *Age and SHAP value of age with education number superimposed*

In Figure 5-23, the age and education numbers follow a similar pattern as the SHAP value for age.

```
shap.plots.scatter(shap_values[:,"Age"], color=shap_values[:,"Capital
Gain"])
```

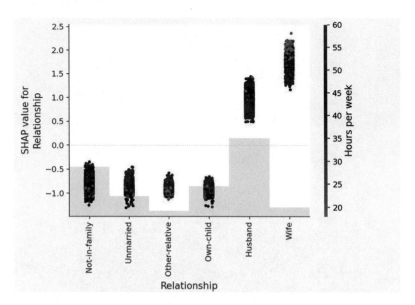

Figure 5-24. *Relationship and SHAP values for relationship with hours per week*

In Figure 5-24, there is a clear difference in husband, wife, and the rest of the relationship status values. The SHAP values for husband and wife are positive; however, for other four relationships the SHAP values are negative.

Using SHAP to Explain Categorical Boosting Models

When the features of a classification model contain categorical variables, we usually do one hot encoding for the features in order to identify the impact of each feature on the target column. In this example, you are going to use the CatBoost Python library along with SHAP to generate explanations.

To install the CatBoost library you can use the pip installation command.

```
!pip install catboost
shap.initjs()
import catboost
from catboost.datasets import *
import shap
```

This census income data set has categorical features such as relationship, sex, occupation, and marital status. These categorical features cannot be directly passed to the machine learning training algorithms using sklearn or any other pipeline like Keras,

TensorFlow, etc. These categorical features first need to be converted to label encoder and then converted to one hot encoder. This becomes very cumbersome if you have more than a hundred features that are categorical. Hence you need a library that can handle this process automatically. This need is answered by the CatBoost library.

The Initjs() function loads the JavaScript visualization code to a Jupyter notebook. Hence we use the above syntax to load the JS functionality.

The CatBoost regression model or classification model works on top of a gradient boosting model, hence the name is the CatBoost model.

```
X,y = shap.datasets.boston()

model = CatBoostRegressor(iterations=300, learning_rate=0.1, random_seed=123)
model.fit(X, y, verbose=False, plot=False)

explainer = shap.TreeExplainer(model)
shap_values = explainer.shap_values(X)

# visualize the first prediction's explanation
shap.force_plot(explainer.expected_value, shap_values[0,:], X.iloc[0,:])
```

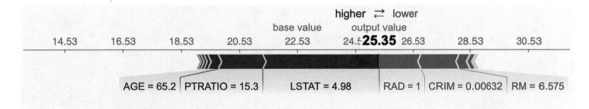

Figure 5-25. *Force plot for prediction for a record*

In Figure 5-25 you are trying to explain a local prediction. For record 0 from the training dataset you are showing the prediction explanation. As an example, you have taken the Boston housing prices dataset, trained a CatBoost model using the default parameters, and saved the model. As a next step, an explainer object is generated using a tree explainer and the explainer object is again used to generate the SHAP values using training dataset X as input. Finally, the force plot visualization is created using the predicted value and the SHAP value for the input first record from the training dataset. For the first record, the predicted housing price is 25.35, which is $25,350. The average of the predicted house prices is 22.53, which is $22,530. Features such as age, PTRATIO, and LSTAT push the prediction higher (the red arrow facing towards the right). Features such as RAD, CRIM, and RM push the prediction down which means pushing the prediction towards the left, shown by the blue arrow showing backwards. The values shown on the horizontal axis in grey are the predicted values for all of the samples.

```
# visualize the training set predictions
shap.force_plot(explainer.expected_value, shap_values, X)
```

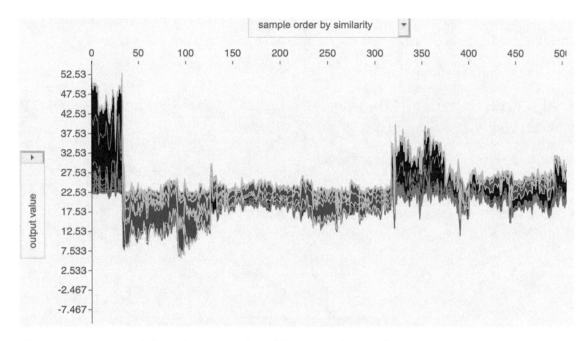

Figure 5-26. *Model explainer ordered by sample similarity*

In Figure 5-26, the samples are ordered by sample similarity. The horizontal axis shows the samples and the vertical axis shows the predicted output value. This is an interesting visualization; by just hovering your mouse or cursor you should be able to see the features' SHAP values, the exact predicted output value, and the corresponding sample that was selected as an input to the explainer. This chart gives a detailed view about understanding the predicted outcome and the features' contributions.

In order to explain applying the CatBoost classifier, let's use the Amazon dataset. Table 5-6 lists the features in the dataset.

Table 5-6. *Amazon Dataset Data Description*

Feature name	Description
ACTION	ACTION is 1 if the resource was approved, 0 if the resource was not
RESOURCE	An ID for each resource
MGR_ID	The EMPLOYEE ID of the manager of the current EMPLOYEE ID record; an employee may have only one manager at a time
ROLE_ROLLUP_1	Company role grouping category id 1 (e.g., US Engineering)
ROLE_ROLLUP_2	Company role grouping category id 2 (e.g., US Retail)
ROLE_DEPTNAME	Company role department description (e.g., Retail)
ROLE_TITLE	Company role business title description (e.g., Senior Engineering Retail Manager)
ROLE_FAMILY_DESC	Company role family extended description (e.g., Retail Manager, Software Engineering)
ROLE_FAMILY	Company role family description (e.g., Retail Manager)
ROLE_CODE	Company role code; this code is unique to each role (e.g., Manager)

When an employee starts work in a software development department, they need certain access and permissions to fulfil their job requirements. There is a manual process of granting access to the employee but the employee may encounter roadblocks in the process. There is no automated mechanism to grant access to the necessary software systems. The objective of this use case is to model historical data to determine an employee's access need. The target column is ACTION; it is 1 if the resource is approved and 0 if the resource access is denied. The rest of the features are used to predict the target feature.

```
train_df, test_df = catboost.datasets.amazon()
train_df

set(train_df.ACTION)

y_train = train_df.ACTION
X_train = train_df.drop('ACTION',axis=1)
cat_features = list(range(0,X_train.shape[1]))
```

```
from catboost import Pool, CatBoostClassifier, cv
# Initialize CatBoostClassifier
model = CatBoostClassifier(iterations=300,
                                learning_rate=0.1,
                                random_seed=12)
```

```
# Fit model
model.fit(X_train,y_train,cat_features=cat_features,verbose=False,
plot=False)
```

The model training process using the CatBoost classifier has some complexity, which means a complex relationship that cannot be approximated by a single function. If the features have a linear relationship, you can use a straight line to approximate the function. However, if the features are either circular or in a zig-zag pattern, then it is called a complex pattern, as there is no function mathematically that can approximate a circular or zig-zag pattern. In those scenarios, either you need more than one function or data normalization to match to any of the mathematical function.

In the current scenario, the SHAP values are calculated approximately due to the complexity of the features dataset.

```
eval_dataset = [X_train.iloc[0:1]]
eval_dataset
```

```
# Get predicted classes
preds_class = model.predict(X_train)
```

```
# Get predicted probabilities for each class
preds_proba = model.predict_proba(X_train)
```

```
# Get predicted RawFormulaVal
preds_raw = model.predict(X_train,
                        prediction_type='RawFormulaVal')
```

```
preds_class
```

```
preds_proba
```

```
preds_raw
```

The trained model is stored in the model object. You can take two samples as an example to produce the probability for that instance and a raw formula value. The sample can be any data point from the training dataset. In the script, let's take first and 91st record as examples.

```
import numpy as np
np.log(0.9964/(1-0.9964))
np.exp(5.62)/(1+np.exp(5.62))
cat_features
```

The first record shows a predicted probability of 99.64% towards class 1. The log odds value is 5.61. Log odds means log(P/1-P) and here P is the probability of class 1. If you want to get the probability from the raw prediction value, you can use the formula exp(raw prediction) / (1+ exp(raw prediction)). For example, for the first record, exp(5.61) / (1+ exp(5.61)) = 0.9964. In a similar fashion you can interpret the raw prediction value -3.4734 for the 91st record. The CatBoost model provides options to predict different prediction types; see Table 5-7.

Table 5-7. *Prediction Type Generated by the CatBoost Model Object*

prediction_type	Description
Probability	Probability value corresponding to each class
Class	Class label will be produced
RawFormula Value	Log odds value
Exponent	Exponential value of prediction probability
LogProbability	Logarithmic of the probability

Different types of predictions from the CatBoost model give more insights into understanding the prediction value and how the model generates the prediction. The linkage between all types provides better understanding. You convert the raw prediction value to arrive at a probability of class 1.

```
from catboost.datasets import *
train_df, test_df = catboost.datasets.amazon()
y = train_df.ACTION
```

```
X = train_df.drop('ACTION', axis=1)
cat_features = list(range(0, X.shape[1]))

model = CatBoostClassifier(iterations=300, learning_rate=0.1, random_
seed=12)
model.fit(X, y, cat_features=cat_features, verbose=False, plot=False)

explainer = shap.TreeExplainer(model)
shap_values = explainer.shap_values(Pool(X, y, cat_features=cat_features))

test_objects = [X.iloc[7:9], X.iloc[56:58]]

for obj in test_objects:
    print('Probability of class 1 = {:.4f}'.format(model.predict_proba(obj)
    [0][1]))
    print('Formula raw prediction = {:.4f}'.format(model.predict(obj,
    prediction_type='RawFormulaVal')[0]))
    print('\n')

shap.force_plot(explainer.expected_value, shap_values[0,:], X.iloc[0,:])
```

```
shap.force_plot(explainer.expected_value, shap_values[91,:], X.iloc[91,:])
```

Figure 5-27. *Force plot for record 1 from training set*

In Figure 5-27, the force plot shows how the raw prediction value is decided based on pull (blue, lower graph) and push (red, higher graph) feature values. The values reflected on a scale starting from 1.124 to 6.124 are the raw prediction values, which is the log odds ratio of the prediction probability with respect to class 1. The average log odds ratio value is 3.624. The pull values lower the predicted odds ratio using features such as resource, role title, roll, roll-up 2, etc. The push features (role dept name, MGR id, etc.) will increase the predicted odds ratio to the higher level. The final value is 5.61, which is the final predicted raw probability value, also known as the odds ratio.

```
shap.summary_plot(shap_values, X)
```

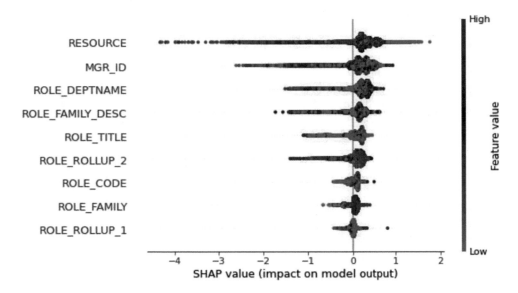

Figure 5-28. *Summary of SHAP values showing impact on model output*

Figure 5-28 shows the features and their importance in impacting the model output. Resource is the most impactful feature, then MGR ID, and so on as shown in the figure.

Using SHAP Multiclass Categorical Boosting Model

The categorical boost classifier model can also be used for training a multiclass classification model. The trained model object can be passed through the SHAP tree explainer to generate SHAP values. See Figure 5-29.

```
model = CatBoostClassifier(loss_function = 'MultiClass', iterations=300,
learning_rate=0.1, random_seed=123)
model.fit(X, y, cat_features=cat_features, verbose=False, plot=False)
```

```
explainer = shap.TreeExplainer(model)
shap_values = explainer.shap_values(Pool(X, y, cat_features=cat_features))

shap.summary_plot(shap_values[0], X)
```

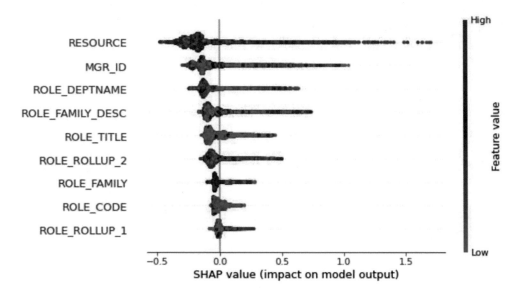

Figure 5-29. *Feature value and SHAP value representation*

A CatBoost classifier or regression has many hyper parameters. Table 5-8 shows some of the important parameters and how they impact the model outcome.

Table 5-8. *The Hyper Parameters of the CatBoost Classifier*

Parameter	Explanation
cat_features	Categorical columns indices that are present in the training dataset
text_features	Text columns indices (specified as integers) or names (specified as strings)
learning_rate	For loss function optimization, used for reducing the gradient step
Iterations	The maximum number of trees that can be built when solving machine learning problems
Max_depth	Depth of the tree

(continued)

Table 5-8. (*continued*)

Parameter	Explanation
leaf_ estimation_ method	The method used to calculate the values in leaves Possible values: Newton Gradient Exact Depends on the mode and the selected loss function: Regression with Quantile or MAE loss functions — One exact iteration Regression with any loss function but Quantile or MAE – One gradient iteration Classification mode – Ten Newton iterations Multi-classification mode – One Newton iteration
boosting_type	Boosting scheme Possible values: Ordered — Usually provides better quality on small datasets, but it may be slower than the Plain scheme Plain — The classic gradient boosting scheme

In order to get better results, the above parameters can be changed or modified and can be explained using the SHAP library.

Using SHAP for Light GBM Model Explanation

As discussed in the CatBoost classifier section, in a similar manner you can use a light gradient boosting model also. The difference between a light gbm model and a CatBoost model is that light GBM is faster to run in a mixed data scenario, where there is a mixed set of features in the training dataset. The CatBoost classifier is useful when you have a high number of categorical features in the dataset. In light GBM you need to encode the categorical features, but in the CatBoost model, the model has an internal mechanism to handle the categorical features.

To install the light gbm model:

```
conda install -c conda-forge lightgbm
```

```
from sklearn.model_selection import train_test_split
import lightgbm as lgb
import shap
```

```
X,y = shap.datasets.adult()
X_display,y_display = shap.datasets.adult(display=True)
```

```
# create a train/test split
X_train, X_test, y_train, y_test = train_test_split(X, y, test_size=0.2,
random_state=7)
d_train = lgb.Dataset(X_train, label=y_train)
d_test = lgb.Dataset(X_test, label=y_test)
```

```
params = {
    "max_bin": 512,
    "learning_rate": 0.05,
    "boosting_type": "gbdt",
    "objective": "binary",
    "metric": "binary_logloss",
    "num_leaves": 10,
    "verbose": -1,
    "min_data": 100,
    "boost_from_average": True
}
```

```
model = lgb.train(params, d_train, 10000, valid_sets=[d_test], early_
stopping_rounds=50, verbose_eval=1000)
```

You can take the same census income classification dataset for training a classifier using the light GBM model and generate the explanations for the predicted outcomes. There are many hyper parameters that can be understood by going through the official documentation page of the light gbm model. Table 5-9 shows the hyper parameters that are used in the following lines of code.

Table 5-9. *Hyper Parameters of a LGB Model*

Parameters	Explanation
Max_bin	Max number of bins that feature values will be bucketed in
	A small number of bins may reduce training accuracy but may increase
	general power (deal with overfitting)
Learning_rate	Shrinkage rate
Boosting_type	gbdt, traditional Gradient Boosting Decision Tree, aliases: gbrt
	rf, Random Forest, aliases: random_forest
	dart, Dropouts meet Multiple Additive Regression Trees
	goss, Gradient-based One-Side Sampling
Objective	Application type such as binary classification, multiclass classification, etc.
Metric	Metric(s) to be evaluated on the evaluation set(s)
Num_leaves	Max number of leaves in one tree
Min_data	Minimal number of data per categorical group

After training the light GBM model, you can go to the SHAP tree explainer to explain the predicted results, and also you can generate the force plot for the SHAP values (Figure 5-30).

```
explainer = shap.TreeExplainer(model)
shap_values = explainer.shap_values(X)

shap.force_plot(explainer.expected_value[1], shap_values[1][0,:], X_
display.iloc[0,:])
```

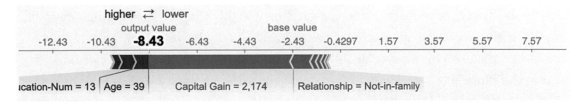

Figure 5-30. *Force plot for predicting the log odds with the SHAP feature values*

In Figure 5-30, the education number and age push the predicted odds ratio to a higher value and the capital gains and relationship pull the predicted odds ratio to a lower value. Hence the final predicted odds ratio for record 1 from the dataset produces -8.43, which is much lower than the average odds ratio as shown by the base value of -2.43.

```
shap.force_plot(explainer.expected_value[1], shap_values[1][:1000,:],
X_display.iloc[:1000,:])
```

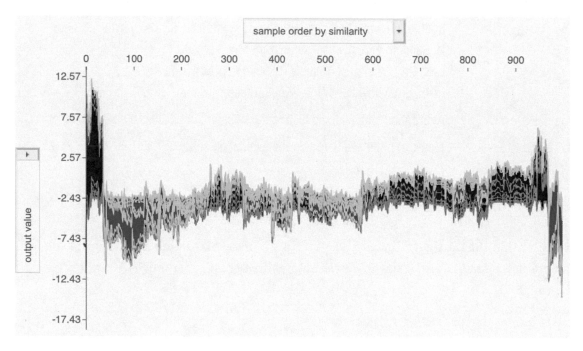

Figure 5-31. *Sample order similarity in producing the output value from the LGBM model*

In Figure 5-31, the odds ratio is the output, and from the odds ratio you can get back the probability values of the target classes as shown in this chapter. This graph shows the samples' similarity and then ordered accordingly. The samples that generate a higher odds ratio are placed between 0-50. Afterwards the rest of the samples generate odds ratios in the range of +3 and -9 up to the 900the record. After that, the odds ratio drops to a very negative range. The red line shows feature values that contribute towards making the predicted odds ratio higher and the blue line indicates the feature values that make the predicted odds ratio lower. The average line corresponds to a -2.43 value. If you take the odds ratio of the entire dataset and then compute the average, the value comes out to be -2.43.

```
shap.summary_plot(shap_values, X)
```

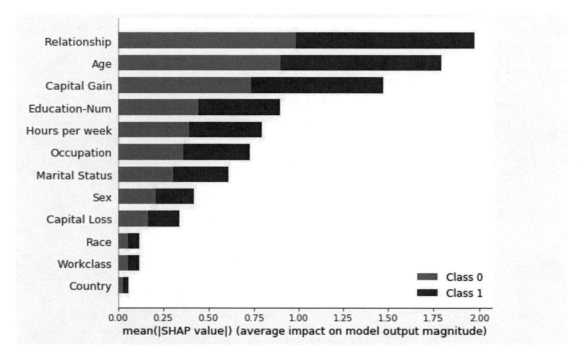

Figure 5-32. *Summary plot*

Figure 5-32 shows the summary plot. It's a very important one. It provides the average SHAP value by different features corresponding to each class for the target column. What is interesting from this graph is that the average value is distributed equally between two classes independent of the feature values.

Conclusion

You covered a few boosting based models for both classification scenarios and regression scenarios. In a similar fashion, the bagging classifiers can be trained and similar graphs as output can be produced. The graphs won't change, but the interpretation of the values will change as you switch from one model to another model. Here are five important things you should take a note of:

- In a regression scenario, you predict the target column and, based on the feature contribution, you can see how the predicted outcome moves up or down. So if you change an input feature, you can easily understand the impact on the target output.

- In a classification scenario, you predict the log odds ratio as a continuous variable and predict the value based on feature input values. You know which features are important, so you have an exact visibility of a predicted outcome based on changes in the input features.

- Be it bagging, boosting, or stacking, a similar framework of PDP, force plot, and summary plot can be generated to understand the decision making by the model. However, the pattern shown in a PDP plot, as an example, will change.

- The changes in the patterns of the graphs happen because the model tries to capture the complex patterns, if any, in the data. As the data complexity increases, the model becomes more complex, and visually it may look difficult to interpret. However, the inference from the values will remain same.

- Hence, based on the analysis in this chapter, it does not matter how many ensemble models you are covering. It is more important to establish a framework that can be followed for other ensemble models.

CHAPTER 6

Explainability for Time Series Models

A time series model is a way of generating a multi-step prediction along a future time period. There are statistical models and machine learning-based models that can be deployed to generate forecasting for the future based on historical data. If the model predictions can be trusted or not, what is the degree of confidence someone can have about the predictions? Models that can be explained and models that cannot be explained are certain things we are going to cover in this chapter.

Time Series Models

The primary objective of a time series model is to estimate the value of a target variable using time as an independent variable. The target variable can be the value of a stock price, it can be the number of units of product, it can be the amount of revenue that would flow into the company account, and it can be the number of unique visitors for a particular website. The predicted values are multi-step because when using a time series model we usually predict multiple time steps. The time series model generates forecast values. The forecast values have certain confidence levels. The higher the confidence level, the better the model is; in lower confidence levels the model lacks stability in generating forecast values. The confidence interval can be calculated as a predicted value of a forecasted value plus and minus 1.96 (the standardized value from statistical table corresponding to 95% confidence) multiplied by the standard error of the residual term calculated from the model. This is based on the condition that the error term is normally distributed.

The time series model requires the data to be recorded at frequent time intervals, without any interruption in the time step. The time series data is ordered in nature as the order determines the implicit time sequence. As a machine learning engineer, it

© Pradeepta Mishra 2022
P. Mishra, *Practical Explainable AI Using Python*, https://doi.org/10.1007/978-1-4842-7158-2_6

is important to create useful features from the data to make the right predictions. In a time series model, time is an independent variable. In a univariate time series model, you have only one variable. In a causal forecasting model, you have a model similar to a regression model. In a univariate time series model, the features are autoregressive terms such as lagged terms, moving average terms (such as three period or five period moving average), and difference terms. The most popular time series forecasting models rely purely on the historical values of the target variable. They are exponential smoothing models and ARIMA (autoregressive integrated moving average model). If you are going to use the above mentioned two models, you must capture the components of a time series in the feature engineering step. The following are the components of a time series:

- **Trend**: It is a sign when the value of the variable increases or decreases or remains constant continuously over a couple of time steps in sequence. When using time series modelling, the trend is considered as a feature.

- **Seasonality**: It is a sign of regular patterns evident in a definite interval, which is periodic in nature. It keeps repeating with a constant time interval. A time series model also takes the seasonal variables in the feature engineering step.

- **Cyclic**: Business cycles usually fluctuate over time. Sometimes it's higher and sometimes it's lower. The cyclicity is a particular feature that helps in predicting the value of the target variable.

Apart from the time series components, other engineered features also can be introduced such as lagged variables; moving average-based variables; dummy variables based on events such as holidays and special events; marketing campaigns; and the existence of outliers in the data. The explainability and interpretability of a time series model is necessary to build trust in the model, to explain the predictions, and also to understand the behavior of the models. The time series components and features and additional features are important to interpret the behavior of the time series model. Figure 6-1 shows what we usually model in a univariate time series forecasting model.

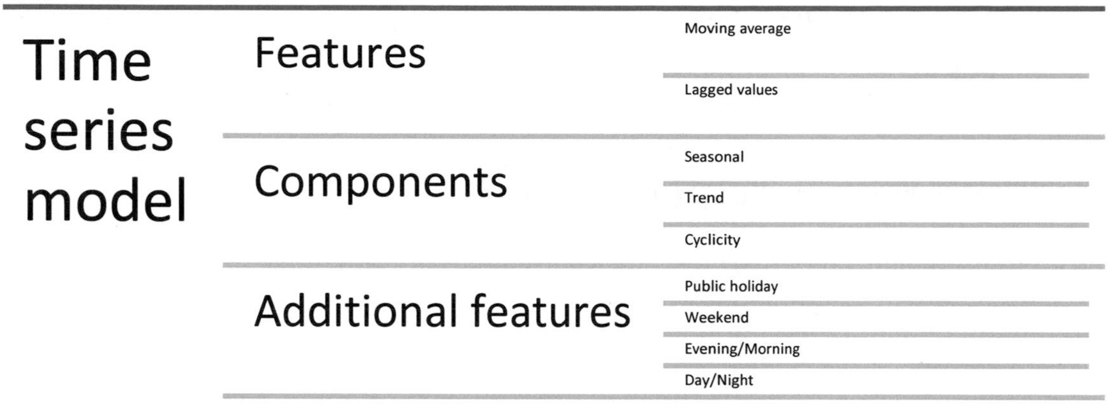

Time series model	Features	Moving average
		Lagged values
	Components	Seasonal
		Trend
		Cyclicity
	Additional features	Public holiday
		Weekend
		Evening/Morning
		Day/Night

Figure 6-1. *What we usually model in a time series forecasting model*

Let's look at some use cases where a time series model is applicable and also model explainability is required:

- Data fetched from sensors of IoT devices installed in various places

- Financial data such as stock prices

- Economic indicators such as GDP, FII, IIP, inflation, and so on

- System logs and error logs from machines

- Demand forecasting in a supply chain industry

To solve the various use cases, we have a list of algorithms that can generate predictions for future. However, the algorithms are not simple to understand. There are complex models as well. Not all of the algorithms possess interpretability and explainability. But it is important to explain the models to the business leaders. The algorithms are as follows:

- Autoregressive integrated moving average model

- Generalized autoregressive conditional heteroskedasticity model

- Baysian probabilistic model

- Vector autoregressive model

- Neural network autoregressive model

- Recurrent neural network model

- Long short term memory model

- Gate recurrent unit model

Knowing Which Model Is Good

The time series models need to be evaluated using metrics and other diagnostics before using the models in a production scenario.

Metrics:

- **Root mean square error (RMSE)**: This is a function of scale. The less it is, the better the model is.

- **Mean absolute percentage error (MAPE)**: This is scale-independent. It's preferred to be less than 10%, as per the industry benchmark.

After the forecasting model has been fit, it is important to know the metrics to determine how well the model fits the data. A concept specific to the time series model is white noise, which means errors that cannot be explained by the model. An error can be considered as white noise if the following properties are met:

- The residual terms are not correlated, which means the autocorrelated function represented by the ACF value is 0.

- The residuals follow a normal distribution.

If the above two are not satisfied, then there is still scope for improving the model.

Strategy for Forecasting

If the business need is to generate a forecast at an upper hierarchy and granular level data is available, then there are two ways the forecasting can be generated:

- Macro level, using the upper hierarchy (example: forecast of sales volume for an apparel category is at a macro level and for each stock-keeping unit (SKU) it is at a micro level)

- Micro level and then performing aggregation, using lowest possible granularity

Confidence Interval of Predictions

Not all time series models provide confidence intervals for the forecasted values. The confidence interval of forecasted values provides a meaningful insight. The higher the confidence interval, the better the model is. If the models do not align to the confidence interval, two scenarios may occur:

- **A black swan event**: The forecasted value confidence interval is breached by an actual value in a significant way, causing havoc.

- **A gray swan event**: It is less than the confidence interval of forecasted value and may result in a suboptimal result.

In Figure 6-2, the daily sales are shown and the historical data is used to predict the forecast ahead. The dotted line shows the forecasted values generated by the model, the two parallel black lines show the confidence interval on the forecasted values, and the confidence interval has an upper threshold at the upper line and a lower threshold at the lower line. If the forecasted values exceed the upper threshold like point A, it is called a black swan event, and if the forecasted values exceed the lower threshold point B, it is called a grey swan event.

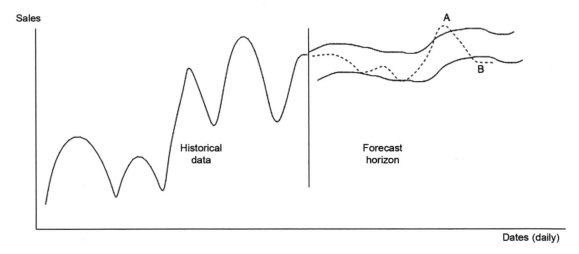

Figure 6-2. *Black swan and grey swan events*

What Happens to Trust?

The objective of XAI is to explain to the end user whether they should believe the prediction or decide on competing models that can be more trustworthy. The above two scenarios, the black swan and gray swan events, are extremely difficult to predict. If they occur once or twice, it's fine. If the model fails to identify such scenarios frequently, then the user will not have faith or trust in the model. One of the ways to control these kinds of events is to generate the confidence interval at a higher threshold value such as a 90% confidence limit. Other scenarios need to be explained using model parameters.

The dataset has a date stamp and a price of some product. This is considered a univariate time series model. You need to generate the forecasted values for the future.

```
import pandas as pd
import numpy as np
import matplotlib.pyplot as plt
%matplotlib inline
df = pd.read_csv('/Users/pradmishra/Downloads/XAI Book Apress/monthly_csv.
csv',index_col=0)
df
# line plot of time series
# line plot of dataset
df.plot()
```

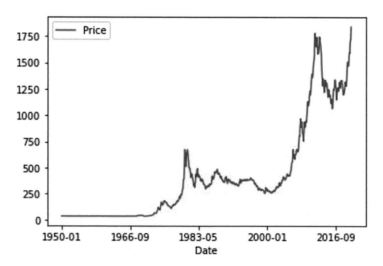

Figure 6-3. *Price over dates*

In Figure 6-3, the data in the dataset shows variations in price, with trends and some degree of jump towards the end of 2016. There is some degree of seasonality in the time series model. Seasonality means the same values of price will occur in a particular time period and there will be repeated events like this. If it is more than one, then it can be confirmed that seasonality exists in the data. To incorporate seasonality in the forecasted values, you can extend the time series model to seasonally adjusted model variants. But if you want to remove the impact of seasonal elements from the forecasted value, you need to adjust the time series by using a difference method. The difference is the time series minus its own values in the past by one period. The seasonally adjusted data can be stored separately.

```
 # seasonal difference
differenced = df.diff(12)
# trim off the first year of empty data
differenced = differenced[12:]
# save differenced dataset to file
differenced.to_csv('seasonally_adjusted.csv', index=False)
# plot differenced dataset
differenced.plot()
plt.show()
```

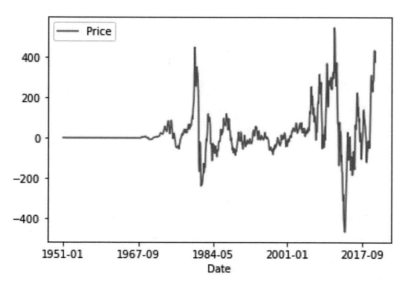

Figure 6-4. *The seasonally differenced time series data*

In Figure 6-4, the same seasonally adjusted time series is represented. The autoregressive integrated moving average (ARIMA) models are most frequently used in the industry. They explain the autocorrelations in the data. A stationary time series can be defined as a series whose values do not depend on when it actually occurred. Any time series with trends and seasonality is not stationary. However, a time series with cyclicity is stationary in nature. One of the ways to make the time series stationary is by applying the differencing method, because stationarity is one of the assumptions of the ARIMA model. The differencing helps to reduce the trends and seasonality in the data and hence make it stationary. The autocorrelation function (ACF) is one of the ways to identify stationarity; the ACF will drop to zero quickly. However, for a non-stationary time series, the value of correlation remains fairly higher and the decay in the correlation value is also very insignificant.

```
from statsmodels.graphics.tsaplots import plot_acf
plot_acf(df)
plt.show()
```

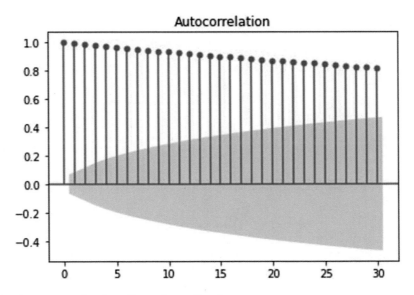

Figure 6-5. *Autocorrelation function of price*

In Figure 6-5, the pattern of the autocorrelation function tells us that the series is non-stationary, because the correlation coefficient up to 30 lags seen to be more than 0.80. The shaded color shows the confidence level of the correlation coefficient value. Since the correlation coefficient is not zero at up to 30 lags, the series is highly non-stationary in nature. Since you know the series is not stationary you cannot apply the standard ARIMA model.

There is an alternative way of turning the problem into an autoregressive supervised machine learning problem to understand if any lag has an impact on the forecast value. This is why you create 12 lag values as independent features to predict the actual price series as a dependent variable.

```
# reframe as supervised learning
dataframe = pd.DataFrame()
for i in range(12,0,-1):
    dataframe['t-'+str(i)] = df.shift(i).values[:,0]
dataframe['t'] = df.values[:,0]
print(dataframe.head(13))
dataframe = dataframe[13:]
# save to new file
dataframe.to_csv('lags_12months_features.csv', index=False)
```

In the above script you calculate the lag values. In Figure 6-6, you can see the lag values as a table.

	t-12	t-11	t-10	t-9	t-8	t-7	t-6	t-5	t-4	t-3
0	NaN	NaN	NaN	NaN	NaN	NaN	NaN	NaN	NaN	NaN
1	NaN	NaN	NaN	NaN	NaN	NaN	NaN	NaN	NaN	NaN
2	NaN	NaN	NaN	NaN	NaN	NaN	NaN	NaN	NaN	NaN
3	NaN	NaN	NaN	NaN	NaN	NaN	NaN	NaN	NaN	34.73
4	NaN	NaN	NaN	NaN	NaN	NaN	NaN	NaN	34.73	34.73
5	NaN	NaN	NaN	NaN	NaN	NaN	NaN	34.73	34.73	34.73
6	NaN	NaN	NaN	NaN	NaN	NaN	34.73	34.73	34.73	34.73
7	NaN	NaN	NaN	NaN	NaN	34.73	34.73	34.73	34.73	34.73
8	NaN	NaN	NaN	NaN	34.73	34.73	34.73	34.73	34.73	34.73
9	NaN	NaN	NaN	34.73	34.73	34.73	34.73	34.73	34.73	34.73
10	NaN	NaN	34.73	34.73	34.73	34.73	34.73	34.73	34.73	34.73
11	NaN	34.73	34.73	34.73	34.73	34.73	34.73	34.73	34.73	34.73
12	34.73	34.73	34.73	34.73	34.73	34.73	34.73	34.73	34.73	34.73

	t-2	t-1	t
0	NaN	NaN	34.73
1	NaN	34.73	34.73
2	34.73	34.73	34.73
3	34.73	34.73	34.73
4	34.73	34.73	34.73
5	34.73	34.73	34.73
6	34.73	34.73	34.73
7	34.73	34.73	34.73
8	34.73	34.73	34.73
9	34.73	34.73	34.73
10	34.73	34.73	34.73
11	34.73	34.73	34.72
12	34.73	34.72	34.72

Figure 6-6. *Processed data after lag variable creation for model development*

The 12 lag values are features, and you can use a random forest regressor to make different combinations of features in order to construct a decision tree and ensemble the model predictions by taking the average of predicted values from all of the trees. In this way you can identify which feature is more important.

```
# split into input and output
df = pd.read_csv('lags_12months_features.csv')
data = df.values
X = data[:,0:-1]
y = data[:,-1]
from sklearn.ensemble import RandomForestRegressor
# fit random forest model
model = RandomForestRegressor(n_estimators=500, random_state=1)
```

```
model.fit(X, y)
# show importance scores
print(model.feature_importances_)
# plot importance scores
names = dataframe.columns.values[0:-1]
ticks = [i for i in range(len(names))]
plt.bar(ticks, model.feature_importances_)
plt.xticks(ticks, names)
plt.show()
```

You have considered 500 decision trees and used the features to train a random forest regression model. Figure 6-7 estimates the feature importance.

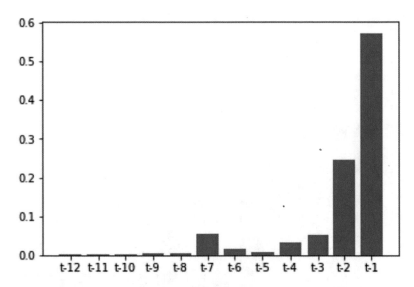

Figure 6-7. *Feature importance of RF model*

In Figure 6-7, you can see that lag 1 (t-1) is the most important feature, lag 2 (t-2) is second important feature, lag 7 (t-7) is the third important feature, followed by lag 3 and lag 4 as shown by (t-3) and (t-4), respectively. Other features are not too important to the model.

```
from sklearn.feature_selection import RFE
# perform feature selection
rfe = RFE(RandomForestRegressor(n_estimators=500, random_state=1),
n_features_to_select=4)
```

```
fit = rfe.fit(X, y)
# report selected features
print('Selected Features:')
names = dataframe.columns.values[0:-1]
for i in range(len(fit.support_)):
    if fit.support_[i]:
        print(names[i])
# plot feature rank
names = dataframe.columns.values[0:-1]
ticks = [i for i in range(len(names))]
plt.bar(ticks, fit.ranking_)
plt.xticks(ticks, names)
plt.show()
```

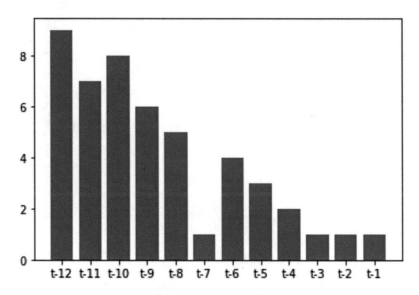

Figure 6-8. *Feature importance from the RFE algorithm*

Recursive feature elimination (RFE) is a popular algorithm to remove redundant features from the list of features in a supervised learning environment (Figure 6-8). There are two different options to configure the RFE: either the number of features to select or the choice of algorithm used to choose the features. RFE acts like a wrapper algorithm on top of a supervised regression-based model or a classification-based model. This means you need a model and then you can apply RFE on top of it. In the above script you use RFE on top of random forest regression model. The most important features selected are lags 7, 3, 2, and 1. The rest of the eight features are not selected by the algorithm. Hence continuous and consistent lags have no impact on the target feature; however, the selected features have an impact on the prediction result. The features of the time series model as discussed earlier in this chapter are only the lag variables and the moving average variables. This is why the time series object can be modelled as AR if only the lagged terms are used. It can be only MA if only the moving average terms are used as features. Autoregression means the lagged values can be used as features to predict the actual time series.

```
# AR example
from statsmodels.tsa.ar_model import AutoReg
from random import random
# fit model
model = AutoReg(y, lags=1)
model_fit = model.fit()
model_fit.summary()
```

The preceding script shows if you use only lag 1 to predict the current time period, it is called an AR 1 model. This is similar to linear regression. See Table 6-1.

Table 6-1. *Autoregression Model Results*

AutoReg Model Results

Dep. Variable:		y	No. Observations:	834
Model:		AutoReg(1)	Log Likelihood	-3864.852
Method:		Conditional MLE	S.D. of innovations	25.047
Date:		Mon, 01 Mar 2021	AIC	6.449
Time:		23:08:04	BIC	6.466
Sample:		1	HQIC	6.455
		834		

	coef	std err	z	P>|z|	[0.025	0.975]
intercept	0.5136	1.186	0.433	0.665	-1.810	2.838
y.L1	1.0039	0.002	522.886	0.000	1.000	1.008

Roots

	Real	Imaginary	Modulus	Frequency
AR.1	0.9961	+0.0000j	0.9961	0.0000

You can write the equation as

$$Yt = 0.5136 + 1.0039*Yt\text{-}1$$

The coefficient 1.0039 has a p-value of 0.000, which is less than 0.05. That means at a 95% confidence level and a 5% statistical level of significance, the first lag term is significant enough to impact the actual time series Yt. This can be interpreted as, *if the lag term changes by 1 unit, the actual value of the series is predicted to change by 0.39%.*

```
# AR example
from statsmodels.tsa.ar_model import AutoReg
from random import random
# fit model
model = AutoReg(y, lags=2)
model_fit = model.fit()
model_fit.summary()
```

Similar analysis can be done by taking into consideration two lags, and the equation becomes

$$Yt = 0.6333 + 1.2182*Yt\text{-}1 - 0.2156*Yt\text{-}2$$

The coefficients 1.2182 and 0.2156 have a p-value of 0.000, which is less than 0.05, which means a 95% confidence level and a 5% statistical level of significance. For the first and second lag terms, this is significant enough to impact the actual time series Yt. This can be interpreted as, *if the lag term changes by one unit, the actual value of the series is predicted to change by 0.22%.* The lag 2 coefficient can be interpreted as, *if lag 2 changes by one unit, the series Yt is going to reduce by 0.2156 times.* See Table 6-2.

Table 6-2. *Autoregression Model with Two Lag Results*

AutoReg Model Results

Dep. Variable:		y	No. Observations:		834
Model:		AutoReg(2)	Log Likelihood		-3841.483
Method:		Conditional MLE	S.D. of innovations		24.489
Date:		Mon, 01 Mar 2021	AIC		6.406
Time:		23:08:14	BIC		6.429
Sample:		2	HQIC		6.415
		834			

	coef	std err	z	P>|z|	[0.025	0.975]
intercept	0.6333	1.161	0.546	0.585	-1.642	2.908
y.L1	1.2182	0.034	35.614	0.000	1.151	1.285
y.L2	-0.2156	0.034	-6.274	0.000	-0.283	-0.148

Roots

	Real	Imaginary	Modulus	Frequency
AR.1	0.9967	+0.0000j	0.9967	0.0000
AR.2	4.6536	+0.0000j	4.6536	0.0000

```
# AR example
from statsmodels.tsa.ar_model import AutoReg
from random import random
# fit model
model = AutoReg(y, lags=12)
model_fit = model.fit()
model_fit.summary()
```

Like the above two-lag scenario, you can extend the model for 12 lag scenarios and a similar interpretation can be made. See Tables 6-3 and 6-4.

Table 6-3. *Autoregression Model Result with 12 Lag Variables*

AutoReg Model Results

Dep. Variable:	y	No. Observations:	834
Model:	AutoReg(12)	Log Likelihood	-3776.103
Method:	Conditional MLE	S.D. of innovations	23.923
Date:	Mon, 01 Mar 2021	AIC	6.384
Time:	23:08:22	BIC	6.464
Sample:	12	HQIC	6.415
	834		

Table 6-4. *Coefficients Table for the Above Model*

	coef	std err	z	P>|z|	[0.025	0.975]
intercept	0.7456	1.147	0.650	0.516	-1.503	2.994
y.L1	1.2473	0.035	35.827	0.000	1.179	1.316
y.L2	-0.3653	0.056	-6.569	0.000	-0.474	-0.256
y.L3	0.1999	0.057	3.504	0.000	0.088	0.312
y.L4	-0.1471	0.057	-2.558	0.011	-0.260	-0.034
y.L5	0.2303	0.058	3.981	0.000	0.117	0.344
y.L6	-0.1920	0.058	-3.290	0.001	-0.306	-0.078
y.L7	0.0802	0.058	1.373	0.170	-0.034	0.195
y.L8	-0.1004	0.058	-1.730	0.084	-0.214	0.013
y.L9	0.0705	0.058	1.215	0.224	-0.043	0.184
y.L10	-0.0587	0.058	-1.016	0.309	-0.172	0.054
y.L11	0.1843	0.056	3.270	0.001	0.074	0.295
y.L12	-0.1475	0.035	-4.155	0.000	-0.217	-0.078

When selecting the ARIMA model, you need to define the order of the model. In the following script, you define the order as (0,0,1) which means (p,d,q) where p is for the autoregressive term, d is for differentiation, and q is for the moving average. So an order of 0, 0, and 1 means only a moving average model.

```
# MA example
from statsmodels.tsa.arima.model import ARIMA
from random import random
# fit model
model = ARIMA(y, order=(0, 0, 1))
model_fit = model.fit()
# make prediction
yhat = model_fit.predict(len(y), len(y))
print(yhat)
model_fit.summary()
```

Table 6-5. *Seasonal ARIMA Model Results*

SARIMAX Results

Dep. Variable:	y	No. Observations:	834
Model:	ARIMA(0, 0, 1)	Log Likelihood	-5736.156
Date:	Mon, 01 Mar 2021	AIC	11478.312
Time:	23:09:14	BIC	11492.490
Sample:	0	HQIC	11483.748
	- 834		
Covariance Type:	opg		

	coef	std err	z	P>|z|	[0.025	0.975]
const	422.8527	28.368	14.906	0.000	367.252	478.453
ma.L1	0.9997	0.007	134.053	0.000	0.985	1.014
sigma2	5.476e+04	3750.622	14.601	0.000	4.74e+04	6.21e+04

Ljung-Box (L1) (Q):	668.38	Jarque-Bera (JB):	383.81
Prob(Q):	0.00	Prob(JB):	0.00
Heteroskedasticity (H):	3.33	Skew:	1.51
Prob(H) (two-sided):	0.00	Kurtosis:	4.40

The following script shows the ARIMA of order 2, 0 and 1, 2 lag autoregressive terms, 0 differentiation, and 1 moving average term:

```
# ARMA example
from statsmodels.tsa.arima.model import ARIMA
from random import random
# fit model
```

```
model = ARIMA(y, order=(2, 0, 1))
model_fit = model.fit()
# make prediction
yhat = model_fit.predict(len(y), len(y))
print(yhat)
model_fit.summary()
```

Table 6-6. *SARIMAX Model Results, the following table displays the autoregressive terms up to 2 lags and moving average up to 1, the coefficients and their statistical significance level also displayed*

SARIMAX Results

Dep. Variable:		y	No. Observations:	834
Model:	ARIMA(2, 0, 1)		Log Likelihood	-3849.432
Date:	Mon, 01 Mar 2021		AIC	7708.864
Time:	23:11:45		BIC	7732.495
Sample:	0		HQIC	7717.924
	- 834			
Covariance Type:	opg			

	coef	std err	z	P>|z|	[0.025	0.975]
const	422.5370	3593.885	0.118	0.906	-6621.347	7466.421
ar.L1	0.4603	0.043	10.759	0.000	0.376	0.544
ar.L2	0.5390	0.043	12.585	0.000	0.455	0.623
ma.L1	0.7660	0.032	23.996	0.000	0.703	0.829
sigma2	592.5712	11.593	51.113	0.000	569.849	615.294

Ljung-Box (L1) (Q):	0.93	Jarque-Bera (JB):	5757.42
Prob(Q):	0.34	Prob(JB):	0.00
Heteroskedasticity (H):	178.08	Skew:	1.17
Prob(H) (two-sided):	0.00	Kurtosis:	15.66

The results summary of all the models can be interpreted in a very similar manner as you did above. If you want to introduce the seasonal components to the ARIMA model, it becomes a SARIMA model. The seasonal order can also be defined per Table 6-7.

Table 6-7. *SARIMA Model Parameter Explanation, the following table is a representation of parameters and their explanation*

Parameters	Explanation
Endog	The observed time-series process y
Order	The (p,d,q) order of the model for the number of AR parameters, differences, and MA parameters
seasonal_order	The (p,d,q) order of the seasonal component of the model for the AR parameters, differences, MA parameters, and periodicity
Trend	Parameter controlling the deterministic trend polynomial $A(t)$.
enforce_stationarity	Whether or not to transform the AR parameters to enforce stationarity in the autoregressive component of the model. Default is True.

```
# ARMA example
from statsmodels.tsa.arima.model import ARIMA
from random import random
# fit model
model = ARIMA(y, order=(2, 1, 1))
model_fit = model.fit()
# make prediction
yhat = model_fit.predict(len(y), len(y))
print(yhat)
model_fit.summary()

# SARIMA example
from statsmodels.tsa.statespace.sarimax import SARIMAX
from random import random
# fit model
model = SARIMAX(y, order=(1, 1, 1), seasonal_order=(0, 0, 0, 0))
model_fit = model.fit(disp=False)
# make prediction
yhat = model_fit.predict(len(y), len(y))
print(yhat)
model_fit.summary()
```

Table 6-8. *SARIMA Model Results*

SARIMAX Results

Dep. Variable:	y	No. Observations:	834
Model:	SARIMAX(1, 1, 1)	Log Likelihood	-3841.210
Date:	Mon, 01 Mar 2021	AIC	7688.419
Time:	23:13:53	BIC	7702.594
Sample:	0	HQIC	7693.854
	- 834		
Covariance Type:	opg		

	coef	std err	z	P>|z|	[0.025	0.975]
ar.L1	-0.5398	0.043	-12.639	0.000	-0.624	-0.456
ma.L1	0.7664	0.032	24.047	0.000	0.704	0.829
sigma2	592.5977	11.206	52.880	0.000	570.633	614.562

Ljung-Box (L1) (Q):	0.87	Jarque-Bera (JB):	5724.72
Prob(Q):	0.35	Prob(JB):	0.00
Heteroskedasticity (H):	184.64	Skew:	1.13
Prob(H) (two-sided):	0.00	Kurtosis:	15.64

The p-values of the coefficients from Table 6-8 are statistically significant at a 5% level of significance as the values are less than 0.05. The summary of the model output produced above uses primarily the OLS as a measurement technique, and the OLS method is very similar to the multiple linear regression model. Hence the model coefficients, their relevance, and an interpretation can be made easily.

Time Series: LIME

Using the LIME explainable library, you can take the 12 lags as features and train a regression model and explain the predictions as shown below. As a first step, you need to install the LIME library if you have not installed it:

```
!pip install Lime
 import lime
import lime.lime_tabular
explainer = lime.lime_tabular.LimeTabularExplainer(np.array(X),
                                            mode='regression',
```

```
                                    feature_names=X.columns,
                                    class_names=['t'],
                                    verbose=True)
explainer.feature_frequencies
# asking for explanation for LIME model
i = 60
exp = explainer.explain_instance(np.array(X)[i],
                        new_model.predict,
                        num_features=12
                        )
exp.show_in_notebook(show_table=True)
```

In the above script, you consider the time series model as a supervised learning model and used 12 lags as features. From the LIME library you use the LIME tabular explainer. Figure 6-9 shows an explanation of record number 60.

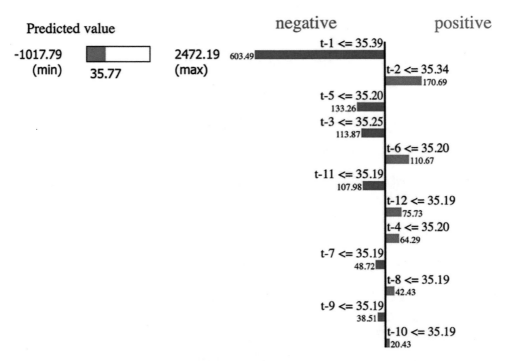

Figure 6-9. *LIME explanation for record 60*

The predicted value is 35.77, and the lower threshold value and upper threshold value reflect the confidence band of the predicted outcome. The positive factors and negative factors contributing towards the prediction are shown in Figure 6-9. Lag 1 is a very important feature; the second important feature is lag 2, then lag 5, lag 3, lag 6, and so on. The lag values as features and their contribution towards the predicted value is shown in Figure 6-10.

t-1	34.99
t-2	34.97
t-5	34.98
t-3	34.98
t-6	35.03
t-11	35.06
t-12	35.05
t-4	34.98
t-7	35.05
t-8	35.04
t-9	35.05
t-10	35.05

Figure 6-10. *Feature importance for the model*

```
 # Code for SP-LIME
import warnings
from lime import submodular_pick

# Remember to convert the dataframe to matrix values
# SP-LIME returns exaplanations on a sample set to provide a non redundant
global decision boundary of original model
sp_obj = submodular_pick.SubmodularPick(explainer, np.array(X),
                                        new_model.predict,
                                        num_features=12,
                                        num_exps_desired=10)
```

```
import matplotlib.pyplot as plt
plt.savefig('[exp.as_pyplot_figure() for exp in sp_obj.sp_explanations
].png', dpi=300)
images = [exp.as_pyplot_figure() for exp in sp_obj.sp_explanations ]
exp.predicted_value
```

The submodular pick for explaining models provides a global understanding of the model by a set of instances from the data. In the above script, you consider all 12 lag-based features, 10 instances for the user to inspect or show explanations.

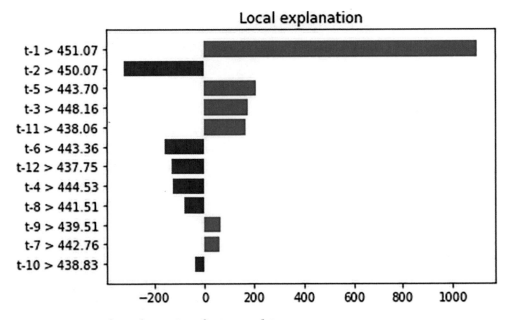

Figure 6-11. *Local explanation for record 0*

In Figure 6-11, lag 1 is very important in predicting the output value. The green bars improve the prediction and the red bars reduce the predicted value. This is the local explanation for the first record. In a similar way you can consider other sample records and generate such explanations.

Conclusion

In this chapter, you learned how to interpret the time series model. You considered the time series model as a supervised learning model and interpreted the feature importance for all of the features. You explored the autoregressive models, moving average models, and autoregressive and integrated moving average models. Using LIME as an explainability library, you looked at the lags' importance in predicting the target value. Also, you looked at the positive lag and negative lag features that contribute towards the predicted outcome.

CHAPTER 7

Explainability for NLP

This chapter explains the use of ELI5 and SHAP-explainable AI-based Python libraries with natural language processing (NLP) based tasks such as text classification models. The prediction decisions made by machine learning models for supervised learning tasks are of unstructured data. Text classification is a task where you need to consider text sentences or phrases as input and classify them into discrete categories. An example is news classification, where the content is used as the input and the output is classified into politics, business, sports, technology, and so on. A similar use case is spam detection in email classification, where the email content is used as the input and classified into spam or not spam. In this scenario, it is important to know if an email is classified into spam, then why? Which tokens present in the content actually lead to the prediction? This is of interest to the end user. When I say NLP tasks here, there any many tasks, but I'll limit it to text classification use cases and similar use cases like entity recognition, parts of speech tagging, and sentiment analysis.

© Pradeepta Mishra 2022
P. Mishra, *Practical Explainable AI Using Python*, https://doi.org/10.1007/978-1-4842-7158-2_7

Natural Language Processing Tasks

Today the entire world is connected through the World Wide Web. Unstructured textual data is everywhere. It's in social media, email conversations, chats through various applications, HTML-based pages, word documents, customer service center support tickets, online survey responses, and more. The following are some use cases associated with unstructured data:

- Document classification, where the input is a text document and the output can be a binary class or a multiclass label.

- Sometimes if the sentiments are labelled, then the sentiments also follow a document classification use case. Otherwise, the sentiment classification would be a lexicon-based classification.

- Named entity recognition (NER) models, where the input is a text document and the output is a named entity class.

- Text summarization, where a large text is compressed and represented in a compact form.

In NLP text classification, NER models, next word prediction is common, where the input is a sentence or word vectors and the output is a label that needs to be classified or predicted. Before the machine learning era, the text classification task was fairly manual, where a group of annotators used to read, understand the meaning of the text expressed in a document, and attach it to one class. With the massive explosion of unstructured data, this manual way of classifying the data became very difficult. Now some annotated data can be fed into a machine and a learning algorithm can be trained so that in the future the trained model can be used to make predictions.

Explainability for Text Classification

The unstructured documents or input text vectors are highly dimensional. The predictive models used to classify the documents need to be explained because the reasons behind a prediction or the features behind the predicted class need to be shown to the end user. In case of text classification, the model predicts class 1 against class 2, so it is important to know the keywords that are actually positive for class 1 vs. negative for class 1. In a multi-class classification, this becomes more complex since you need to explain all the keywords that lead to a prediction of a particular class. In this chapter, you will look at both scenarios.

Figure 7-1 shows the steps that are required to engage the XAI into text classification models.

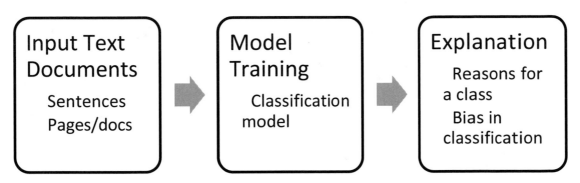

Input Text Documents

Sentences
Pages/docs

Model Training

Classification model

Explanation

Reasons for a class
Bias in classification

Figure 7-1. *Steps in a text explanation where an AI model is involved*

The input texts are represented in the form of a vector and the document term matrix is used to develop the classification model and finally the predicted class needs to be explained using the explainability library just to know the features or words that are responsible for predicting the specific class label.

Dataset for Text Classification

In this chapter you are going to use the Large Movie Review Dataset from http:// ai.stanford.edu/~amaas/data/sentiment/. This dataset has 50,000 reviews, and 25,000 are already labelled with a binary classification tag, such as a positive or negative review. It has another 25,000 reviews for testing purposes. You are going to use this dataset to create a text classification model to predict movie reviews. Post prediction you are going to analyze the reasons for the predictions and further explain the importance of features and other explainability elements from this text classification machine learning model. In this task, you provide the review sentences to the machine learning model and the model predicts the emotion as positive or negative. Hence the ML model is considered here as a black box model. It subsequently raises the question, how can someone trust results from a black box model?

```
import warnings
warnings.filterwarnings("ignore")
import pandas as pd
from keras.datasets import imdb
imdb = pd.read_csv('IMDB Dataset.csv')
imdb.head()
```

The IMDB movie dataset contains reviews and sentiments. The sentiments are labelled as positive and negative, which is a binary class label system. The review gets cleaned up, stop words are removed, and the text is converted into vectors. The following script shows the splitting of the dataset into train and test datasets using the sklearn library's function `train-test-split`:

```
from sklearn.model_selection import train_test_split
from sklearn.feature_extraction.text import CountVectorizer
from sklearn.linear_model import LogisticRegressionCV
from sklearn.pipeline import make_pipeline
vec = CountVectorizer()
clf = LogisticRegressionCV()
clf.fit(vec,imdb.sentiment)
```

To distribute the data into train and test sets, you use the `train-test-split` function from the sklearn library. The count vectorizer converts the tokens and represents the tokens as vectors, which is a document term matrix representation from the corpus. The count vector is initialized and stored in `vec` and then the logistic regression model with cross validation is initialized to develop a training model. The initialized object is stored in `clf`. The last step is to train the model using the `fit` method.

A pipeline is a method where all of the preprocessing steps, model training steps, and validation steps can be sequenced and triggered once. In this pipeline, you convert the textual data from words to the count vector and then pass through a classifier. The textual sentences are first converted into a structured data table. This happens using the count of the words present in each sentence. In the above example, the reviews are considered as documents. Each document is parsed into words. A unique list of words is collected from all of the reviews and then each word is considered as a feature. If you take the count of each word in various reviews, it is called count vectorizer. Since this is a movie review sentiment analysis dataset, it is classified into a positive class and a negative class, which leads towards a binary classification problem. The pipeline stores the sequence of transformations and training steps and gets executed by calling the fit method from the sklearn library.

```
from sklearn import metrics

def print_report(pipe):
    y_test = imdb.sentiment
    y_pred = pipe.predict(imdb.review)
    report = metrics.classification_report(y_test, y_pred)
    print(report)
    print("accuracy: {:0.3f}".format(metrics.accuracy_score(y_test,
    y_pred)))

print_report(pipe)
```

In the above piece of script, you predict the sentiments on the test dataset and compute the error metric for the classification accuracy. In this example, the classification accuracy is 95%, which is a very good accuracy.

Explaining Using ELI5

In order to explain the text classification model, you need to install the explainable AI (XAI) library ELI5. It is known as *explain it like I am 5*. This library can be installed either using pip install or using conda install from an Anaconda distribution.

```
!pip install eli5
import eli5
eli5.show_weights(clf, top=10) #this result is not meaningful, as weight
and feature names are not there
```

Once the library is installed, you can write an import statement to call the library.

```
eli5.show_weights(clf,feature_names=vec.get_feature_names(),
target_names=set(imdb.sentiment))
#make sense
```

The results from the ELI5 module for a base linear classifier are not meaningful. It provides weights and features. The feature names are not meaningful. To make them meaningful, you can pass the name of the feature names and target names.

y=positive top features

Weight[?]	Feature
+0.875	excellent
+0.753	refreshing
+0.733	perfect
+0.716	superb
... 51892 more positive ...	
... 49984 more negative ...	
-0.713	lacks
-0.718	poor
-0.726	forgettable
-0.728	laughable
-0.757	lame
-0.764	horrible
-0.771	dull
-0.775	fails
-0.793	disappointing
-0.813	terrible
-0.858	poorly
-0.889	boring
-0.970	disappointment
-1.071	awful
-1.334	waste
-1.375	worst

Figure 7-2. *Features extracted from the model for the positive sentiment class*

The features in Figure 7-2 in green are positive features for the target class positive and red ones are negative features, which support the other class. The feature weight along with the weight value indicates the relative importance of the features in classifying the sentiments to one category.

Calculating the Feature Weights for Local Explanation

The feature weights are calculated using the decision path. The decision path follows a series of if/else/then statements that connect the predicted class from the root of the tree through the branches of the tree. In the above example, logistic regression is used as a model to train the sentiment classifier, hence the weights are the coefficients of the logistic regression model. For a complex model like a random forest or a gradient boosting model, the decision path of the tree is followed. Basically the weights are estimator parameters that you use in the model training phase.

Local Explanation Example 1

```
eli5.show_prediction(clf, imdb.review[0], vec=vec,
                     target_names=set(imdb.sentiment))         # explain
                     local prediction
```

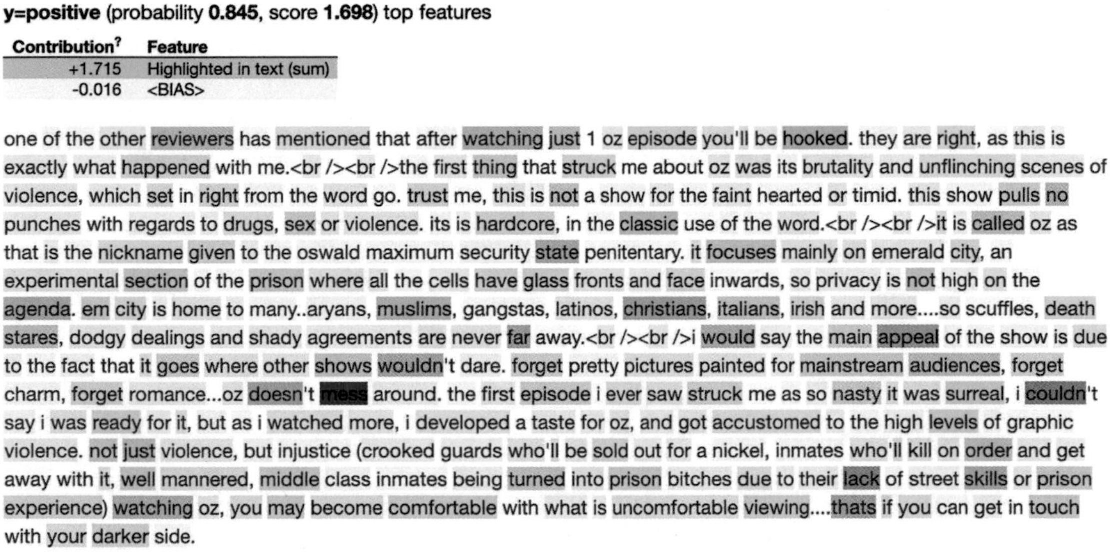

y=positive (probability **0.845**, score **1.698**) top features

Contribution[?]	Feature
+1.715	Highlighted in text (sum)
-0.016	<BIAS>

one of the other reviewers has mentioned that after watching just 1 oz episode you'll be hooked. they are right, as this is exactly what happened with me.

the first thing that struck me about oz was its brutality and unflinching scenes of violence, which set in right from the word go. trust me, this is not a show for the faint hearted or timid. this show pulls no punches with regards to drugs, sex or violence. its is hardcore, in the classic use of the word.

it is called oz as that is the nickname given to the oswald maximum security state penitentary. it focuses mainly on emerald city, an experimental section of the prison where all the cells have glass fronts and face inwards, so privacy is not high on the agenda. em city is home to many..aryans, muslims, gangstas, latinos, christians, italians, irish and more....so scuffles, death stares, dodgy dealings and shady agreements are never far away.

i would say the main appeal of the show is due to the fact that it goes where other shows wouldn't dare. forget pretty pictures painted for mainstream audiences, forget charm, forget romance...oz doesn't mess around. the first episode i ever saw struck me as so nasty it was surreal, i couldn't say i was ready for it, but as i watched more, i developed a taste for oz, and got accustomed to the high levels of graphic violence. not just violence, but injustice (crooked guards who'll be sold out for a nickel, inmates who'll kill on order and get away with it, well mannered, middle class inmates being turned into prison bitches due to their lack of street skills or prison experience) watching oz, you may become comfortable with what is uncomfortable viewing....thats if you can get in touch with your darker side.

Figure 7-3. *Plotting the important features of the sentences for better clarity*

BIAS is the intercept term from the logistic regression classifier. We can use the count vectorizer and linear classifier, hence the mapping is quite clear as each word's weight corresponds to the coefficients of the linear classifier. In order to explain a single movie review, which is called local interpretation, you can pass that through the show prediction function. Since it is a binary classifier, the log odds can be calculated. The log odds is 1.698. If you use the formula exp(log odds)/1+exp(log odds) then you get back the probability value 0.845. There is 84.5% chance is that the review[0] belongs to the positive sentiment. The highlighted text in green in Figure 7-3 leads towards the positive log odds score and the text in red reduces the log odds score. The total contribution is the sum of contributions from each text in green and red, and the net result is the log odds score.

Local Explanation Example 2

In a similar way you can explain reviews number 123 and 100. Review 123 is classified as negative and the probability for the negative class is 0.980. Review number 100 is classified as positive with a probability value of 0.670. See Figure 7-4.

```
eli5.show_prediction(clf, imdb.review[123], vec=vec,
                     target_names=set(imdb.sentiment)) # explain local
                     prediction
```

y=negative (probability **0.980**, score **-3.877**) top features

Contribution[?]	Feature
+3.861	Highlighted in text (sum)
+0.016	<BIAS>

ah yes the 1980s , a time of reaganomics and sly , chuck and a host of other action stars hiding in a remote jungle blowing away commies . at the time i couldn't believe how movies like rambo , missing in action and uncommon valor (and who can forget the ridiculous red dawn ?) made money at the box office , they're turgid action crap fests with a rather off putting right wing agenda and they have dated very badly . troma's war is a tongue in cheek take on these type of movies but you've got to ask yourself did they need spoofing in the first place ? of course not . troma's war lacks any sort of sophistication - though it does make the point that there's no real difference between right wing tyrants and left wing ones - and sometimes feels more like a grade z movie than a send up . maybe it is ?

Figure 7-4. *Local explanation for a negative class prediction*

Local Explanation Example 3

In example 1 you looked at the first record, where the probability of a positive class is more than 80%. In example 2, the probability of a negative class is 98%. The words highlighted in green contribute towards the negative class of the prediction. See Figure 7-5.

```
eli5.show_prediction(clf, imdb.review[100], vec=vec,
                     target_names=set(imdb.sentiment)) # explain local
                     prediction
```

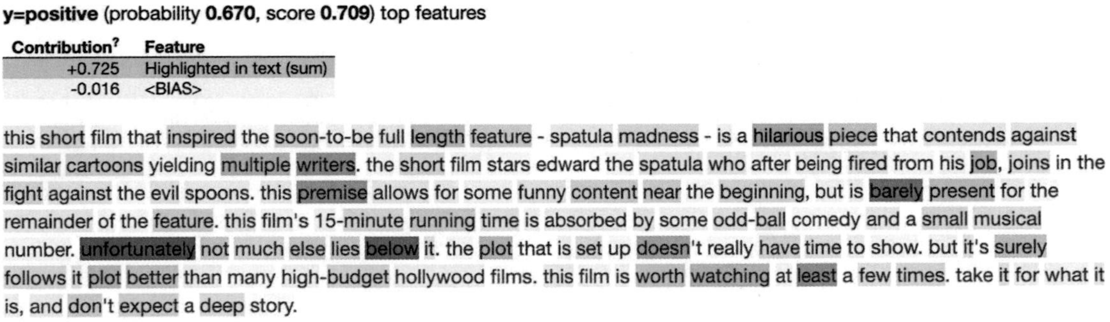

y=positive (probability **0.670**, score **0.709**) top features

Contribution[7]	Feature
+0.725	Highlighted in text (sum)
-0.016	<BIAS>

this short film that inspired the soon-to-be full length feature - spatula madness - is a hilarious piece that contends against similar cartoons yielding multiple writers. the short film stars edward the spatula who after being fired from his job, joins in the fight against the evil spoons. this premise allows for some funny content near the beginning, but is barely present for the remainder of the feature. this film's 15-minute running time is absorbed by some odd-ball comedy and a small musical number. unfortunately not much else lies below it. the plot that is set up doesn't really have time to show. but it's surely follows it plot better than many high-budget hollywood films. this film is worth watching at least a few times. take it for what it is, and don't expect a deep story.

Figure 7-5. *Feature highlight for both positive and negative classes*

Explanation After Stop Word Removal

The above analysis is done just by keeping the stop words in order to retain the context of the text input. If you remove the stop words from the input text, then a few redundant features will be removed from the input vector. You will be able to get more meaningful features for the explanation. The bias is the intercept term from the model. In the above script, you looked at the bag of words without stop word removal.

```
vec = CountVectorizer(stop_words='english')
clf = LogisticRegressionCV()
pipe = make_pipeline(vec, clf)
pipe.fit(imdb.review, imdb.sentiment)

print_report(pipe)
```

Table 7-1. *The Classifier Model Accuracy After Refinement process is shown in Table 7-1*

	precision	recall	f1-score	support
negative	0.95	0.94	0.95	25000
positive	0.94	0.95	0.95	25000
accuracy			0.95	50000
macro avg	0.95	0.95	0.95	50000
weighted avg	0.95	0.95	0.95	50000

accuracy: 0.948

You tried the linear classifier. As you increase the model complexity, you get more refined tokens and more refined context. See Table 7-1. As an example, you updated the logistic regression model to a logistic regression model with cross validation. You can see that review number 0 has a more refined probability score which, at 78.7%, is little lower than the earlier model.

```
eli5.show_prediction(clf, imdb.review[0], vec=vec,
                     target_names=set(imdb.sentiment),
                     targets=['positive'])
```

y=positive (probability **0.787**, score **1.307**) top features

Contribution?	Feature
+1.315	Highlighted in text (sum)
-0.008	<BIAS>

one of the other reviewers has mentioned that after watching just 1 oz episode you'll be hooked. they are right, as this is exactly what happened with me.

the first thing that struck me about oz was its brutality and unflinching scenes of violence, which set in right from the word go. trust me, this is not a show for the faint hearted or timid. this show pulls no punches with regards to drugs, sex or violence. its is hardcore, in the classic use of the word.

it is called oz as that is the nickname given to the oswald maximum security state penitentiary. it focuses mainly on emerald city, an experimental section of the prison where all the cells have glass fronts and face inwards, so privacy is not high on the agenda. em city is home to many..aryans, muslims, gangstas, latinos, christians, italians, irish and more....so scuffles, death stares, dodgy dealings and shady agreements are never far away.

i would say the main appeal of the show is due to the fact that it goes where other shows wouldn't dare. forget pretty pictures painted for mainstream audiences, forget charm, forget romance...oz doesn't mess around. the first episode i ever saw struck me as so nasty it was surreal, i couldn't say i was ready for it, but as i watched more, i developed a taste for oz, and got accustomed to the high levels of graphic violence. not just violence, but injustice (crooked guards who'll be sold out for a nickel, inmates who'll kill on order and get away with it, well mannered, middle class inmates being turned into prison bitches due to their lack of street skills or prison experience) watching oz, you may become comfortable with what is uncomfortable viewing....thats if you can get in touch with your darker side.

Figure 7-6. *Highlighted feature importance for the positive class*

The movie review text (Figure 7-6) shows repetition of some key words. If there is too much repetition, then the counts will be inflated in the count vectorizer. If there are many words whose counts are inflated, then it would reflect the feature in the feature importance list. In order to avoid the influence of a higher count of words in a count vectorizer, you must apply a normalization method so that all features get equal importance in the classification process. In order to do that, you can introduce a new vectorizer which is called *term frequency and inverse document frequency*, popularly known as a (tf-idf) vectorizer. The following formula can be used to calculate the value of tf-idf:

Tf-idf value of ith word in jth document = term frequency of ith word in jth document * log (total number of documents / number of documents containing the ith word)

The tf-idf function is readily available from the sklearn library in feature extraction from a text module. You do not have to compute for a corpus the tf-idf values; you can apply the following method:

```
from sklearn.feature_extraction.text import TfidfVectorizer

vec = TfidfVectorizer()
clf = LogisticRegressionCV()
pipe = make_pipeline(vec, clf)
pipe.fit(imdb.review, imdb.sentiment)

print_report(pipe)
```

Table 7-2. *Classification Report for the tf-idf Vectorizer-Based Model*

	precision	recall	f1-score	support
negative	0.96	0.95	0.95	25000
positive	0.95	0.96	0.95	25000
accuracy			0.95	50000
macro avg	0.95	0.95	0.95	50000
weighted avg	0.95	0.95	0.95	50000

```
accuracy: 0.954
```

Per Table 7-2 and Figure 7-7, there is no visible difference in the model accuracy after the application of the tf-idf transformation. However, the probability value changes marginally and the score also changes marginally.

```
eli5.show_prediction(clf, imdb.review[0], vec=vec,
                 target_names=set(imdb.sentiment),
                 targets=['positive'])
```

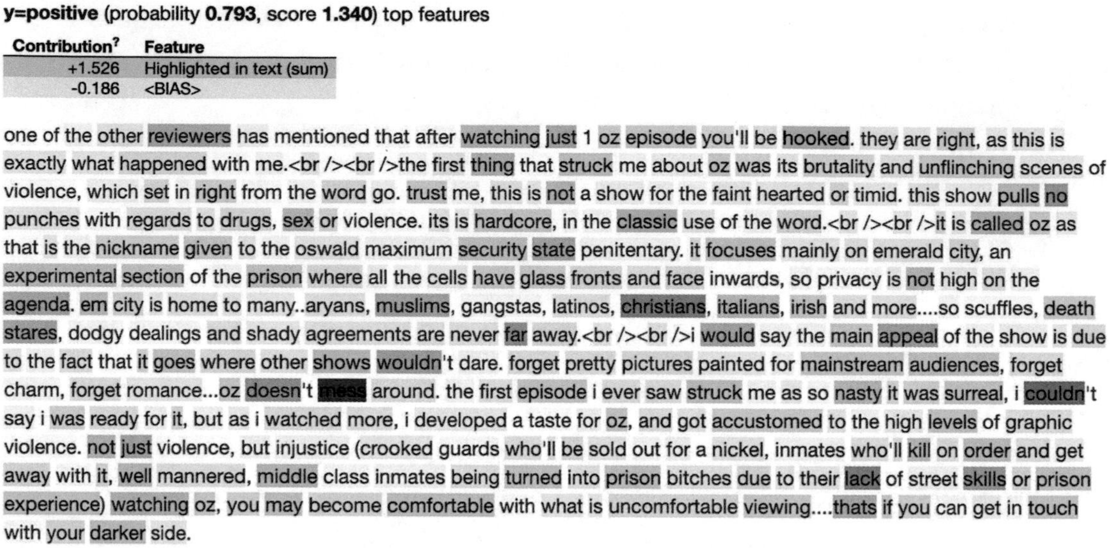

y=positive (probability **0.793**, score **1.340**) top features

Contribution?	Feature
+1.526	Highlighted in text (sum)
-0.186	<BIAS>

one of the other reviewers has mentioned that after watching just 1 oz episode you'll be hooked. they are right, as this is exactly what happened with me.

the first thing that struck me about oz was its brutality and unflinching scenes of violence, which set in right from the word go. trust me, this is not a show for the faint hearted or timid. this show pulls no punches with regards to drugs, sex or violence. its is hardcore, in the classic use of the word.

it is called oz as that is the nickname given to the oswald maximum security state penitentiary. it focuses mainly on emerald city, an experimental section of the prison where all the cells have glass fronts and face inwards, so privacy is not high on the agenda. em city is home to many..aryans, muslims, gangstas, latinos, christians, italians, irish and more....so scuffles, death stares, dodgy dealings and shady agreements are never far away.

i would say the main appeal of the show is due to the fact that it goes where other shows wouldn't dare. forget pretty pictures painted for mainstream audiences, forget charm, forget romance...oz doesn't mess around. the first episode i ever saw struck me as so nasty it was surreal, i couldn't say i was ready for it, but as i watched more, i developed a taste for oz, and got accustomed to the high levels of graphic violence. not just violence, but injustice (crooked guards who'll be sold out for a nickel, inmates who'll kill on order and get away with it, well mannered, middle class inmates being turned into prison bitches due to their lack of street skills or prison experience) watching oz, you may become comfortable with what is uncomfortable viewing....thats if you can get in touch with your darker side.

Figure 7-7. *Feature highlights for the positive class after tf-idf application*

```
vec = TfidfVectorizer(stop_words='english')
clf = LogisticRegressionCV()
pipe = make_pipeline(vec, clf)
pipe.fit(imdb.review, imdb.sentiment)

print_report(pipe)
```

Table 7-3. *Classification Report After Stop Word Removal from tf-idf vec Approach*

	precision	recall	f1-score	support
negative	0.96	0.95	0.96	25000
positive	0.95	0.96	0.96	25000
accuracy			0.96	50000
macro avg	0.96	0.96	0.96	50000
weighted avg	0.96	0.96	0.96	50000

```
accuracy: 0.956
```

Tf-idf is a vector-based representation of textual data. This is very useful when the count-based features have high frequencies. In order to avoid the influence of high frequency words on the classification algorithm, it is preferable to use the tf-idf-based vectorizer. When initializing the tf-idf vectorizer, if you provide the stop word option, then for the stop words the vectors will not be created. Also, for the tf-idf calculation the stop word count will not be considered. Stop words are defined as words that do not have any meaning themselves but help us understand the context along with other words. As a feature, they do not add much value to the text classification task; rather, they increase the dimensionality of the data. Hence stop word removal will help you get better accuracy by reducing the data dimensions. See Figure 7-8.

```
eli5.show_prediction(clf, imdb.review[0], vec=vec,
                     target_names=set(imdb.sentiment),
                     targets=['positive'])
```

y=positive (probability **0.755**, score **1.125**) top features

Contribution?	Feature
+1.227	Highlighted in text (sum)
-0.102	<BIAS>

one of the other reviewers has mentioned that after watching just 1 oz episode you'll be hooked. they are right, as this is exactly what happened with me.

the first thing that struck me about oz was its brutality and unflinching scenes of violence, which set in right from the word go. trust me, this is not a show for the faint hearted or timid. this show pulls no punches with regards to drugs, sex or violence. its is hardcore, in the classic use of the word.

it is called oz as that is the nickname given to the oswald maximum security state penitentiary. it focuses mainly on emerald city, an experimental section of the prison where all the cells have glass fronts and face inwards, so privacy is not high on the agenda. em city is home to many..aryans, muslims, gangstas, latinos, christians, italians, irish and more....so scuffles, death stares, dodgy dealings and shady agreements are never far away.

i would say the main appeal of the show is due to the fact that it goes where other shows wouldn't dare. forget pretty pictures painted for mainstream audiences, forget charm, forget romance...oz doesn't mess around. the first episode i ever saw struck me as so nasty it was surreal, i couldn't say i was ready for it, but as i watched more, i developed a taste for oz, and got accustomed to the high levels of graphic violence. not just violence, but injustice (crooked guards who'll be sold out for a nickel, inmates who'll kill on order and get away with it, well mannered, middle class inmates being turned into prison bitches due to their lack of street skills or prison experience) watching oz, you may become comfortable with what is uncomfortable viewing....thats if you can get in touch with your darker side.

Figure 7-8. *Important features highlighted from a more refined model*

N-gram-Based Text Classification

Let's consider two new approaches to developing the text classification model. For text classification, either you can use words or you can use characters. The following script analyses the characters and picks up the bigrams until five grams and keeps those n-grams as features in the tf-idf vectorizers. After the vector creation, the data for review is fed to the pipeline and model training happens. The training accuracy for sentiment classification is 99.8%, which is good. Now you can explain the individual prediction and see what factors contribute to positive sentiment and what contribute to negative sentiment (see Table 7-4 and Figure 7-9).

```
vec = TfidfVectorizer(stop_words='english', analyzer='char',
                      ngram_range=(2,5))
clf = LogisticRegressionCV()
pipe = make_pipeline(vec, clf)
pipe.fit(imdb.review, imdb.sentiment)
print_report(pipe)
```

Table 7-4. *N-gram-Based Vectorizer is taken as a pre-processing method and n-gram 2 till n-gram 5 is considered to create the training model using TF-IDF vectorizer and following Table 7-4 shows the Classification Report*

```
                 precision      recall  f1-score      support

    negative          1.00        1.00      1.00        25000
    positive          1.00        1.00      1.00        25000

    accuracy                                1.00        50000
   macro avg          1.00        1.00      1.00        50000
weighted avg          1.00        1.00      1.00        50000


accuracy: 0.998
```

```
eli5.show_prediction(clf, imdb.review[0], vec=vec,
                     target_names=set(imdb.sentiment),
                     targets=['positive'])
```

y=positive (probability **0.949**, score **2.914**) top features

Contribution?	Feature
+3.106	Highlighted in text (sum)
-0.192	<BIAS>

one of the other reviewers has mentioned that after watching just 1 oz episode you'll be hooked. they are right, as this is exactly what happened with me.

the first thing that struck me about oz was its brutality and unflinching scenes of violence, which set in right from the word go. trust me, this is not a show for the faint hearted or timid. this show pulls no punches with regards to drugs, sex or violence. its is hardcore, in the classic use of the word.

it is called oz as that is the nickname given to the oswald maximum security state penitentary. it focuses mainly on emerald city, an experimental section of the prison where all the cells have glass fronts and face inwards, so privacy is not high on the agenda. em city is home to many..aryans, muslims, gangstas, latinos, christians, italians, irish and more....so scuffles, death stares, dodgy dealings and shady agreements are never far away.

i would say the main appeal of the show is due to the fact that it goes where other shows wouldn't dare. forget pretty pictures painted for mainstream audiences, forget charm, forget romance...oz doesn't mess around. the first episode i ever saw struck me as so nasty it was surreal, i couldn't say i was ready for it, but as i watched more, i developed a taste for oz, and got accustomed to the high levels of graphic violence. not just violence, but injustice (crooked guards who'll be sold out for a nickel, inmates who'll kill on order and get away with it, well mannered, middle class inmates being turned into prison bitches due to their lack of street skills or prison experience) watching oz, you may become comfortable with what is uncomfortable viewing....thats if you can get in touch with your darker side.

Figure 7-9. *2 gram and 5 gram feature highlights from the model*

In the above script, you picked up the first review's total contribution, which is the net result of green plus red highlighted text elements, and that is +3.106. Since the net result is +3.106, it is classified as a positive sentiment, which is also shown as the probability of positive sentiment is 0.949 and log odds for the classification is 2.914. -0.192 is the bias, which is also known as the intercept term for the logistic regression model.

The count vectorizer is appropriate when the length of the text documents is shorter. If the length of the text is longer, which means each word has a high frequency or is repeated multiple times in the text, then you should use the tf-idf vectorizer. The count vectorizer is just the words and their frequencies represented in a tabular format or array. From the following script, a count vectorizer with stop word removal reduces the number of features and makes it very relevant. After training the model, you can see that the accuracy is 94.8%.

Also, when you explain the first review, the sum of the net result of green plus red highlighted text is +1.315, and since the net result is positive, the sentiment is tagged as a positive sentiment with a probability score of 78.7% and a log odds score of 1.307. You can keep updating the feature extraction and keep updating the model type to make the prediction better. The better the model, the better the explanation of the classification of sentiments. The following script shows the tf-idf vector as a feature without the stop word removal process.

You can see in the highlighted text in Figure 7-10 there are few stop words and bigrams and trigrams, which are not correctly labelled with color. In order to take care of this, you can use the option in the analyzer as char_wb. char as an analyzer you have seen before because it parses the text into characters as n-grams, but this process takes time. In addition, char_wb is more to fine-tune, to take those n-grams as features where the n-grams are not overlapping each other.

```
vec = TfidfVectorizer(stop_words='english', analyzer='char_wb',
                    ngram_range=(2,5))
clf = LogisticRegressionCV()
pipe = make_pipeline(vec, clf)
pipe.fit(imdb.review, imdb.sentiment)

print_report(pipe)
```

```
eli5.show_prediction(clf, imdb.review[0], vec=vec,
                     target_names=set(imdb.sentiment),
                     targets=['positive'])
```

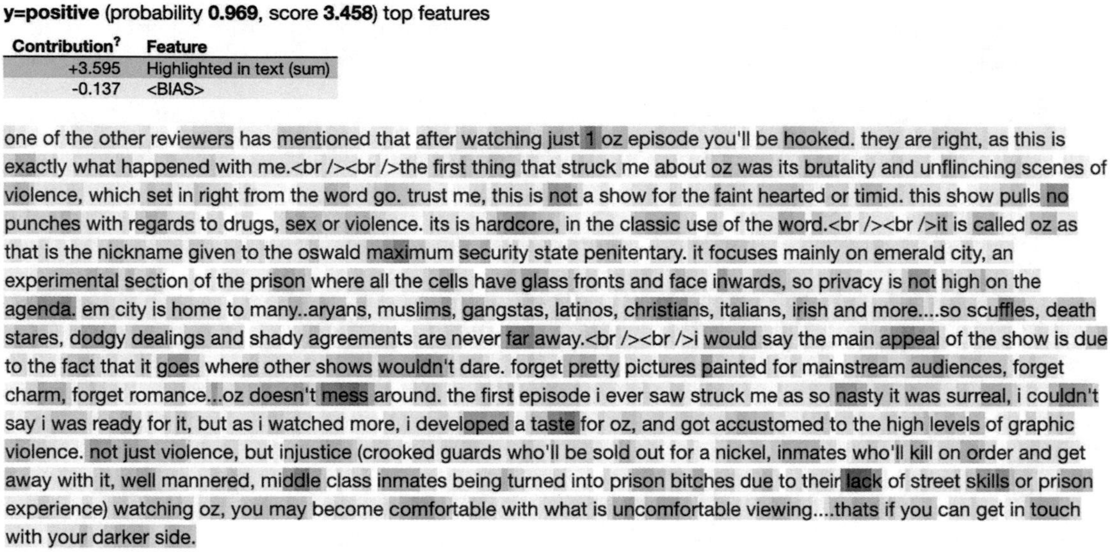

y=positive (probability **0.969**, score **3.458**) top features

Contribution[?]	Feature
+3.595	Highlighted in text (sum)
-0.137	<BIAS>

one of the other reviewers has mentioned that after watching just 1 oz episode you'll be hooked. they are right, as this is exactly what happened with me.

the first thing that struck me about oz was its brutality and unflinching scenes of violence, which set in right from the word go. trust me, this is not a show for the faint hearted or timid. this show pulls no punches with regards to drugs, sex or violence. its is hardcore, in the classic use of the word.

it is called oz as that is the nickname given to the oswald maximum security state penitentiary. it focuses mainly on emerald city, an experimental section of the prison where all the cells have glass fronts and face inwards, so privacy is not high on the agenda. em city is home to many..aryans, muslims, gangstas, latinos, christians, italians, irish and more....so scuffles, death stares, dodgy dealings and shady agreements are never far away.

i would say the main appeal of the show is due to the fact that it goes where other shows wouldn't dare. forget pretty pictures painted for mainstream audiences, forget charm, forget romance...oz doesn't mess around. the first episode i ever saw struck me as so nasty it was surreal, i couldn't say i was ready for it, but as i watched more, i developed a taste for oz, and got accustomed to the high levels of graphic violence. not just violence, but injustice (crooked guards who'll be sold out for a nickel, inmates who'll kill on order and get away with it, well mannered, middle class inmates being turned into prison bitches due to their lack of street skills or prison experience) watching oz, you may become comfortable with what is uncomfortable viewing....thats if you can get in touch with your darker side.

Figure 7-10. *Non-overlapping character N-grams as feature importance*

This time the results look better. As an example, "watching just 1" is a negative n-gram that is not overlapping with any other n-gram, which is meaningful. Similarly, other n-grams are more refined. If the movie review is limited to a few lines of words you can use a count vectorizer or tf-idf vectorizer, but if the reviews become lengthy, then a hashing vectorizer comes to the rescue. When the review length goes up, the vocabulary size increases, hence a hashing vectorizer is quite useful. In the following script, the hashing vectorizer with one of the advanced ML model stochastic gradient descent classifiers is introduced. This produces a better model than the earlier model (Figure 7-11). This is because earlier models were slightly overfitting as well. To explore explainability, you can take the same first review text and explain the classification label and also look at the words that contributed to the positive sentiment and the negative sentiment.

```
from sklearn.feature_extraction.text import HashingVectorizer
from sklearn.linear_model import SGDClassifier
```

```
vec = HashingVectorizer(stop_words='english', ngram_range=(1,2))
clf = SGDClassifier(random_state=42)
pipe = make_pipeline(vec, clf)
pipe.fit(imdb.review, imdb.sentiment)

print_report(pipe)

eli5.show_prediction(clf, imdb.review[0], vec=vec,
                     target_names=set(imdb.sentiment),
                     targets=['positive'])
```

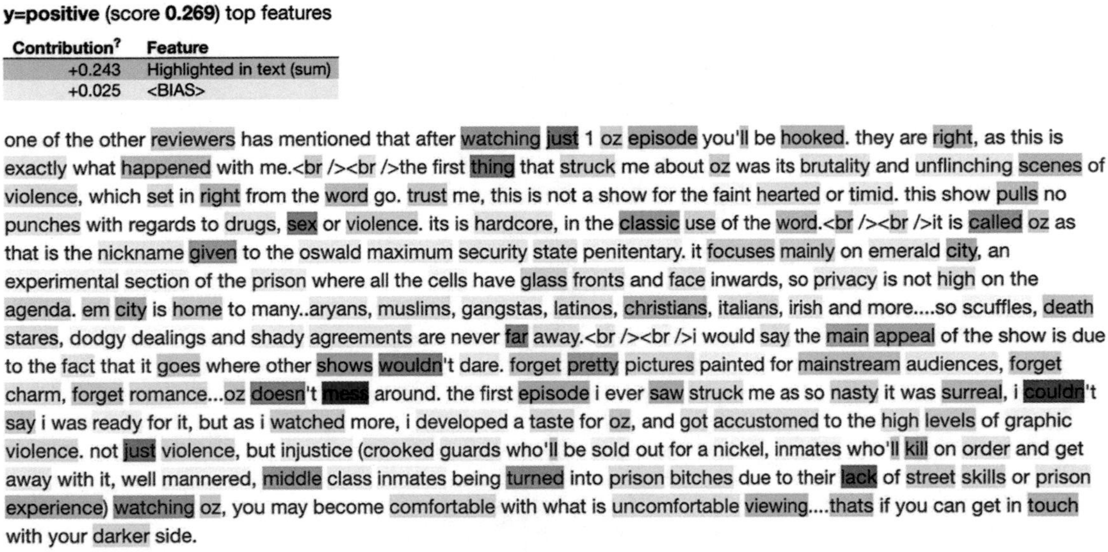

y=positive (score **0.269**) top features

Contribution[7]	Feature
+0.243	Highlighted in text (sum)
+0.025	<BIAS>

one of the other reviewers has mentioned that after watching just 1 oz episode you'll be hooked. they are right, as this is exactly what happened with me.

the first thing that struck me about oz was its brutality and unflinching scenes of violence, which set in right from the word go. trust me, this is not a show for the faint hearted or timid. this show pulls no punches with regards to drugs, sex or violence. its is hardcore, in the classic use of the word.

it is called oz as that is the nickname given to the oswald maximum security state penitentiary. it focuses mainly on emerald city, an experimental section of the prison where all the cells have glass fronts and face inwards, so privacy is not high on the agenda. em city is home to many..aryans, muslims, gangstas, latinos, christians, italians, irish and more....so scuffles, death stares, dodgy dealings and shady agreements are never far away.

i would say the main appeal of the show is due to the fact that it goes where other shows wouldn't dare. forget pretty pictures painted for mainstream audiences, forget charm, forget romance...oz doesn't mess around. the first episode i ever saw struck me as so nasty it was surreal, i couldn't say i was ready for it, but as i watched more, i developed a taste for oz, and got accustomed to the high levels of graphic violence. not just violence, but injustice (crooked guards who'll be sold out for a nickel, inmates who'll kill on order and get away with it, well mannered, middle class inmates being turned into prison bitches due to their lack of street skills or prison experience) watching oz, you may become comfortable with what is uncomfortable viewing....thats if you can get in touch with your darker side.

Figure 7-11. *Very refined highlighted features explain the prediction better*

The first review comment is a positive sentiment, the overall positive score is +0.243, and the score is 0.269. It only considered relevant features as highlighted by the green and red colored text.

```
from eli5.sklearn import InvertableHashingVectorizer
import numpy as np
ivec = InvertableHashingVectorizer(vec)
sample_size = len(imdb.review) // 10
X_sample = np.random.choice(imdb.review, size=sample_size)
ivec.fit(X_sample)
```

```
eli5.show_weights(clf, vec=ivec, top=20,
                target_names=set(imdb.sentiment))
```

The invertible hashing vectorizer helps in featuring the weights along with the feature names from the hashing vectorizer without fitting a huge vocabulary. The notebook output in Figure 7-12 shows the positive and negative features.

y=positive top features

Weight[?]	Feature
+4.547	excellent
+3.812	great
+3.293	wonderful ...
+3.270	perfect ...
+3.195	amazing ...
+3.066	brilliant ...
+3.038	best
... 456783 more positive ...	
... 454840 more negative ...	
-3.070	supposed ...
-3.109	unfortunately
-3.110	minutes
-3.269	stupid
-3.408	worse ...
-3.502	dull ...
-3.819	terrible
-4.213	poor
-4.268	waste
-4.479	bad
-4.562	boring ...
-5.084	awful ...
-6.464	worst

Figure 7-12. *Top features for the positive class prediction*

Multi-Class Label Text Classification Explainability

Let's look at the multi-class classification model, where you have more than two categories in the target column. Multi-class classification is another use case where the dependent variable or target column can have more than two categories or labels. The explainability required here is for each corresponding class label so the important positive and negative features need to be shown. Let's use a customer complaints data set, where the objective is to predict the customer complaints category or type of customer complaints.

```
import pandas as pd
df = pd.read_csv('complaints.csv')
df.shape
df.info()
# Create a new dataframe with two columns
df1 = df[['Product', 'Consumer complaint narrative']].copy()

# Remove missing values (NaN)
df1 = df1[pd.notnull(df1['Consumer complaint narrative'])]

# Renaming second column for a simpler name
df1.columns = ['Product', 'Consumer_complaint']

df1.shape

# Because the computation is time consuming (in terms of CPU), the data was
sampled
df2 = df1.sample(20000, random_state=1).copy()

# Renaming categories
df2.replace({'Product':
            {'Credit reporting, credit repair services, or other personal
            consumer reports':
             'Credit reporting, repair, or other',
             'Credit reporting': 'Credit reporting, repair, or other',
            'Credit card': 'Credit card or prepaid card',
            'Prepaid card': 'Credit card or prepaid card',
            'Payday loan': 'Payday loan, title loan, or personal loan',
            'Money transfer': 'Money transfer, virtual currency, or money
            service',
             'Virtual currency': 'Money transfer, virtual currency, or
            money service'}},
           inplace= True)
df2.head()

pd.DataFrame(df2.Product.unique())
```

The source of dataset is `https://catalog.data.gov/dataset/consumer-complaint-database`. The dataset is cleaned and prepared to predict the complaint category. After reading the data, the Python object DF is created. The following output shows the first few records from the dataset.

From DF you have a copy with only the customer complaint narrative and the product column, for the developing of the multi-class classification model, which is assigned to the DF1 object. Then the data frame is cleaned up by removing the NaNs and putting in simpler names for the variables.

The longer descriptions having more text are cleaned up using shorter and more appropriate names so that you can analyze the data better. There are 13 unique categories of products against which the customer complaint narrative has been mentioned.

```
# Create a new column 'category_id' with encoded categories
df2['category_id'] = df2['Product'].factorize()[0]
category_id_df = df2[['Product', 'category_id']].drop_duplicates()

# Dictionaries for future use
category_to_id = dict(category_id_df.values)
id_to_category = dict(category_id_df[['category_id', 'Product']].values)

# New dataframe
df2.head()

df2.Product.value_counts()
```

For the model training purpose, you need to encode the target column text into numbers. Hence you create the column `category_id` by factorizing the product column. The next two lines of code in the above script create a mapping between the encoded number and the class description. This is useful for reverse transformation after generating predictions. In the following lines of code you create a tf-idf vector with n-grams taken from 1 to 2 and remove the stop words, keeping the sublinear TF and minimum document frequency as 5. If you want to reduce the bias generated by the length of the document, then you have to use the sublinear term frequency TRUE. As you know from Zipf's Law, the frequency of any word is inversely proportional to its rank. The minimum document frequency implies that while developing the vocabulary you should ignore terms that have a document frequency lower than the defined threshold. In the following script it is 5, which means that any term with a frequency less than 5 will not be part of the vocabulary.

The output from the following script shows the count of each class in the multi-class classification target column. The following script fits a logistic regression for a multi-class model using a count vectorizer as a starting point.

```
from sklearn.feature_extraction.text import CountVectorizer
from sklearn.linear_model import LogisticRegressionCV
from sklearn.pipeline import make_pipeline

vec = CountVectorizer()
clf = LogisticRegressionCV()
pipe = make_pipeline(vec, clf)
pipe.fit(df2.Consumer_complaint,df2.Product)

from sklearn import metrics

def print_report(pipe):
    y_test = df2.Product
    y_pred = pipe.predict(df2.Consumer_complaint)
    report = metrics.classification_report(y_test, y_pred)
    print(report)
    print("accuracy: {:0.3f}".format(metrics.accuracy_score(y_test,
    y_pred)))

print_report(pipe)
```

	precision	recall	f1-score	support
Bank account or service	0.97	0.74	0.84	441
Checking or savings account	0.91	0.87	0.89	849
Consumer Loan	0.98	0.59	0.74	296
Credit card or prepaid card	0.91	0.85	0.88	2000
Credit reporting, repair, or other	0.87	0.95	0.91	8231
Debt collection	0.87	0.85	0.86	4075
Money transfer, virtual currency, or money service	0.92	0.80	0.86	358
Money transfers	1.00	0.70	0.82	53
Mortgage	0.96	0.95	0.95	2216
Other financial service	1.00	0.57	0.73	7
Payday loan, title loan, or personal loan	0.93	0.67	0.78	312
Student loan	0.94	0.85	0.89	788
Vehicle loan or lease	0.93	0.68	0.79	374
accuracy			0.89	20000
macro avg	0.94	0.78	0.84	20000
weighted avg	0.89	0.89	0.89	20000

```
accuracy: 0.890
```

Figure 7-13. *Classification accuracy for a multi-class text classification model*

Per Figure 7-13, the model accuracy seems to be fine as it is 89%. In a multi-class classification problem, you typically look at the f1-score, which is a harmonic mean of the precision and recall. The acceptable limit of an f1-score is 75% or more. You can see for a consumer loan and other financial services it is less than 75%. As a starting point, let's have a look at the terms as weights for each class in the classification problem. The result is not meaningful as the feature term names are not available (Figure 7-14).

```
import eli5
eli5.show_weights(clf, top=10)
#this result is not meaningful, as weight and feature names are not there
```

y=Mortgage top features		y=Other financial service top features		y=Payday loan, title loan, or personal loan top features		y=Student loan top features		y=Vehicle loan or lease top features	
Weight?	Feature	Weight?	Feature	Weight?	Feature	Weight?	Feature	Weight?	Feature
+1.119	x15196	+0.229	x14201	+0.578	x14062	+1.081	x15458	+0.607	x4596
+0.777	<BIAS>	+0.201	x6495	+0.535	x16848	+0.776	x22119	+0.597	x24811
+0.769	x9037	+0.191	x11457	+0.362	x10873	+0.735	x14077	+0.524	x3171
+0.621	x15082	+0.167	x2853	+0.358	x4665	+0.473	x19395	+0.395	x20363
+0.533	x20813	+0.167	x15115	+0.311	x13958	+0.436	x1888	+0.352	x1467
+0.506	x18974	+0.153	x13149	+0.296	x1987	+0.427	x8458	+0.318	x13715
+0.486	x7980	+0.150	x22755	... 2746 more positive ...		+0.419	x14062	+0.310	x15678
+0.463	x5262	... 424 more positive ...		... 23451 more negative ...		+0.410	x20478	+0.301	x23501
... 7456 more positive ...		... 25773 more negative ...		-0.295	x15196	+0.380	x10211	... 3355 more positive ...	
... 18741 more negative ...		-0.157	x1528	-0.315	x22119	... 4286 more positive ...		... 22842 more negative ...	
-0.475	x4600	-0.164	x23119	-0.315	x4600	... 21911 more negative ...		-0.295	x25367
-0.481	x24811	-2.364	<BIAS>	-0.537	<BIAS>	-0.381	x3427	-0.610	<BIAS>

Figure 7-14. *Sample feature important for each class*

Since the feature names as terms are not available in Figure 7-14, you cannot make sense out of this. You need to change the script slightly, as below, to include the feature names from the vec object and also to include target names as unique names. Hence you can see the terms that positively impact the class label are in green and the terms that negatively impact it are in red. For each category, such as bank account, service, or consumer loan, you can see the top features. Since you have more than 10 categories, you cannot accommodate all positive and negative terms in one screen, hence you take different snapshots for at least 5 labels at a time in order to accommodate readability of the terms.

```
eli5.show_weights(clf,feature_names=vec.get_feature_names(),target_
names=set(df2.Product))
#make sense
```

y=Bank account or service top features		y=Checking or savings account top features		y=Consumer Loan top features		y=Credit card or prepaid card top features		y=Credit reporting, repair, or other top features	
Weight?	Feature	Weight?	Feature	Weight?	Feature	Weight?	Feature	Weight?	Feature
+0.613	scottrade	+0.423	schwab	+0.604	vehicle	+0.899	<BIAS>	+2.290	<BIAS>
+0.373	2016	+0.387	citibank	+0.556	car	+0.763	card	+1.208	equifax
+0.372	overdraft	+0.365	bank	+0.400	loan	+0.445	capital	+1.078	experian
+0.369	greentree	+0.341	<BIAS>	+0.352	2016	+0.427	purchase	+0.999	transunion
+0.368	debit	+0.340	deposit	+0.351	financial	+0.420	limit	+0.607	inquiries
+0.362	bank	+0.314	overdraft	+0.300	finance	+0.417	minimum	+0.565	freeze
+0.327	requirements	+0.311	bonus	+0.285	dealer	+0.388	rewards	+0.540	mortgage
+0.323	2015	+0.307	debit	+0.265	contract	+0.386	visa	+0.483	inaccurate
+0.310	branch	+0.289	charged	+0.253	corporation	+0.381	unemployment	+0.464	report
+0.306	deposited	+0.288	branch	+0.252	paying	+0.378	issued	+0.447	remove
+0.295	club	+0.287	won	+0.251	credit	+0.376	netspend	+0.444	background
+0.289	hold	+0.287	access	+0.229	tree	+0.366	capitol	+0.432	trans
+0.279	atm	+0.279	link	... 2767 more positive ...		+0.359	found	+0.421	mine
+0.277	fee	+0.275	funds	... 23420 more negative ...		+0.344	citibank	+0.398	inquiry
... 3662 more positive ...		... 4762 more positive ...		-0.231	2018	+0.340	citi	+0.387	removed
... 22525 more negative ...		... 21425 more negative ...		-0.245	problem	+0.337	discover	+0.379	delinquent
-0.287	<BIAS>	-0.365	2016	-0.267	2020	... 6420 more positive ...		+0.372	victim
-0.287	company	-0.371	payments	-0.272	2019	... 19767 more negative ...		... 8710 more positive ...	
-0.297	2019	-0.397	2015	-0.273	don	-0.387	loans	... 17477 more negative ...	
-0.341	payment	-0.417	credit	-0.283	didn	-0.416	mortgage	-0.381	calls
-0.351	tried	-0.444	payment	-0.284	accounts	-0.437	debit	-0.384	servicer
-0.378	2018	-0.484	debt	-0.585	<BIAS>	-0.727	loan	-0.416	american

Figure 7-15. *Top features for each class with the feature names*

The output in Figure 7-15 shows the first five classes from the target column shows five classes and their top features, positive and negative.

What are the key takeaways from these tables? Let's take the mortgage class. Words such as mortgage, escrow, refinance, modification, servicer, and ditech are the top positive features that helped in predicting the class mortgage. In a similar fashion you can interpret and explain all other classes and words from the consumer complaints that actually help a text document predict the particular class as a product category the customer is complaining about. So it's not just the identification of top features but the entire context that leads to the prediction of the class label.

Local Explanation Example 1

The following script and Figure 7-16 look at the first consumer complaint. The prediction for bank account or service has a very low probability of 0.008, which means the first complaint does not belong to this class.

```
eli5.show_prediction(clf, np.array(df2.Consumer_complaint)[0], vec=vec,
                target_names=set(df2.Product)) # explain local
                prediction
np.array(df2.Consumer_complaint)[0]
```

y=Bank account or service (probability **0.008**, score **0.383**) top features

Contribution[7]	Feature
+0.670	Highlighted in text (sum)
-0.287	<BIAS>

dear cfpb, i currently have a bank of america mortgage and am unable to contact " customer service '' for any assistance on my loan or impound account. on xxxx xxxx, xxxx, i was " on hold '' xxxx hours trying to reach a representative to ask a simple question about my impound account and finally got disconnected from their phone bank. this is unacceptable. i am calling about my home. i am a customer. the use of a so called " customer service '' number by bank of america is hypocrisy because what is going on is instead customer abuse. why should i have to wait xxxx hours during my work week to try to speak with a representative about my home mortgage? they should be required to have a call back service or something that does not hold customers xxxx for hours to their negligence, disregard and abuse of customers. please advise what you plan to do about this. sincerely, customer

Figure 7-16. *Class prediction explanation for the first complaint*

Since the probability is 0.083, the first complaint does not belong to checking or service account (Figure 7-17).

y=Checking or savings account (probability **0.083**, score **2.686**) top features

Contribution[7]	Feature
+2.345	Highlighted in text (sum)
+0.341	<BIAS>

dear cfpb, i currently have a bank of america mortgage and am unable to contact " customer service '' for any assistance on my loan or impound account. on xxxx xxxx, xxxx, i was " on hold '' xxxx hours trying to reach a representative to ask a simple question about my impound account and finally got disconnected from their phone bank. this is unacceptable. i am calling about my home. i am a customer. the use of a so called " customer service '' number by bank of america is hypocrisy because what is going on is instead customer abuse. why should i have to wait xxxx hours during my work week to try to speak with a representative about my home mortgage? they should be required to have a call back service or something that does not hold customers xxxx for hours to their negligence, disregard and abuse of customers. please advise what you plan to do about this. sincerely, customer

Figure 7-17. *Feature importance for checking or savings account*

Figure 7-18 shows that the first consumer complaint belongs to the mortgage category as the probability is 84.3% or 0.843. The words that actually contributed to the prediction are in green.

y=Mortgage (probability **0.843**, score **5.006**) top features

Contribution[7]	Feature
+4.229	Highlighted in text (sum)
+0.777	<BIAS>

dear cfpb, i currently have a bank of america mortgage and am unable to contact " customer service " for any assistance on my loan or impound account. on xxxx xxxx, xxxx, i was " on hold " xxxx hours trying to reach a representative to ask a simple question about my impound account and finally got disconnected from their phone bank. this is unacceptable. i am calling about my home. i am a customer. the use of a so called " customer service " number by bank of america is hypocrisy because what is going on is instead customer abuse. why should i have to wait xxxx hours during my work week to try to speak with a representative about my home mortgage? they should be required to have a call back service or something that does not hold customers xxxx for hours to their negligence, disregard and abuse of customers. please advise what you plan to do about this. sincerely, customer

Figure 7-18. *Feature importance for mortgage class prediction*

The following output shows the actual text of the first consumer complaint:

```
'Dear CFPB, I currently have a Bank of America mortgage and am unable to contact " customer s
ervice \'\' for any assistance on my loan or impound account. On XXXX XXXX, XXXX, I was " on
hold \'\' XXXX hours trying to reach a representative to ask a simple question about my impou
nd account and finally got disconnected from their phone bank. \nTHIS IS UNACCEPTABLE. I am c
alling about my home. I am a customer. The use of a so called " customer service \'\' number
by Bank of America is hypocrisy because what is going on is instead customer ABUSE. \nWhy sho
uld I have to wait XXXX hours during my work week to try to speak with a representative about
my home mortgage? They should be required to have a call back service or something that does
not hold customers XXXX for hours to their negligence, disregard and abuse of customers. \nPl
ease advise what you plan to do about this. \nSincerely, Customer'
```

In a similar way you can check complaint no 123 and see that the complaint belongs to the debt collection class. The probability of the text belonging to the debt collection is 0.740 (74%). If you explain the predictions in terms of the exact text that contributed, it is called local interpretation.

Local Explanation Example 2

Let's look at another example, record number 123 from the consumer complaint dataset. The feature importance for each class is shown below. The following script takes complaint no 123, and the local prediction generated shows it belongs to the credit reporting repair or other class. The probability is 0.515 (51.5%). See Figure 7-19.

```
eli5.show_prediction(clf, np.array(df2.Consumer_complaint)[100], vec=vec,
                target_names=set(df2.Product)) # explain local
                prediction
```

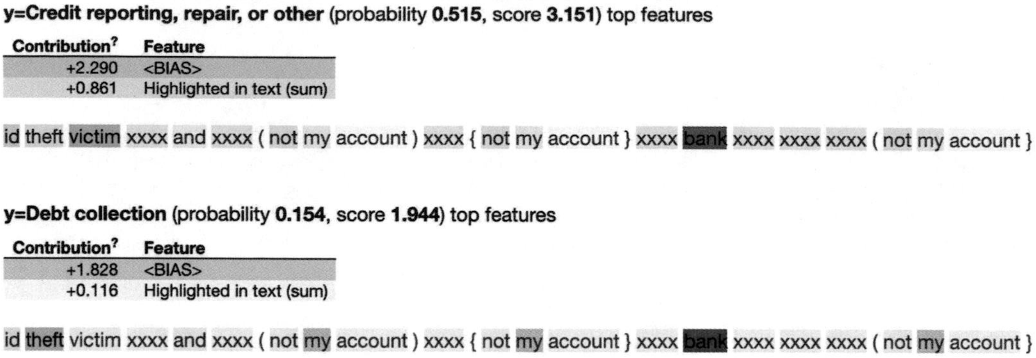

y=Credit reporting, repair, or other (probability **0.515**, score **3.151**) top features

Contribution?	Feature
+2.290	<BIAS>
+0.861	Highlighted in text (sum)

id theft victim xxxx and xxxx (not my account) xxxx { not my account } xxxx bank xxxx xxxx xxxx (not my account }

y=Debt collection (probability **0.154**, score **1.944**) top features

Contribution?	Feature
+1.828	<BIAS>
+0.116	Highlighted in text (sum)

id theft victim xxxx and xxxx (not my account) xxxx { not my account } xxxx bank xxxx xxxx xxxx (not my account }

Figure 7-19. *Feature importance with positive and negative words*

The above output as explained is without any preprocessing or fine tuning. A more refined result can be expected if you further fine-tune and preprocess the text. The standard practice is to remove the stop words. The following script removes the stop words and again triggers the model training pipeline:

```
vec = CountVectorizer(stop_words='english')
clf = LogisticRegressionCV()
pipe = make_pipeline(vec, clf)
pipe.fit(df2.Consumer_complaint, df2.Product)

print_report(pipe)

eli5.show_prediction(clf, np.array(df2.Consumer_complaint)[0], vec=vec,
                    target_names=set(df2.Product))
```

Since many of the complaints don't have enough text, after the removal of stop words, you lost many features, which is why the accuracy dropped slightly to 88.1%, as shown in Table 7-5.

Table 7-5. *Classification Report for Multiple Classes from a Refined Model*

	precision	recall	f1-score	support
Bank account or service	0.95	0.71	0.81	441
Checking or savings account	0.90	0.85	0.87	849
Consumer Loan	0.96	0.52	0.68	296
Credit card or prepaid card	0.89	0.84	0.86	2000
Credit reporting, repair, or other	0.86	0.95	0.90	8231
Debt collection	0.86	0.84	0.85	4075
Money transfer, virtual currency, or money service	0.92	0.80	0.85	358
Money transfers	0.97	0.62	0.76	53
Mortgage	0.95	0.94	0.95	2216
Other financial service	1.00	0.43	0.60	7
Payday loan, title loan, or personal loan	0.93	0.62	0.75	312
Student loan	0.94	0.84	0.89	788
Vehicle loan or lease	0.93	0.67	0.78	374
accuracy			0.88	20000
macro avg	0.93	0.74	0.81	20000
weighted avg	0.88	0.88	0.88	20000

accuracy: 0.881

Local Explanation Example 1

You can take the refined model and generate the local interpretations for consumer complaint number 0. The probability score is now little refined; it is 76.4%, as shown in Figure 7-20.

```
eli5.show_prediction(clf, np.array(df2.Consumer_complaint)[0], vec=vec,
                     target_names=set(df2.Product))
```

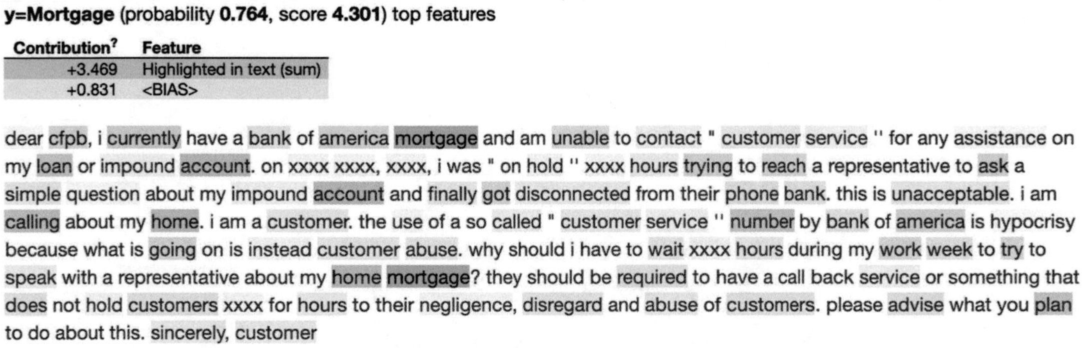

y=Mortgage (probability **0.764**, score **4.301**) top features

Contribution[?]	Feature
+3.469	Highlighted in text (sum)
+0.831	<BIAS>

dear cfpb, i currently have a bank of america mortgage and am unable to contact " customer service " for any assistance on my loan or impound account. on xxxx xxxx, xxxx, i was " on hold " xxxx hours trying to reach a representative to ask a simple question about my impound account and finally got disconnected from their phone bank. this is unacceptable. i am calling about my home. i am a customer. the use of a so called " customer service " number by bank of america is hypocrisy because what is going on is instead customer abuse. why should i have to wait xxxx hours during my work week to try to speak with a representative about my home mortgage? they should be required to have a call back service or something that does not hold customers xxxx for hours to their negligence, disregard and abuse of customers. please advise what you plan to do about this. sincerely, customer

Figure 7-20. *Local explanation for a single complaint prediction*

In a similar manner, change the vectorizer from count vector to tf-idf vector, without removing the stop words, and see what impact it will have on the local interpretation. You can see this from the following script:

```
from sklearn.feature_extraction.text import TfidfVectorizer

vec = TfidfVectorizer()
clf = LogisticRegressionCV()
pipe = make_pipeline(vec, clf)
pipe.fit(df2.Consumer_complaint, df2.Product)
print_report(pipe)
```

Table 7-6. *Classification Report from tf-idf Vectorizer Model*

	precision	recall	f1-score	support
Bank account or service	0.95	0.73	0.82	441
Checking or savings account	0.86	0.90	0.88	849
Consumer Loan	0.92	0.53	0.68	296
Credit card or prepaid card	0.88	0.89	0.89	2000
Credit reporting, repair, or other	0.91	0.94	0.92	8231
Debt collection	0.88	0.88	0.88	4075
Money transfer, virtual currency, or money service	0.88	0.83	0.86	358
Money transfers	0.96	0.49	0.65	53
Mortgage	0.93	0.97	0.95	2216
Other financial service	0.00	0.00	0.00	7
Payday loan, title loan, or personal loan	0.91	0.66	0.76	312
Student loan	0.93	0.90	0.92	788
Vehicle loan or lease	0.85	0.74	0.79	374
accuracy			0.90	20000
macro avg	0.84	0.73	0.77	20000
weighted avg	0.90	0.90	0.90	20000

```
accuracy: 0.901
```

Per Table 7-6, it looks like the tf-idf approach increases the overall accuracy to 90.1% and the local interpretation for the first complaint has a better probability score of 72.5%.

```
eli5.show_prediction(clf, np.array(df2.Consumer_complaint)[0], vec=vec,
                target_names=set(df2.Product))
```

As a next step, experiment with tf-idf with stop word removal to see any difference in the local explainability of the prediction for first consumer complaint. See Table 7-7.

```
vec = TfidfVectorizer(stop_words='english')
clf = LogisticRegressionCV()
pipe = make_pipeline(vec, clf)
```

```
pipe.fit(df2.Consumer_complaint, df2.Product)
print_report(pipe)
```

Table 7-7. *Classification Report for Multi-Class Classification Model*

	precision	recall	f1-score	support
Bank account or service	0.93	0.76	0.83	441
Checking or savings account	0.87	0.90	0.88	849
Consumer Loan	0.94	0.60	0.74	296
Credit card or prepaid card	0.88	0.90	0.89	2000
Credit reporting, repair, or other	0.91	0.94	0.93	8231
Debt collection	0.89	0.88	0.89	4075
Money transfer, virtual currency, or money service	0.89	0.85	0.87	358
Money transfers	0.96	0.49	0.65	53
Mortgage	0.94	0.97	0.96	2216
Other financial service	0.00	0.00	0.00	7
Payday loan, title loan, or personal loan	0.92	0.70	0.80	312
Student loan	0.93	0.91	0.92	788
Vehicle loan or lease	0.86	0.73	0.79	374
accuracy			0.91	20000
macro avg	0.84	0.74	0.78	20000
weighted avg	0.91	0.91	0.90	20000

```
accuracy: 0.906
```

Stop word removal has no major impact on the overall model accuracy. It increased marginally from 90.1% to 90.6%. Also, the probability score for the `mortgage` class changed to 73.5%.

```
eli5.show_prediction(clf, np.array(df2.Consumer_complaint)[0], vec=vec,
                    target_names=set(df2.Product))
```

y=Mortgage (probability **0.735**, score **4.000**) top features

Contribution[?]	Feature
+3.153	Highlighted in text (sum)
+0.847	<BIAS>

dear cfpb, i currently have a bank of america mortgage and am unable to contact " customer service " for any assistance on my loan or impound account. on xxxx xxxx, xxxx, i was " on hold " xxxx hours trying to reach a representative to ask a simple question about my impound account and finally got disconnected from their phone bank. this is unacceptable. i am calling about my home. i am a customer. the use of a so called " customer service " number by bank of america is hypocrisy because what is going on is instead customer abuse. why should i have to wait xxxx hours during my work week to try to speak with a representative about my home mortgage? they should be required to have a call back service or something that does not hold customers xxxx for hours to their negligence, disregard and abuse of customers. please advise what you plan to do about this. sincerely, customer

Figure 7-21. *The feature importance is necessary to understand the Positive and negative contribution of factors to the classification, the following Figure 7-21 highlights the positive one's in green and negative feature importance in red background color*

As a further improvement step, you can take the characters as an analyzer and take the bigrams up to five grams for feature creation. The accuracy increases to 91.4% marginally over the previous results.

```
vec = TfidfVectorizer(stop_words='english', analyzer='char',
                      ngram_range=(2,5))
clf = LogisticRegressionCV()
pipe = make_pipeline(vec, clf)
pipe.fit(df2.Consumer_complaint, df2.Product)

print_report(pipe)
```

Table 7-8. *After iteration the following Table 7-8 shows Multi-Class Classification Report Probability for Mortgage Class Again Increased to 74.2%*

	precision	recall	f1-score	support
Bank account or service	0.95	0.75	0.84	441
Checking or savings account	0.88	0.91	0.90	849
Consumer Loan	0.98	0.56	0.71	296
Credit card or prepaid card	0.89	0.91	0.90	2000
Credit reporting, repair, or other	0.92	0.95	0.94	8231
Debt collection	0.89	0.90	0.90	4075
Money transfer, virtual currency, or money service	0.90	0.85	0.87	358
Money transfers	1.00	0.38	0.55	53
Mortgage	0.94	0.97	0.95	2216
Other financial service	0.00	0.00	0.00	7
Payday loan, title loan, or personal loan	0.91	0.63	0.75	312
Student loan	0.94	0.90	0.92	788
Vehicle loan or lease	0.91	0.74	0.81	374
accuracy			0.91	20000
macro avg	0.86	0.73	0.77	20000
weighted avg	0.91	0.91	0.91	20000

```
accuracy: 0.914
```

```
eli5.show_prediction(clf, np.array(df2.Consumer_complaint)[0], vec=vec,
                     target_names=set(df2.Product))
```

y=Mortgage (probability **0.742**, score **3.989**) top features

Contribution[?]	Feature
+3.370	Highlighted in text (sum)
+0.619	<BIAS>

dear cfpb, i currently have a bank of america mortgage and am unable to contact " customer service " for any assistance on my loan or impound account. on xxxx xxxx, xxxx, i was " on hold " xxxx hours trying to reach a representative to ask a simple question about my impound account and finally got disconnected from their phone bank. this is unacceptable. i am calling about my home. i am a customer. the use of a so called " customer service " number by bank of america is hypocrisy because what is going on is instead customer abuse. why should i have to wait xxxx hours during my work week to try to speak with a representative about my home mortgage? they should be required to have a call back service or something that does not hold customers xxxx for hours to their negligence, disregard and abuse of customers. please advise what you plan to do about this. sincerely, customer

Figure 7-22. *The Figure 7-22 indicates the positive words as features Highlighted in green and negative words as features highlighted in red background, for the mortgage class*

In a similar fashion, you can take char and a non-overlapping bigram for feature creation, with bigrams up to five grams. It reduces the overall accuracy to the lowest level of 88.4%, but you can check the local explanation to see if it improved the explainability or not.

```
vec = TfidfVectorizer(stop_words='english', analyzer='char_wb',
                        ngram_range=(2,5))
clf = LogisticRegressionCV()
pipe = make_pipeline(vec, clf)
pipe.fit(df2.Consumer_complaint, df2.Product)

print_report(pipe)
```

It actually did not improve the explanation. As you can see in Figure 7-23, only the mortgage word is important. The other words are highlighted with very light green color. Even the red colored text is very feeble.

```
eli5.show_prediction(clf, np.array(df2.Consumer_complaint)[0], vec=vec,
                        target_names=set(df2.Product))
```

y=Mortgage (probability **0.720**, score **3.996**) top features

Contribution?	Feature
+3.422	Highlighted in text (sum)
+0.575	<BIAS>

dear cfpb, i currently have a bank of america mortgage and am unable to contact " customer service " for any assistance on my loan or impound account. on xxxx xxxx, xxxx, i was " on hold " xxxx hours trying to reach a representative to ask a simple question about my impound account and finally got disconnected from their phone bank. this is unacceptable. i am calling about my home. i am a customer. the use of a so called " customer service " number by bank of america is hypocrisy because what is going on is instead customer abuse. why should i have to wait xxxx hours during my work week to try to speak with a representative about my home mortgage? they should be required to have a call back service or something that does not hold customers xxxx for hours to their negligence, disregard and abuse of customers. please advise what you plan to do about this. sincerely, customer

Figure 7-23. *Highlighted feature text*

In order to take care of vocabulary length, you can introduce the hashing vectorizer with the stochastic gradient boosting model as a classifier. The accuracy further dropped to 85.7%. Still you can check the interpretation.

```
from sklearn.feature_extraction.text import HashingVectorizer
from sklearn.linear_model import SGDClassifier

vec = HashingVectorizer(stop_words='english', ngram_range=(1,2))
clf = SGDClassifier(random_state=42)
pipe = make_pipeline(vec, clf)
pipe.fit(df2.Consumer_complaint, df2.Product)
print_report(pipe)
```

Table 7-9. *The following Table 7-9 shows the accuracy of the Multi-Class Classification Report*

	precision	recall	f1-score	support
Bank account or service	0.97	0.47	0.63	441
Checking or savings account	0.77	0.79	0.78	849
Consumer Loan	0.98	0.49	0.66	296
Credit card or prepaid card	0.82	0.83	0.83	2000
Credit reporting, repair, or other	0.86	0.93	0.89	8231
Debt collection	0.86	0.82	0.84	4075
Money transfer, virtual currency, or money service	0.91	0.73	0.81	358
Money transfers	1.00	0.68	0.81	53
Mortgage	0.86	0.96	0.91	2216
Other financial service	0.50	0.14	0.22	7
Payday loan, title loan, or personal loan	0.95	0.54	0.69	312
Student loan	0.91	0.84	0.87	788
Vehicle loan or lease	0.93	0.52	0.66	374
accuracy			0.86	20000
macro avg	0.87	0.67	0.74	20000
weighted avg	0.86	0.86	0.85	20000

accuracy: 0.857

Although the overall model accuracy dropped, the probability score increases to 78%. However, only the dominant feature mortgage leads the classification. The other features are not of importance. This is a biased model. Other key words have very low weights. The strength of the green and red defines the value of the weight. For example, the mortgage has a high weight because it is dark green. All other words are light green (Figure 7-24).

```
eli5.show_prediction(clf, np.array(df2.Consumer_complaint)[0], vec=vec,
                     target_names=set(df2.Product))
```

y=Mortgage (score **0.780**) top features

Contribution[7]	Feature
+2.050	Highlighted in text (sum)
-1.270	<BIAS>

dear cfpb, i currently have a bank of america mortgage and am unable to contact " customer service " for any assistance on my loan or impound account. on xxxx xxxx, xxxx, i was " on hold " xxxx hours trying to reach a representative to ask a simple question about my impound account and finally got disconnected from their phone bank. this is unacceptable. i am calling about my home. i am a customer. the use of a so called " customer service " number by bank of america is hypocrisy because what is going on is instead customer abuse. why should i have to wait xxxx hours during my work week to try to speak with a representative about my home mortgage? they should be required to have a call back service or something that does not hold customers xxxx for hours to their negligence, disregard and abuse of customers. please advise what you plan to do about this. sincerely, customer

Figure 7-24. *A more refined and better highlighted feature to predict the mortgage class*

```
from eli5.sklearn import InvertableHashingVectorizer
import numpy as np

ivec = InvertableHashingVectorizer(vec)
sample_size = len(df2.Consumer_complaint) // 10
X_sample = np.random.choice(df2.Consumer_complaint, size=sample_size)
ivec.fit(X_sample)

eli5.show_weights(clf, vec=ivec, top=20,
                  target_names=set(df2.Product))
```

Using the invertible hashing vectorizer you can get the name of the features and their relative weights in a class prediction. See Figures 7-25 through 7-27.

y=Bank account or service top features		y=Checking or savings account top features		y=Consumer Loan top features		y=Credit card or prepaid card top features	
Weight?	Feature	Weight?	Feature	Weight?	Feature	Weight?	Feature
+1.096	requirements	+2.169	branch	+0.432	vehicle	+4.756	card
+0.725	promotion	+2.145	deposit	+0.409	finance ...	+2.565	purchase
+0.661	citigold	+1.696	bonus	+0.404	car	+2.422	capital
+0.658	overdraft	+1.641	bank	+0.403	auto loan	+2.404	minimum
+0.649	miles	+1.591	deposited	+0.394	dealer	+2.228	discover
+0.633	met	+1.447	funds	+0.380	vehicle xxxx ...	+2.187	synchrony
+0.629	fee	+1.433	checking ...	+0.375	FEATURE[503180]	+2.154	express
+0.608	citi	+1.414	atm	+0.350	bmw	+2.144	cards
+0.573	FEATURE[428730]	+1.351	savings account	+0.346	corporation	+2.015	citi
+0.570	2016			+0.336	xxxx vehicle	+1.987	amex
+0.520	debit	+1.341	savings	+0.325	contract	+1.934	charges
+0.519	bank	+1.294	debit	+0.291	door ...	+1.921	visa
+0.511	xx 2016	+1.283	chase	+0.273	come	+1.825	purchases
+0.505	checks	+1.229	debit card	+0.271	car repossessed	+1.816	american express ...
+0.504	negative	... 68301 more positive ...		+0.263	westlake financial		
+0.499	charge	... 75832 more negative ...		... 45800 more positive ...		+1.779	citibank
+0.497	branch	-1.147	mortgage	... 60839 more negative ...		... 108317 more positive ...	
... 51135 more positive ...		-1.156	transfer ...	-0.294	don ...	... 117322 more negative ...	
... 64901 more negative ...		-1.311	paypal	-0.319	didn	-2.063	experian ...
-0.516	didn	-1.469	2016	-0.340	im	-2.299	mortgage
-1.254	<BIAS>	-1.506	<BIAS>	-0.341	mortgage	-2.373	debit card
-2.153	FEATURE[301946]	-1.676	credit	-1.134	<BIAS>	-2.492	loan
		-1.929	payment ...			-2.579	debit

Figure 7-25. *Positive and negative features with their weights corresponding to each class in a multi-class classification problem*

y=Credit reporting, repair, or other top features		y=Debt collection top features		y=Money transfer, virtual currency, or money service top features		y=Money transfers top features	
Weight?	Feature	Weight?	Feature	Weight?	Feature	Weight?	Feature
+6.313	experian ...	+5.378	debt ...	+4.269	coinbase	+0.411	wire
+6.148	equifax	+3.592	collection	+1.652	app	+0.398	western
+5.390	transunion	+3.478	collect	+1.593	paypal	+0.394	western union
+3.496	inquiries	+3.426	owe	+1.314	transfer ...	+0.369	sent money
+2.969	report	+2.883	calling ...	+1.228	cash app	+0.306	money ...
+2.916	reporting	+2.685	collections	+1.150	tickets	+0.302	union
+2.775	inquiry	+2.553	hospital	+0.898	transaction ...	+0.267	service
+2.500	00 xxxx ...	+2.477	owed ...	+0.881	wallet ...	+0.265	paypal
+2.330	xxxx account	+2.324	recovery	+0.846	buyer	+0.264	ebay
+2.128	removed	+2.192	medical	+0.823	moneygram	+0.257	refused ...
+1.998	freeze	+2.078	calls	+0.798	support	+0.254	send
+1.965	late	+1.972	midland ...	+0.766	withdraw	+0.238	bank xxxx
+1.939	inaccurate	+1.676	llc	+0.735	cash	+0.236	tracking
... 135798 more positive ...		... 123540 more positive ...		+0.706	money ...	+0.234	sent ...
... 146309 more negative ...		... 136030 more negative ...		+0.692	usd	+0.215	seller
-2.006	capital	-1.656	car	+0.670	use xxxx	+0.210	transfer ...
-2.017	notice	-1.665	customer	... 40678 more positive ...		... 10299 more positive ...	
-2.039	calls	-2.380	mortgage	... 51535 more negative ...		... 16171 more negative ...	
-2.057	bank	-2.525	loan	-0.756	card	-0.224	FEATURE[628860]
-2.110	owe	-2.910	transunion	-0.758	credit	-0.252	case ...
-2.185	collection	-3.192	equifax	-0.792	FEATURE[537929]	-0.256	FEATURE[14521]
-3.499	debt ...	-3.751	experian ...	-1.228	<BIAS>	-1.182	<BIAS>

Figure 7-26. *Positive and negative features with their weights corresponding to each class in a multi-class classification problem*

y=Mortgage top features		y=Other financial service top features		y=Payday loan, title loan, or personal loan top features		y=Student loan top features		y=Vehicle loan or lease top features	
Weight[?]	Feature	Weight[?]	Feature	Weight[?]	Feature	Weight[?]	Feature	Weight[?]	Feature
+7.850	mortgage	+0.180	lower	+0.836	00 loan	+6.329	navient	+0.971	car
+5.020	escrow	+0.120	help	+0.810	payday	+3.108	loans	+0.688	santander
+4.525	modification	+0.114	money ...	+0.510	cash	+3.027	student	+0.611	toyota
+3.341	home	+0.104	irs	+0.484	loan	+2.066	repayment	+0.603	dmv
+2.990	foreclosure	+0.087	karma	+0.465	lending	+1.920	aes	+0.557	auto
+2.959	closing	+0.087	credit karma	+0.459	borrowed	+1.877	school	+0.548	vehicle
+2.955	appraisal	+0.086	credit score	+0.459	taking	+1.758	student loan	+0.526	nissan
+2.848	refinance ...	+0.081	return	+0.429	apr	+1.575	private	+0.492	ally
+2.627	ocwen	+0.081	process	+0.415	payday loan	+1.436	forbearance	+0.485	motor
+2.621	ditech	+0.079	forced	+0.377	store	+1.397	forgiveness	+0.471	lease ...
+2.548	servicing	+0.079	creditors	+0.376	payoff	+1.375	education	+0.452	title
+2.403	property	+0.078	promised	+0.357	state	+1.190	nelnet	+0.431	acceptance
+2.231	lender	+0.076	hard ...	+0.336	800	+1.177	paying	+0.390	FEATURE[800554]
+2.132	house	+0.076	said	+0.335	800 00	+1.176	income	+0.385	ford
+2.055	sale	+0.073	credit	+0.335	personal loan	+1.144	plan	+0.379	dealer
+1.914	nationstar	+0.071	td	+0.334	working	... 61062 more positive ...		+0.374	extra
... 110314 more positive ...		+0.071	attorney	+0.334	lady	... 70420 more negative ...		+0.373	financial
... 118461 more negative ...		+0.071	power attorney	... 44935 more positive ...		-1.090	modification	... 51906 more positive ...	
-1.921	student			... 59073 more negative ...		-1.194	report	... 64554 more negative ...	
-1.981	car	+0.071	power	-0.457	student	-1.221	<BIAS>	-0.414	home
-2.054	debt ...	... 1925 more positive ...		-0.585	mortgage	-1.309	credit	-0.506	mortgage
-2.092	reporting	... 3705 more negative ...		-1.184	<BIAS>	-2.083	mortgage	-1.203	<BIAS>
		-1.098	<BIAS>						

Figure 7-27. *Positive and negative features with their weights corresponding to each class in a multi-class classification problem*

Conclusion

Text classification is the most important use case in the domain of natural language processing. It is useful for the classification of consumer complaints, the classification of raw text into various entities, and the classification of sentiments into positive and negative. We are talking about both binary classification and multi-class classification. Other use cases are topic modelling and summarization, which was included in this chapter as these tasks are not supervised machine learning models. You only considered the supervised machine learning models because the interpretation is usually lost when you generate the predicted class result. The user will obviously think about which tokens or features are considered and why the predicted class is so and so, etc. However, for unsupervised learning-based tasks from the NLP domain, there are easier ways to understand the relations, but there is no prediction in unsupervised learning that needs to be explained to the end user. In this chapter, you focused more on different preprocessing methods and models and their explainability.

## CHAPTER 8

AI Model Fairness Using a What-If Scenario

This chapter explains the use of a What-If Tool (WIT) to explain biases in AI models, such as machine learning-based regression models, classification models, and multi-class classification models. As a data scientist, you are responsible for not only developing a machine learning model, but also for ensuring that the model is not biased and that new observations are treated fairly. It is imperative to probe the decisions and verify the algorithmic fairness. Google has developed the What-If Tool (WIT) to address model fairness issue in machine learning models. You will look at the implementation of WIT in three possible ML models: ML for regression-based tasks, ML for binary classification models, and ML for multi-nominal models.

What Is the WIT?

The What-If Tool (WIT) is an open source tool released by Google in 2019 to probe machine learning models. It was developed to understand the cause-and-effect relationship between drivers and outcome variables and changes in data points and outcome variables. The drivers here imply the independent predictors for the outcome variables. Due to its ease of use, attractive visualization, and explainability, the WIT tool has a broad acceptance and adoption. With minimal coding, a user can visually probe the learned behavior of any machine learning model. Simulation of various inputs to a trained machine learning model is necessary for developing explainable AI and responsible AI. This WIT tool is available in three formats: regular Jupyter Notebook from Anaconda Navigator window, Google Colab Notebook, and TensorBoard-based visualizations for any deep learning-based model. The currently available version of the tool is 1.8.0, and this version overcomes certain limitations of earlier versions. See Figure 8-1 for the flow.

© Pradeepta Mishra 2022
P. Mishra, *Practical Explainable AI Using Python*, https://doi.org/10.1007/978-1-4842-7158-2_8

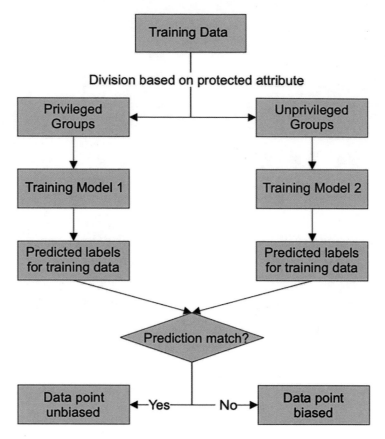

Figure 8-1. *Bias identification flow chart*

The training data can be divided based on certain protected attributes based on your question. As an example, say you have race and gender as two attributes and you want an answer from an explainability point of view such as

- Is the model biased towards a particular race?

- Is the model biased towards a particular gender, assuming male and female?

Let's take the second point, gender as a protected variable. The first gender is privileged and the second is unprivileged. You can prepare two training models, and using the two models you will generate predictions for the training data. If for any particular record the predictions match from both models, then the record or data point is unbiased; if it differs, then it is biased. Based on that, you can conclude whether the model is biased towards a gender or race.

Installing the WIT

Here is the code to install the What-If Tool:

```
import pandas as pd
import warnings
warnings.filterwarnings("ignore")

!pip install witwidget

from witwidget.notebook.visualization import WitConfigBuilder
from witwidget.notebook.visualization import WitWidget
```

Before running the WitWidget() function from the notebook environment, please run the following two lines from the command line:

```
jupyter nbextension install --py --symlink --sys-prefix witwidget
jupyter nbextension enable --py --sys-prefix witwidget
```

Once the installation is complete, the following functions need to be created to prepare the input data for model creation and visualization. The following script creates feature specifications based on the TensorFlow specification, as the WIT tool is dependent on the TensorFlow backend to format the input data:

```
!pip install xgboost

# if you get error in xgboost
# run

conda install -c conda-forge xgboost

import pandas as pd
import xgboost as xgb
import numpy as np
import collections
import witwidget

from sklearn.model_selection import train_test_split
from sklearn.metrics import accuracy_score, confusion_matrix
from sklearn.utils import shuffle
from witwidget.notebook.visualization import WitWidget, WitConfigBuilder
```

You are going to use the churn dataset because you used it in other chapters.

```
df = pd.read_csv('ChurnData.csv')
df.head()

del df['Unnamed: 0']
df.head()

import pandas as pd
import numpy as np
import tensorflow as tf
import functools

 # Creates a tf feature spec from the dataframe and columns specified.
def create_feature_spec(df, columns=None):
    feature_spec = {}
    if columns == None:
        columns = df.columns.values.tolist()
    for f in columns:
        if df[f].dtype is np.dtype(np.int64):
            feature_spec[f] = tf.io.FixedLenFeature(shape=(), dtype=tf.
                int64)
        elif df[f].dtype is np.dtype(np.float64):
            feature_spec[f] = tf.io.FixedLenFeature(shape=(), dtype=tf.
                float32)
        else:
            feature_spec[f] = tf.io.FixedLenFeature(shape=(), dtype=tf.
                string)
    return feature_spec
# Creates simple numeric and categorical feature columns from a feature
spec and a
# list of columns from that spec to use.
#
# NOTE: Models might perform better with some feature engineering such as
bucketed
# numeric columns and hash-bucket/embedding columns for categorical
features.
```

```
def create_feature_columns(columns, feature_spec):
    ret = []
    for col in columns:
        if feature_spec[col].dtype is tf.int64 or feature_spec[col].dtype
        is tf.float32:
            ret.append(tf.feature_column.numeric_column(col))
        else:
            ret.append(tf.feature_column.indicator_column(
                tf.feature_column.categorical_column_with_vocabulary_
                list(col, list(df[col].unique())))))
    return ret
```

In the above function, given a data set, you validate the input data and format the integer, float, and string-based columns.

The following utility function generates input from TensorFlow-based examples for use in the model training step:

```
# An input function for providing input to a model from tf.Examples
def tfexamples_input_fn(examples, feature_spec, label, mode=tf.estimator.
ModeKeys.EVAL,
                        num_epochs=None,
                        batch_size=64):
    def ex_generator():
        for i in range(len(examples)):
            yield examples[i].SerializeToString()
    dataset = tf.data.Dataset.from_generator(
      ex_generator, tf.dtypes.string, tf.TensorShape([]))
    if mode == tf.estimator.ModeKeys.TRAIN:
        dataset = dataset.shuffle(buffer_size=2 * batch_size + 1)
    dataset = dataset.batch(batch_size)
    dataset = dataset.map(lambda tf_example: parse_tf_example(tf_example,
    label, feature_spec))
    dataset = dataset.repeat(num_epochs)
    return dataset
```

The following function parses the TensorFlow example function using feature specifications as defined by the feature specification function:

```
# Parses Tf.Example protos into features for the input function.
def parse_tf_example(example_proto, label, feature_spec):
    parsed_features = tf.io.parse_example(serialized=example_proto,
    features=feature_spec)
    target = parsed_features.pop(label)
    return parsed_features, target
```

The TensorFlow-based model requires batch feeding of the input data to the training step.

```
# Converts a dataframe into a list of tf.Example protos.
def df_to_examples(df, columns=None):
    examples = []
    if columns == None:
        columns = df.columns.values.tolist()
    for index, row in df.iterrows():
        example = tf.train.Example()
        for col in columns:
            if df[col].dtype is np.dtype(np.int64):
                example.features.feature[col].int64_list.value.
                append(int(row[col]))
            elif df[col].dtype is np.dtype(np.float64):
                example.features.feature[col].float_list.value.
                append(row[col])
            elif row[col] == row[col]:
                example.features.feature[col].bytes_list.value.
                append(row[col].encode('utf-8'))
        examples.append(example)
    return examples
```

The following function converts a data frame provided by the user into a column of binary values (0s and 1s). The function forces the label column to be numeric for the binary classification model. Similarly, for the multi-class classification model, the label or the target column also changes to a label encoder column by applying the label encoder function.

```
# Converts a dataframe column into a column of 0's and 1's based on the
provided test.
# Used to force label columns to be numeric for binary classification using
a TF estimator.
def make_label_column_numeric(df, label_column, test):
    df[label_column] = np.where(test(df[label_column]), 1, 0)
```

The use case that you are looking at in this chapter is a telecom churn classification scenario. The telecom customers' usage history is being taken into consideration, such as account length, area code from where the customer is based, state code, international plan enabled or not, voice mail plan, number of voice mail messages, total day talk time in minutes, total daytime calls, and total daytime charges. Similar to day, the evening and night usage details are also considered as features. These features help you in predicting the possibility of churn in the future. If you can predict the correct outcome in advance, then the factors leading to a possible churn can be addressed and the customer can be retained. Retaining a customer is always preferable to acquiring a new one. Acquiring new customers is always costly, and retaining existing customers is significantly less expensive. Thus, in the churn prediction process, you can develop relevant strategies to keep a customer from churning by identifying the reasons for churn and validating the biases and what-if scenarios in advance.

```
import numpy as np

# Set the column in the dataset you wish for the model to predict
label_column = 'churn'

# Make the label column numeric (0 and 1), for use in our model.
# In this case, examples with a target value of 'yes' are considered to be in
# the '1' (positive) class and all other examples are considered to be in the
# '0' (negative) class.
make_label_column_numeric(df, label_column, lambda val: val == 'yes')

# Set list of all columns from the dataset we will use for model input.
input_features = [
    'account_length', 'area_code', 'international_plan',
        'voice_mail_plan', 'number_vmail_messages', 'total_day_minutes',
        'total_day_calls', 'total_day_charge', 'total_eve_minutes',
        'total_eve_calls', 'total_eve_charge', 'total_night_minutes',
```

```
        'total_night_calls', 'total_night_charge', 'total_intl_minutes',
        'total_intl_calls', 'total_intl_charge',
        'number_customer_service_calls']

# Create a list containing all input features and the label column
features_and_labels = input_features + [label_column]

features_and_labels

examples = df_to_examples(df)

num_steps = 5000   #@param {type: "number"}

# Create a feature spec for the classifier
feature_spec = create_feature_spec(df, features_and_labels)

# Define and train the classifier
train_inpf = functools.partial(tfexamples_input_fn, examples, feature_spec,
label_column)
classifier = tf.estimator.LinearClassifier(
    feature_columns=create_feature_columns(input_features, feature_spec))
classifier.train(train_inpf, steps=num_steps)

test_df = pd.read_csv('churnTest.csv')

num_datapoints = 2000
tool_height_in_px = 700

from witwidget.notebook.visualization import WitConfigBuilder
from witwidget.notebook.visualization import WitWidget

make_label_column_numeric(test_df, label_column, lambda val: val == 'yes')
test_examples = df_to_examples(test_df[0:num_datapoints])

# Setup the tool with the test examples and the trained classifier
config_builder = WitConfigBuilder(test_examples).set_estimator_and_feature_
spec(
    classifier, feature_spec).set_label_vocab(['Churn', 'No Churn'])
WitWidget(config_builder, height=tool_height_in_px)
```

The test data set contains 1667 samples, which you will visualize using Google's What-If Tool. The above script generates a visualization with two panels. The left panel shows various options such as a data point editor, performance, and fairness of model and features. The right panel shows the visualization and other options.

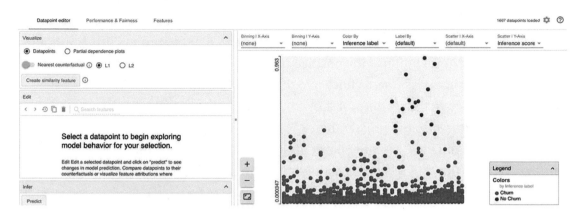

Figure 8-2. *Exploring model behavior through the WIT*

In Figure 8-2, the left-hand block has data points and partial dependency plots, which come under the data point editor. The second tab has performance and fairness options, and the third tab has features. On the right-hand side the y-axis shows the inference score, and it is ordered by inference label. The red dots are the no-churn customers and the blue dots are the churn customers. Here the label by option is the default.

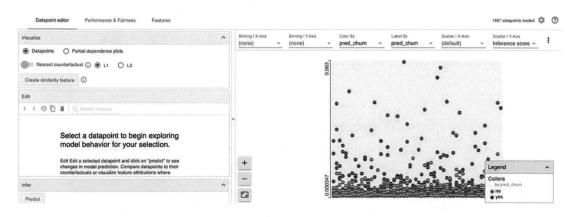

Figure 8-3. *Representing churn and no-churn by prediction type*

In Figure 8-3, the blue points are no-churn cases and the red points are churn cases. From the test dataset, if you consider the record number 1073, the churn probability is 0.016% and the no-churn probability is 98.4%, which is a good prediction. However, when you look at the example number 799, the probability of churn is 49.2% and the probability of no churn is 50.8%. These types of cases are quite ambiguous for the model. Your predictive model does not know how to differentiate the churn and no-churn cases. By default the WIT tool uses a classification threshold of 0.5. If the probability threshold exceeds more than 0.5 it predicts the positive class; otherwise, it predicts the negative class. Here the positive class is no churn and the negative class is churn. On the right-hand side of the panel, the scatterplot shows the inference score, which is the probability score. If the inference score is greater than 0.5, then it is the positive class; otherwise, it is the negative class. There are some borderline cases, so additional model fine-tuning is required. Thus, to obtain a better result, it is critical to fine-tune the model using various hyperparameters. See Figure 8-4.

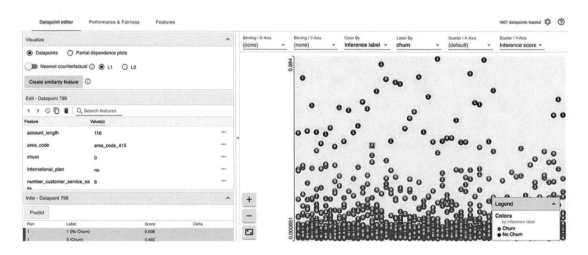

Figure 8-4. *Data point 799 analysis*

The data point editor on the left-hand panel shows the viewing and editing of the individual values of the records and shows what happens to the prediction inference. This shows the power of model inference and the detailed explanation of the prediction results. For the same 799 example number, when you change the individual values of account length to 210, total day calls to 227, and certain other parameters, and then click the Predict button on the left-hand side menu, you can see that the churn inference score decreases from 49.2% to 25.8% and the probability of no churn increases from 50.8% to 74.2%, which corresponds to run 2 of the simulation. See Figure 8-5.

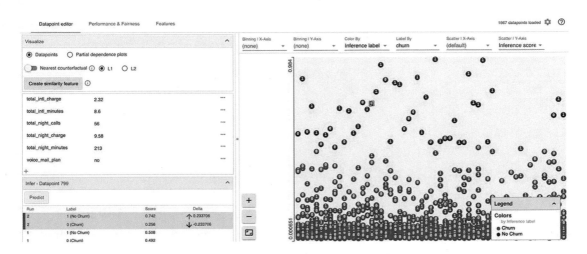

Figure 8-5. *Change in the inference score due to a small value change in the features*

You can also see a partial dependence plot (PDP) of individual features. The PDP plot, in short, shows the marginal contribution of one or two features on the predicted outcome of the machine learning model.

Figure 8-6 shows the distribution of churn and no-churn cases as predicted by the model. By taking into account the inference score on the X-axis, the inference score is less than 10%. All cases are predicted to be churn. The point to note here is that with an inference score of 49% to 59% you can see the presence of both churn and no-churn cases, which indicates lack of predictive power of the model because your model does not learn the difference between churn and no-churn classes in this bucket.

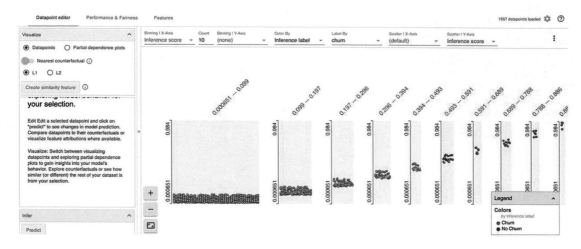

Figure 8-6. *Inference score bucket view for churn prediction*

In Figure 8-6, the inference score is bucketed into 10 groups and the view shows the existence of two classes in each bucket. This view helps you select a threshold that should be used to classify the target class. The threshold is applied on the probability value.

The partial dependence plot for all of the independent variables used as input variables in the model is given in Figure 8-7. The PDPs are sorted by variation.

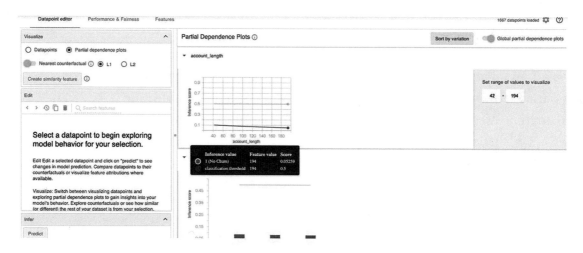

Figure 8-7. *Partial dependency plot for account length*

As the account length increases, the inference score gradually decreases. See Figure 8-8.

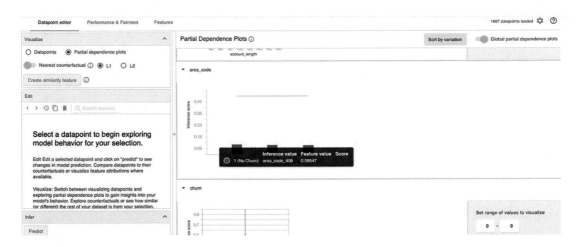

Figure 8-8. *PDP for area code variable*

While evaluating the overall performance of a model, you can consider the confusion matrix that illustrates the match and mismatch between the churn and no-churn cases in your model.

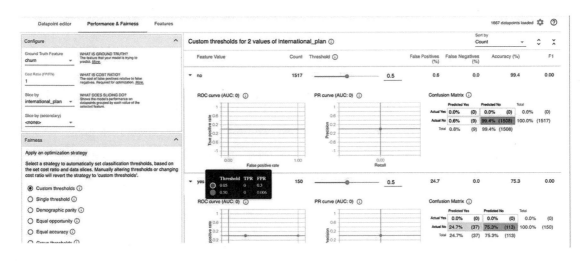

Figure 8-9. *Performance and fairness screen*

In the performance and fairness screen shown in Figure 8-9, you can see the ROC curve, the AUC curve, the confusion matrix, and the cost ratio. You can change the threshold probability value to change the classification matrix.

Evaluation Metric

Precision: How often your model correctly predicts the positive label

Recall: How many of the positive classes in the data set does the model correctly predict?

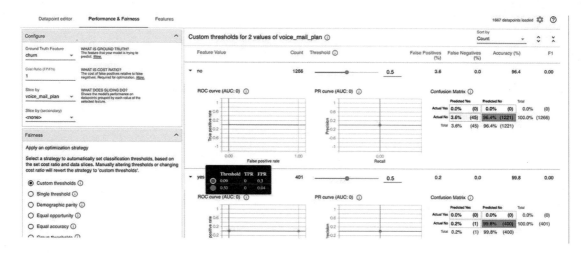

Figure 8-10. *Evaluation screen showing the accuracy of the model*

Conclusion

This chapter discussed how to interpret the inference for the results of a classification model using the What-If Tool and how to identify the features that play a crucial role in classifying the churn and no-churn cases. Also, you used methods for local interpretation of individual data points.

## CHAPTER 9

Explainability for Deep Learning Models

Deep neural network-based models are gradually becoming the backbone of artificial intelligence and machine learning implementations. The future of data mining will be governed by usage of artificial neural network-based advanced modelling techniques. So why are neural networks gaining so much importance when they were invented in the 1950s? Borrowed from the computer science domain, neural networks can be defined as a parallel information processing system where the inputs are connected with each other much like neurons in a human brain to transmit information so that activities like face recognition and image recognition can be performed. In theory, neural networks have existed for more than 50 years, but the execution of neural network projects in practical scenarios became possible after certain advancements in computation, specifically the evolution of GPUs and TPUs in performing high-end calculations, large-scale matrix multiplications, and so on. In this chapter, you are going to learn about the application of neural network-based methods on various data mining tasks like classification, regression, forecasting, and feature reduction. An artificial neural network (ANN) functions similarly to the way the human brain functions, where billions of neurons link to each other for information processing and insight generation.

Explaining DL Models

The brain's biological network provides the basis for connecting elements in a real-life scenario for information processing and insight generation. A hierarchy of neurons is connected through layers, where the output of one layer becomes the input for another layer. The information passes from one layer to another layer as weights. The weights associated with each neuron contain insights so that recognition and reasoning become easier for the next level. An artificial neural network is a very popular and effective

© Pradeepta Mishra 2022
P. Mishra, *Practical Explainable AI Using Python*, https://doi.org/10.1007/978-1-4842-7158-2_9

method that consists of layers associated with weights. The association between different layers is governed by a mathematical equation that passes information from one layer to another. In fact, a bunch of mathematical equations are at work inside one artificial neural network model. Figure 9-1 shows the general architecture for a neural network-based model where the input layer, the output layer, and the hidden layer are displayed.

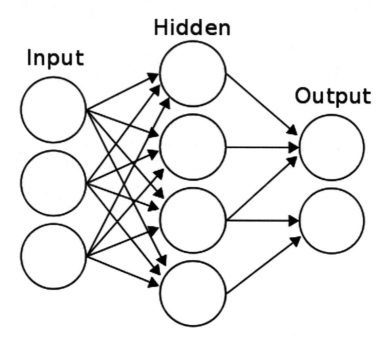

Figure 9-1. *Sample neural network structure*

There are three layers (input, hidden, and output) and they are the core of any neural network-based architecture. ANNs are a powerful technique to solve many real-world problems such as classification, regression, and feature selection. ANNs have the ability to learn from new experiences in the form of new input data in order to improve the performance of classification or regression-based tasks and to adapt themselves to changes in the input environment. Each circle in Figure 9-1 represents a neuron. One of the major advantages of deep learning is that we do not have to focus on creating handcrafted features for model training. Feature interactions need not be created by human beings; they should be automatically created during the training process itself.

There are different variants of neural networks from an algorithmic or computational point of view that are used in multiple different scenarios. I am going to explain a few of them conceptually below so that you can understand their usage in practical applications.

- **Single hidden layer neural network**: This is the simplest form of a neural network, as shown in Figure 9-1. There is only one hidden layer in it.

- **Multiple hidden layer neural networks**: In this form, more than one hidden layer connects the input data with the output data. The complexity of calculations increases in this form and it requires more computational power by the system to process information.

- **Feed forward neural networks**: In this form of neural network architecture, the information is passed in one direction from one layer to another layer; there is no iteration from the first level of learning.

- **Back propagation neural networks**: In this form of a neural network, there are two important steps. The feed forward works by passing information from the input layer to the hidden layer and from the hidden layer to the output layer. Secondly, it calculates the error and propagates it back to the previous layers.

There is another kind of classification based on usage and structure, which can be explained as follows:

- **Recurrent neural network (RNN)**: This is mostly used for sequential information processing, such as audio processing, text classification, and so on.

- **Deep neural network (DNN)**: This is used for high dimensional structured data problems where feature interactions are so complex that it is very tedious to construct each feature manually.

- **Convolutional neural network (CNN)**: This is mostly useful for image data, where the pixel sizes produce a high dimensional matrix. There is a need to synthesize the information in a convoluted manner to classify images.

The feed forward neural network model architecture is shown in Figure 9-2 and the back propagation method is explained in the next section.

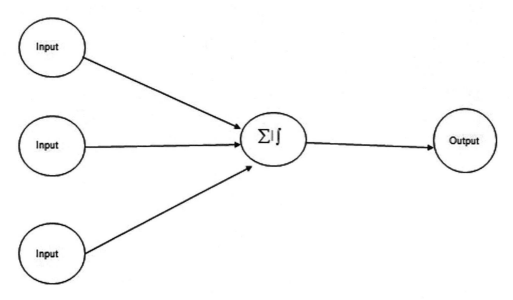

Figure 9-2. *Basic feed forward NN structure*

Using SHAP with DL

As mentioned in earlier chapters, SHAP is a great library for all kinds of model explanations, local model interpretation, global model interpretation, and the interpretation comes from the Shapely value. It is important to know what the Shapely value is; this Shapely value is completely dependent on the game theoretic approach. The following formula explains how the computation of the Shapely value happens inside the library:

$$\phi_i(v) = \frac{1}{|N|!} \sum_R \left[v(P_i^R \cup \{i\}) - v(P_i^R) \right]$$

Φ: Shapley value
N: Number of player (feature)
P_i^R: Set of player with order
$V(P_i^R)$: Contribution of set of player with order
$V(P_i^R \cup \{i\})$: Contribution of set of player with order and player i

Using Deep SHAP

Deep SHAP is a framework to derive SHAP values from a deep learning-based model, developed either using Keras-based models or TensorFlow-based models. You can take the example of the MNIST dataset, where a sample data point shows the pixel values of the number and a deep learning model is being trained to classify the image. The SHAP values are shown below.

If we compare machine learning models with deep learning models, the ML models are still interpretable, but the neural network models, especially the deep neural network models, are black box in nature, which is an obstacle in the adoption of AI models in the industry because no one can interpret the application of deep learning model prediction. Deep Learning Important Features (DeepLIFT) is a framework that came into the picture in October 2019. It is designed to apply a method for decomposing the output prediction of a deep neural network model. This is done by backpropagating the contribution of all neurons in the deep neural network to every feature of the input. The DeepLIFT framework makes it possible by comparing the activation of each neuron to their corresponding activation and assigns a score, which is known as the contribution score.

Using Alibi

Apart from DeepLIFT and Deep SHAP, there is another open source library named Alibi. It's a Python-based library aimed at explaining the machine learning models. The following code explains how to install Alibi and how to speed up the search for Alibi using another library called Ray.

```
!pip install alibi
```

The above code installs the Alibi library for explaining the models.

```
!pip install alibi[ray]
```

The alibi[ray] library is a dependency library and needs to be installed as well.

```
!pip install tensorflow_datasets
```

You can use `tensorflow_datasets` to collect few datasets from the library for usage in this chapter.

```
!pip install keras
```

The Keras library is for training deep learning models.

```
from __future__ import print_function
import keras
from keras.datasets import mnist
from keras.models import Sequential
from keras.layers import Dense, Dropout, Flatten
from keras.layers import Conv2D, MaxPooling2D
from keras import backend as K
import matplotlib.pyplot as plt
%matplotlib inline

batch_size = 128
num_classes = 10
epochs = 12

# input image dimensions
img_rows, img_cols = 28, 28
```

MNIST is a digit classification dataset that has pictures of digits written by hand and labelled by experts to let the model learn the patterns. Conv2D is a convolutional two-dimensional layer that transforms the weights and performs spatial convolution over image pixels. The values that you provide within Conv2D are the numbers of filters that the convolutional layers will learn from. Post convolution, the max pooling is required for a compressed representation of the pixels in a lower-dimensional space. Hence each convoluted layer needs a max pool layer. The max pool layer requires a output matrix size also. In the following script, you are using 32 filters in the Conv2D layer and the kernel size or the filter size is (3,3). Max pooling is generally used to reduce the spatial dimensions of the output volume. The kernel size must be an odd number combination such as (1,1), (3,3) or (5,5) in order to ensure that the kernel filter traverses the spatial space smoothly. Stride is the value that makes the filters move in the pixel space. stride =1 means the filter moves one place to the right in the matrix of pixels. Once it reaches the edge of the pixel matrix, it goes down and keeps moving to the lowest possible row and then it moves towards left. When you move an odd numbered kernel in the pixel space to collect all the convoluted features, sometimes the filter does not go to the edges of the pixel matrix. In order to make that happen, you add a row and column around the original pixel matrix. This is called padding. Padding can be zero padding and same padding.

```
# the data, split between train and test sets
(x_train, y_train), (x_test, y_test) = mnist.load_data()
if K.image_data_format() == 'channels_first':
    x_train = x_train.reshape(x_train.shape[0], 1, img_rows, img_cols)
    x_test = x_test.reshape(x_test.shape[0], 1, img_rows, img_cols)
    input_shape = (1, img_rows, img_cols)
else:
    x_train = x_train.reshape(x_train.shape[0], img_rows, img_cols, 1)
    x_test = x_test.reshape(x_test.shape[0], img_rows, img_cols, 1)
    input_shape = (img_rows, img_cols, 1)

x_train = x_train.astype('float32')
x_test = x_test.astype('float32')
x_train /= 255
x_test /= 255

print('x_train shape:', x_train.shape)
print(x_train.shape[0], 'train samples')
print(x_test.shape[0], 'test samples')
```

The above script shows the general steps for fetching the data from the Keras library and using the loaded data to normalize the training samples and test samples. This is done by dividing each individual pixel value with its highest pixel value. After that, 60,000 samples are parked for training and 10,000 are parked for testing. The image size here is 28 x 28 pixels, the batch size is 128, and the number of classes is 10 for each digit one class image. Also, you are using 10 iterations or epochs to train the model.

```
# convert class vectors to binary class matrices
y_train = keras.utils.to_categorical(y_train, num_classes)
y_test = keras.utils.to_categorical(y_test, num_classes)

model = Sequential()
model.add(Conv2D(32, kernel_size=(3, 3),
                activation='relu',
                input_shape=input_shape))
model.add(Conv2D(64, (3, 3), activation='relu'))
model.add(MaxPooling2D(pool_size=(2, 2)))
model.add(Dropout(0.25))
```

```
model.add(Flatten())
model.add(Dense(128, activation='relu'))
model.add(Dropout(0.5))
model.add(Dense(num_classes, activation='softmax'))
```

The image classification model that you are using here as an example has three parts to it, plus the application of convolution and max pooling to reduce the dimensions. Use of Dropout and Flatten is to remove low probability weights in order to restrict the model from overfitting. Flatten adds layers to reshape the data for further matrix multiplications. You also use a dense layer to create a fully connected neural network model that operates in a low-dimensional space to classify the target class with better accuracy. The activation functions are the transfer functions that are used after the dot product multiplication of weights and features received from the previous layer. In order to get the probability for each class, you need to use the softmax activation function at the final layer of the neural network model.

```
model.compile(loss=keras.losses.categorical_crossentropy,
              optimizer=keras.optimizers.Adadelta(),
              metrics=['accuracy'])
```

Once the model structure is designed, the next step is to compile the model. The compile step in the Keras library has certain parameters; the important ones are loss function, optimizer, and metrics. Apart from them, there are other parameters that can be used to fine-tune a model and retrain it to restrict the model from being overfitted. The selection of the error function or loss function should be based on the task. If the target column has more than two classes, then you can use categorical cross entropy. The role of the optimizer is to optimize the loss function and identify the step where the loss function is minimum. The function of metrics is to calculate the accuracy of the model corresponding to each epoch.

```
model.fit(x_train, y_train,
          batch_size=batch_size,
          epochs=epochs,
          verbose=1,
          validation_data=(x_test, y_test))
```

The results for all the epochs cannot be represented in the logs, hence it is truncated, but keep a watch on the logs to identify the iterations after which the model is learning or accuracy becomes flat, etc. From the following result, the test accuracy of the classification model is 85.28%.

```
score = model.evaluate(x_test, y_test, verbose=0)
print('Test loss:', score[0])
print('Test accuracy:', score[1])

import tensorflow as tf
tf.compat.v1.disable_v2_behavior() # run this if you get tensor related
error
```

SHAP Explainer for Deep Learning

The SHAP library has a deep explainer module which contains a representation to showcase the positive and negative attributes or contributions towards a classification task in general and specific to each class in particular.

```
background = x_train[np.random.choice(x_train.shape[0],100, replace=False)]
explainer = shap.DeepExplainer(model,background)

shap_values = explainer.shap_values(x_test[1:5])

# plot the feature attributions
shap.image_plot(shap_values, -x_test[1:5])
```

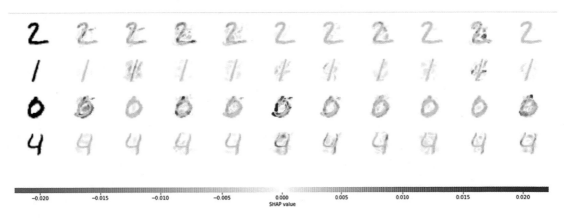

Figure 9-3. *DeepExplainer for image classification*

In Figure 9-3, the values in red are positive classes for the predicted class and the values in blue are the negative classes for the predicted class. The figure displays SHAP values of 2, 1, 0, and 4. The model generates 10 predictions corresponding to those four values of images. The red values make the predictions close to the input image on the extreme left, and the negative values make the predictions decrease in comparison to the input image, which is on the left side. Deep SHAP was developed on the basis of a paper published in NIPS.

DeepLIFT makes an estimation of the SHAP values using an approach similar to backpropagation after the prediction is generated for a classification and regression model.

```
# plot the feature attributions
shap.image_plot(shap_values, -x_test[5:9])
```

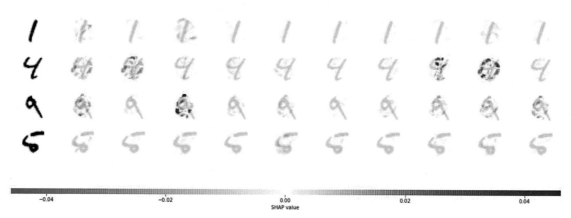

Figure 9-4. *DeepExplainer for a few more records*

In Figure 9-4, another four digits are printed and their corresponding SHAP scores are also plotted. There is a consistency in the pattern if you look at numbers 5 and 1. However, when you look at numbers 4 and 9, there is ambiguity as there are places when the SHAP score does not clearly help predict that class.

```
# plot the feature attributions
shap.image_plot(shap_values, -x_test[9:13])
```

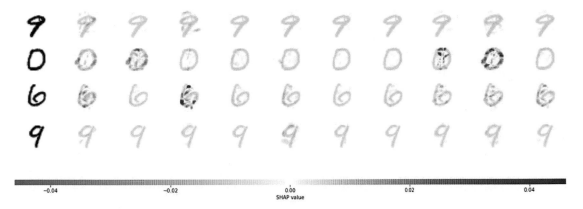

Figure 9-5. *DeepExplainer for another four digits*

In Figure 9-5, a similar view again can be seen in numbers 0 and 6, as both seems to be written in a very similar way. However, the number 9 is fairly clear.

Another Example of Image Classification

The CIFAR-10 dataset is taken from www.cs.toronto.edu/~kriz/cifar.html. You have a sample of 60,000 images consisting of 32x32 color images with 10 classes that need to be predicted or classified. These classes are airplane, automobile, bird, etc. Deep learning models can be explained using two explainers, DeepExplainer and GradientExplainer.

```
from keras.datasets import cifar10
from keras.utils import np_utils
from keras.models import Sequential
from keras.layers.core import Dense, Dropout, Activation, Flatten
from keras.layers.convolutional import Conv2D, MaxPooling2D
from keras.optimizers import SGD, Adam, RMSprop

import matplotlib.pyplot as plt

#from quiver_engine import server
# CIFAR_10 is a set of 60K images 32x32 pixels on 3 channels
IMG_CHANNELS = 3
IMG_ROWS = 32
IMG_COLS = 32
```

```
#constant
BATCH_SIZE = 128
NB_EPOCH = 20
NB_CLASSES = 10
VERBOSE = 1
VALIDATION_SPLIT = 0.2
OPTIM = RMSprop()
```

You cannot take an entire set of samples and run them through the convolutional layer and the dense layer. This process is very slow and time consuming and also computationally intensive. Hence there is a need to use small batches of the sample from the training set and incrementally update the weights after each epoch. Hence the batch size is 128, the number of epochs is 20, the optimizer is RMSPROP, and the validation sample size is 20%. These are the hyper parameters that has been considered as an example, is this the best set of hyper parameter configuration, may not be, as these can be set after many iterations. The best hyper parameter selection either can be done using a grid search approach or multiple iterations.

```
#load dataset
(X_train, y_train), (X_test, y_test) = cifar10.load_data()
print('X_train shape:', X_train.shape)
print(X_train.shape[0], 'train samples')
print(X_test.shape[0], 'test samples')

# convert to categorical
Y_train = np_utils.to_categorical(y_train, NB_CLASSES)
Y_test = np_utils.to_categorical(y_test, NB_CLASSES)

# float and normalization
X_train = X_train.astype('float32')
X_test = X_test.astype('float32')
X_train /= 255
X_test /= 255

# network

model = Sequential()
model.add(Conv2D(32, (3, 3), padding='same',
                 input_shape=(IMG_ROWS, IMG_COLS, IMG_CHANNELS)))
```

```
model.add(Activation('relu'))
model.add(MaxPooling2D(pool_size=(2, 2)))
model.add(Dropout(0.25))

model.add(Flatten())
model.add(Dense(512))
model.add(Activation('relu'))
model.add(Dropout(0.5))
model.add(Dense(NB_CLASSES))
model.add(Activation('softmax'))

model.summary()
```

The summary of the number of neurons is shown in the param column. There are 4,200,842 parameters being trained and there is no non-trainable parameter.

```
# train
#optim = SGD(lr=0.01, decay=1e-6, momentum=0.9, nesterov=True)
model.compile(loss='categorical_crossentropy', optimizer=OPTIM,
        metrics=['accuracy'])

history = model.fit(X_train, Y_train, batch_size=BATCH_SIZE,
        epochs=NB_EPOCH, validation_split=VALIDATION_SPLIT,
        verbose=VERBOSE)

print('Testing...')
score = model.evaluate(X_test, Y_test,
                    batch_size=BATCH_SIZE, verbose=VERBOSE)
print("\nTest score:", score[0])
print('Test accuracy:', score[1])
```

Once a better model to classify is trained, you can save the model object for further usage at a later time for inference generation.

```
#save model
model_json = model.to_json()
open('cifar10_architecture.json', 'w').write(model_json)
model.save_weights('cifar10_weights.h5', overwrite=True)

# list all data in history
print(history.history.keys())
```

```
# summarize history for accuracy
#plt.plot(mo)
plt.plot(history.history['val_acc'])
plt.title('model accuracy')
plt.ylabel('accuracy')
plt.xlabel('epoch')
plt.legend(['train', 'test'], loc='upper left')
plt.show()
```

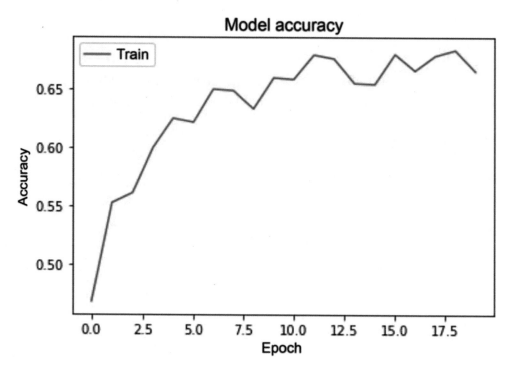

Figure 9-6. *Training model accuracy for each epoch*

From Figure 9-6 it is clear that the highest training accuracy is achieved around the 10th epoch. After that the training accuracy is quite unstable. There is a zigzag pattern.

```
# summarize history for loss
plt.plot(history.history['loss'])
plt.plot(history.history['val_loss'])
plt.title('model loss')
plt.ylabel('loss')
plt.xlabel('epoch')
```

```
plt.legend(['train', 'test'], loc='upper left')
plt.show()
```

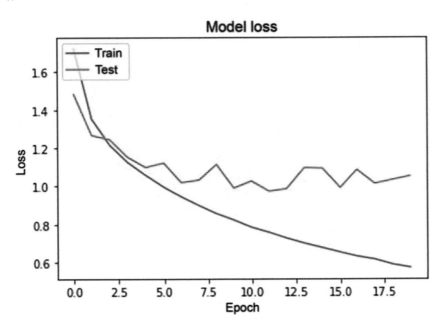

Figure 9-7. *Model training loss and model test loss representation*

From Figure 9-7, the model training loss and model test loss go hand in hand until the 3rd epoch. After that, the loss values diverge and the test loss shows a zigzag pattern, clearly showing unstable loss, and the training loss goes on dropping, which is a clear sign of over-fitting.

Before generating model explanations, it is important to ensure a stable, accurate, and reliable model. Otherwise, it is very difficult to justify the inference, as the model will produce random inferences and explanations.

Using SHAP

After getting a decent deep learning model with a good accuracy, it is important to explain the model predictions. Also, it would be quite interesting to know how the SHAP scores lead to the class prediction. See Figure 9-8 and Table 9-1.

```
background = X_train[np.random.choice(X_train.shape[0],100, replace=False)]
explainer = shap.DeepExplainer(model,background)

shap_values = explainer.shap_values(X_test[10:15])
```

```
# plot the feature attributions
shap.image_plot(shap_values, -X_test[10:15])
import pandas as pd
pd.DataFrame(model.predict_classes(X_test)).head(10)
```

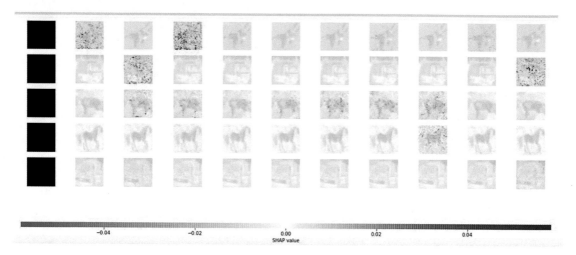

Figure 9-8. *SHAP feature attributions*

Table 9-1. *Predicted Class for the First 10 Records*

Row Number	Predicted Class
0	3
1	8
2	8
3	0
4	6
5	6
6	1
7	6
8	3
9	1

Table 9-2. *The Name of the Objects, the Sample Images, and the Numbers in the Bracket Show How It Is Coded in the Target Class in the Above Model*

Airplane(0)									
Automobile (1)									
Bird (2)									
Cat (3)									
Deer (4)									
Dog (5)									
Frog (6)									
Horse (7)									
Ship (8)									
Truck (9)									

```
import pandas as pd

pd.DataFrame(np.round(model.predict_proba(X_test),3)).head(10)
```

Table 9-3. *Probability Value for Each of the Nine Classes Shown in Table 9-2*

	0	1	2	3	4	5	6	7	8	9
0	0.000	0.001	0.002	0.928	0.007	0.053	0.000	0.000	0.008	0.000
1	0.000	0.005	0.000	0.000	0.000	0.000	0.000	0.000	0.995	0.000
2	0.164	0.013	0.005	0.001	0.001	0.000	0.000	0.001	0.797	0.019
3	0.661	0.002	0.105	0.001	0.003	0.000	0.001	0.000	0.226	0.000
4	0.000	0.000	0.037	0.073	0.289	0.002	0.598	0.000	0.000	0.000
5	0.001	0.000	0.035	0.033	0.023	0.024	0.877	0.003	0.000	0.003
6	0.000	1.000	0.000	0.000	0.000	0.000	0.000	0.000	0.000	0.000
7	0.009	0.000	0.036	0.001	0.000	0.000	0.954	0.000	0.000	0.000
8	0.003	0.000	0.029	0.665	0.121	0.147	0.008	0.025	0.001	0.000
9	0.001	0.936	0.000	0.000	0.000	0.000	0.000	0.000	0.001	0.061

Deep Explainer for Tabular Data

Let's apply a deep learning model on a complex dataset. It's called a wine quality prediction. The best accuracy one can get from this dataset is 62% because of feature complexity and ambiguity. No algorithm can increase the accuracy beyond 70% or 80%. Hence, this is a complex dataset. There are different wine classes that need to be classified. The dataset comes from the UCI machine learning repository at https:// archive.ics.uci.edu/ml/datasets/wine+quality. Two datasets are included, related to red and white wine samples from the north of Portugal. The goal is to model the wine quality based on physicochemical tests. The two datasets are related to red and white variants of the Portuguese Vinho Verde wine. Due to privacy and logistic issues, only physicochemical (input) and sensory (output) variables are available (e.g., there is no data about grape types, wine brand, wine selling price, etc.). These datasets can be viewed as classification or regression tasks. The classes are ordered and not balanced (e.g., there are many more normal wines than excellent or poor ones).

```
from tensorflow import keras
from sklearn.model_selection import cross_val_score, KFold
from keras.wrappers.scikit_learn import KerasRegressor
from keras.layers import Dense, Dropout
```

```
from keras.models import Sequential
from sklearn.metrics import accuracy_score
from sklearn.preprocessing import StandardScaler
import pandas as pd
import numpy as np
import matplotlib.pyplot as plt
```

The above script imports the necessary libraries to create a deep learning model for a tabular dataset. The following script names the features that can be used to predict the wine quality target:

```
feature_names = [
    "fixed acidity",
    "volatile acidity",
    "citric acid",
    "residual sugar",
    "chlorides",
    "free sulfur dioxide",
    "total sulfur dioxide",
    "density",
    "pH",
    "sulphates",
    "alcohol",
    "quality",
]
```

The following script reads the two datasets from the UCI machine learning repository:

```
red_wine_data = pd.read_csv(
    'https://archive.ics.uci.edu/ml/machine-learning-databases/wine-
    quality/winequality-red.csv', names=feature_names, sep=";", header=1)
white_wine_data = pd.read_csv(
    'https://archive.ics.uci.edu/ml/machine-learning-databases/wine-
    quality/winequality-white.csv', names=feature_names, sep=";", header=1)
```

```
wine_data = red_wine_data.append(white_wine_data)
wine_features = wine_data[feature_names].drop('quality', axis=1).values
wine_quality = wine_data['quality'].values

scaler = StandardScaler().fit(wine_features)
wine_features = scaler.transform(wine_features)
```

The deep learning model has input from 11 features. It is a three-layered deep neural network model.

```
model = Sequential()
model.add(Dense(1024, input_dim=11, activation='tanh'))
model.add(Dense(512, activation='tanh'))
model.add(Dense(64,  activation='tanh'))
model.add(Dense(1))
model.compile(loss='mse', optimizer='adam', metrics=['accuracy'])

model.summary()

history = model.fit(wine_features, wine_quality,
                    batch_size=BATCH_SIZE,
                    epochs=NB_EPOCH,
                    validation_split=VALIDATION_SPLIT,
                    verbose=VERBOSE)

background = wine_features[np.random.choice(wine_features.shape[0],100,
replace=False)]
explainer = shap.DeepExplainer(model,background)
shap_values = explainer.shap_values(wine_features)

pd.DataFrame(np.array(shap_values).reshape(6495,11))

np.round(model.predict(wine_features),0)
```

The positive SHAP values help make the prediction and the negative SHAP values decrease the power of prediction.

Conclusion

In this chapter, you learned how to interpret the inference for a classification model result using three datasets: MNIST digit dataset, CIFAR dataset, and wine quality dataset. Using a deep learning model, the training was completed and you explained the model predictions using DeepExplainer from the SHAP library. The role of DeepExplainer is to showcase the positive SHAP values and negative SHAP values of the image to explain any ambiguity or overlap in the classification task. In a structured data problem like the wine quality classification scenario, it also explains what features positively impact the predictions and what features negatively impact the predictions. The difference between the machine learning model and deep learning model is that in deep learning, feature selection happens automatically and there is an iterative process in training a deep neural network. Because of this, it is difficult to explain the model predictions to anyone. The task is much simpler now with the use of DeepExplainer to explain the model predictions.

## CHAPTER 10

Counterfactual Explanations for XAI Models

This chapter explains the use of the What-If Tool (WIT) to explain counterfactual definitions in AI models, such as machine learning-based regression models, classification models, and multi-class classification models. As a data scientist, you don't just develop a machine learning model; you make sure that your model is not biased and that it is fair about the decisions it makes for new observations that it predicts for the future. It is very important to probe the decisions and verify the algorithmic fairness. Google developed the What-If Tool to address the model fairness issue in machine learning models. You will look at the implementation of the WIT in three ML models: ML for regression-based tasks, ML for binomial classification models, and ML for multi-nominal models.

What Are CFEs?

Counterfactual explanations (CFEs) are causal relationships in the prediction process of ML models. I will illustrate the prediction or classification by using one example. Counterfactual explanations are a way of creating hypothetical scenarios and generating predictions under those hypothetical scenarios. This is understandable to business users, non-data scientists, and common individuals who are not from predictive modelling background. Sometimes we find that the relationship between input and output is not causal but still we want to establish a causal relationship to generate predictions. Counterfactual explanations are local explanations for predictions, which means for individual predictions they generate relevant explanations.

P. Mishra, *Practical Explainable AI Using Python*, https://doi.org/10.1007/978-1-4842-7158-2_10

Implementation of CFEs

Counterfactual explanations can be generated for both regression and classification tasks. You are going to use the Python-based library Alibi. Alibi works on Python version 3.6+ and higher. The following commands can be used for installation:

```
!pip install alibi
!pip install alibi[ray]
import alibi
alibi.__version__
```

After installation, please check the version using the following lines of code, just to ensure that the installation is complete: `alibi.__version__`

CFEs Using Alibi

Counterfactual explanations for model predictions can be generated using Alibi. Post installation, you can follow the similar process of initializing, fitting, and predicting using Alibi functions. The Alibi library requires a trained model and a new data set for which predictions need to be generated. As an example, you can use the extreme gradient boosting model to get a trained model object, which can further be used with the Alibi library to generate the counterfactual explanations. The following script installs the xgboost model and the witwidget library. If the xgboost model shows an error, the conda command given below can be used to install the Python-based xgboost library.

```
import pandas as pd
!pip install xgboost

import pandas as pd
import xgboost as xgb
import numpy as np
import collections
import witwidget

from sklearn.model_selection import train_test_split
from sklearn.metrics import accuracy_score, confusion_matrix
from sklearn.utils import shuffle
from witwidget.notebook.visualization import WitWidget, WitConfigBuilder
```

```
# if you get error in xgboost
# run
# conda install -c conda-forge xgboost

data = pd.read_csv('diabetes.csv')
data.head()
data.columns

from sklearn.model_selection import train_test_split
```

You are using the diabetes.csv dataset. Using the features shown in Table 10-1, you must predict whether someone will be diabetic or not. The features are shown in Table 10-1.

Table 10-1. *Data Dictionary for the Features*

Feature Name	Description
Pregnancies	Number of times pregnant
Glucose	Blood glucose level
Blood pressure	Diastolic blood pressure level
Skin thickness	Skin thickness measured in mm
Insulin	Insulin doses administered
BMI	Body mass index of the subject
Diabetes pedigree	Diabetes pedigree function of the subject
Age	Age of the subject
Outcome	No Diabetics, 1- Diabetics

```
# Split the data into train / test sets
y = data['Outcome']
x = data[['Pregnancies', 'Glucose', 'BloodPressure', 'SkinThickness',
'Insulin', 'BMI', 'DiabetesPedigreeFunction', 'Age']]
x_train,x_test,y_train,y_test = train_test_split(x,y,random_state=1234)
```

The total data is split into train and test objects, x_train and y_train, to develop a trained model object. In the following script, you train via a logistic regression model using an extreme gradient boosting classifier. The extreme gradient boosting classifier has many hyper parameters, but you will go ahead with the default selection of hyper parameters. The hyper parameters are the parameters that help fine-tuning a model to get the best version of the model.

```
# Train the model, this will take a few minutes to run
bst = xgb.XGBClassifier(
    objective='reg:logistic'
)

bst.fit(x_train, y_train)
# Get predictions on the test set and print the accuracy score
y_pred = bst.predict(x_test)
acc = accuracy_score(np.array(y_test), y_pred)
print(acc, '\n')

# Print a confusion matrix
print('Confusion matrix:')
cm = confusion_matrix(y_test, y_pred)
print(cm)
```

The trained model object is stored as bst. Using the same object, you can generate accuracy for the model. The base accuracy is 72.9%.

The best model accuracy is 72.9%, and you can store or save the best model and upload it to Alibi to generate predictions and use it for populating counterfactual explanations.

```
# Save the model so we can deploy it
bst.save_model('model.bst')
bst
x_train.head()
bst.predict(x_train.head())
y_train.head()
x_train.iloc[3] = x_train.iloc[1]
x_train.head()
bst.predict(x_train.head())
```

For the person at record no. 8, the model predicts diabetes and the actual is also diabetes. Row number 651, which is the third record from the training dataset, has no diabetes, as seen from y_train record number 651.

If you change the values of row number 651 slightly, the predictions for that record change (Table 10-2). In the following script you make the change.

Table 10-2. *Changes in Feature Values Impacts Prediction*

Feature Name	Old_value_651	New_value_651
Pregnancies	1	5
Glucose	117	97
Blood pressure	60	76
Skin thickness	23	27
Insulin	106	0
BMI	33.8	35.6
Diabetes pedigree	0.446	0.378
Age	27	52

The following script shows the importance of features in predicting diabetes in a person. The glucose level is considered to be the most important feature, followed by BMI level, age, and insulin level.

```
bst.predict(x_train.head())
x_train.iloc[3] = [1, 117, 60, 23, 106, 33.8, 0.466, 27]
x_train.head()

result = pd.DataFrame()
result['features_importance'] = bst.feature_importances_
result['feature_names'] = x_train.columns
result.sort_values(by=['features_importance'],ascending=False)
```

You can make small changes to the feature values and observe changes in the outcome variable. With small changes the prediction did not change.

```
# we will make small changes to the values
x_train.iloc[2] = [2, 146, 70, 38, 360, 28.0, 0.337, 29]
x_train.iloc[2]
x_train.columns
```

```
bst.predict(x_train.head())
y_train.head()
# if we change the important features such as Glucose and Age
```

```
x_train.iloc[2] = [3, 117, 76, 36, 245, 31.6, 0.851, 27]
x_train.iloc[2]
x_train.columns
```

```
bst.predict(x_train.head())
y_train.head()
```

With another round of changes in the input feature values, the prediction of the diabetes class did not change. As you keep on changing the feature values, you will find a place where a small change in a feature value could lead to a change in class prediction. Manually repeating all such scenarios is cumbersome and difficult. Even changes in the values of the most important features have no impact on the target class prediction. Hence there is a need for the identification of such borderline cases through some framework. That framework is offered by Alibi.

```
# if we change the important features such as Glucose, BMI and Age
```

```
x_train.iloc[2] = [3, 117, 76, 36, 245, 30.6, 0.851, 29]
x_train.iloc[2]
x_train.columns
```

```
bst.predict(x_train.head())
```

```
y_train.head()
```

```
import tensorflow as tf
tf.get_logger().setLevel(40) # suppress deprecation messages
```

```
tf.compat.v1.disable_v2_behavior() # disable TF2 behaviour as alibi code
still relies on TF1 constructs
from tensorflow.keras.layers import Dense, Input
from tensorflow.keras.models import Model, load_model
from tensorflow.keras.utils import to_categorical
import matplotlib
%matplotlib inline
import matplotlib.pyplot as plt
import numpy as np
import os
from alibi.explainers import CounterFactualProto

print('TF version: ', tf.__version__)
print('Eager execution enabled: ', tf.executing_eagerly()) # False
```

You can use a Keras layer with TensorFlow as a back end to train a neural network model object. Alibi provides the explainers class, which has a module for generating counterfactual protoresults. The following script creates a neural network model class as a user-defined function. This nn_model() function takes the input and applies a rectified linear unit activation function. Then it creates another hidden layer with 40 neurons and applies the same activation function and uses the stochastic gradient descent as the optimizer and a loss function as the categorical cross entropy.

```
x_train.shape, y_train.shape, x_test.shape, y_test.shape
y_train = to_categorical(y_train)
y_test = to_categorical(y_test)

np.random.seed(42)
tf.random.set_seed(42)

def nn_model():
    x_in = Input(shape=(8,))
    x = Dense(40, activation='relu')(x_in)
    x = Dense(40, activation='relu')(x)
    x_out = Dense(2, activation='softmax')(x)
```

```
nn = Model(inputs=x_in, outputs=x_out)
nn.compile(loss='categorical_crossentropy', optimizer='sgd',
metrics=['accuracy'])
return nn
```

The following script shows the neural network model summary. The model training uses a batch size of 64 and 500 epochs. After model training, the model is saved as an h5 format. The h5 format is a portable model object for loading and transferring a model from one platform to another.

```
nn = nn_model()
nn.summary()
nn.fit(x_train, y_train, batch_size=64, epochs=500, verbose=0)
nn.save('nn_diabetes.h5', save_format='h5')
```

The following script loads the trained model object, uses test datasets, and produces a test accuracy of 71.8%:

```
nn = load_model('nn_diabetes.h5')
score = nn.evaluate(x_test, y_test, verbose=0)
print('Test accuracy: ', score[1])
```

The generation of counterfactuals is guided by the nearest class prototype. You take one row from the test set with eight features in it and do the reshaping in such a way that is acceptable to the counterfactual prototype generation function.

```
#Generate counterfactual guided by the nearest class prototype
X = np.array(x_test)[1].reshape((1,) + np.array(x_test)[1].shape)
shape = X.shape
shape
```

The following script takes the neural network model object. Using a lambda function, you create a prediction function. Then you use the counterfactual proto function (Table 10-3).

Table 10-3. *Counterfactual Proto Hyper Parameters*

Parameters	Explanation
predict_fn	Keras or TensorFlow model or any other model's prediction function returning class probabilities
Shape	Shape of input data starting with batch size
use_kdtree	Whether to use k-d trees for the prototype loss term if no encoder is available
Theta	Constant for the prototype search loss term
max_iterations	Maximum number of iterations for finding a counterfactual
feature_range	Tuple with min and max ranges to allow for perturbed instances
c_init, c_steps	Initial value to scale the attack loss term, number of iterations to adjust the constant scaling of the attack loss term

```
# define model
nn = load_model('nn_diabetes.h5')

predict_fn = lambda x: nn.predict(x)

# initialize explainer, fit and generate counterfactual
cf = CounterFactualProto(predict_fn, shape, use_kdtree=False, theta=10.,
max_iterations=1000,
                        feature_range=(np.array(x_train).min(axis=0),
                        np.array(x_train).max(axis=0)),
                        c_init=1., c_steps=10)
cf.fit(x_train)
```

The above result is generated during the counterfactual fit process or during the training process. The following script shows the lowest possible feature values across all features:

```
x_train.min(axis=0)
```

The explain method takes the input data and generates the counterfactual explanations shown in Table 10-4. The explain method also produces the following local explanation output:

```
explanation = cf.explain(X)
print(explanation)
```

Table 10-4. *Interpretation of Counterfactuals*

Output	Interpretation
Cf.X	The counterfactual instance
Cf.class	Predicted class for the counterfactual
Cf.proba	Predicted class probabilities for the counterfactual
Cf. grads_graph	Gradient values computed from the TF graph with respect to the input features at the counterfactual
Cf. grads_num	Numerical gradient values with respect to the input features at the counterfactual
orig_class	Predicted class for the original instance
orig_proba	Predicted class probabilities for the original instance
All	A dictionary with the iterations as keys and for each iteration a list with counterfactuals found in that iteration as values

```
print(f'Original prediction: {explanation.orig_class}')
print('Counterfactual prediction: {}'.format(explanation.cf['class']))

Original prediction: 0
Counterfactual prediction: 1
```

In the above script, all key provides the results of the iterations in finding the counterfactual values. At iteration 3 you get the counterfactual values. The rest of the nine iteration results do not have counterfactual values. The original prediction is no diabetes and the prediction based on the counterfactual information is diabetes.

```
explanation = cf.explain(X)
explanation.all
```

explanation.cf

```
{'X': array([[2.5628092e+00, 1.7726180e+02, 7.6516624e+01, 2.4388657e+01,
        7.2130630e+01, 2.6932917e+01, 7.8000002e-02, 2.2944651e+01]],
      dtype=float32),
 'class': 1,
 'proba': array([[0.4956944, 0.5043056]], dtype=float32),
 'grads_graph': array([[ -0.7179985 ,  -5.005951 ,  23.374054 ,  -0.96334076,
          3.8287811 , -13.371899 ,  -0.38599998,  -5.9150696 ]],
        dtype=float32),
 'grads_num': array([[  18.74566078,   38.92183304, -117.42114276,
   24.19948392, -35.82239151,   62.04843149,   93.54948252,   25.92801861]])}
```

explanation.orig_class
explanation.orig_proba
X

Counterfactual for Regression Tasks

In a regression scenario, the counterfactual explanations can be viewed by looking at the neural network model using the Boston housing prices dataset. Regression is a task when the target column is a continuous variable and you can use a mix of variables such as continuous and categorical variables. The Boston housing prices dataset is a common dataset for learning regression, so I selected it to showcase counterfactuals, as users are more familiar with this dataset.

```
import tensorflow as tf
tf.get_logger().setLevel(40) # suppress deprecation messages
tf.compat.v1.disable_v2_behavior() # disable TF2 behaviour as alibi code
still relies on TF1 constructs
from tensorflow.keras.layers import Dense, Input
from tensorflow.keras.models import Model, load_model
from tensorflow.keras.utils import to_categorical
import matplotlib
%matplotlib inline
```

```
import matplotlib.pyplot as plt
import numpy as np
import os
from sklearn.datasets import load_boston
from alibi.explainers import CounterFactualProto

print('TF version: ', tf.__version__)
print('Eager execution enabled: ', tf.executing_eagerly()) # False

boston = load_boston()
data = boston.data
target = boston.target
feature_names = boston.feature_names

y = np.zeros((target.shape[0],))
y[np.where(target > np.median(target))[0]] = 1

data = np.delete(data, 3, 1)
feature_names = np.delete(feature_names, 3)

mu = data.mean(axis=0)
sigma = data.std(axis=0)
data = (data - mu) / sigma

idx = 475
x_train,y_train = data[:idx,:], y[:idx]
x_test, y_test = data[idx:,:], y[idx:]
y_train = to_categorical(y_train)
y_test = to_categorical(y_test)

np.random.seed(42)
tf.random.set_seed(42)

def nn_model():
    x_in = Input(shape=(12,))
    x = Dense(40, activation='relu')(x_in)
    x = Dense(40, activation='relu')(x)
    x_out = Dense(2, activation='softmax')(x)
    nn = Model(inputs=x_in, outputs=x_out)
```

```
nn.compile(loss='categorical_crossentropy', optimizer='sgd',
metrics=['accuracy'])
   return nn
```

The script above is a neural network model for regression. The script below is the neural network architecture summary:

```
nn = nn_model()
nn.summary()
nn.fit(x_train, y_train, batch_size=64, epochs=500, verbose=0)
nn.save('nn_boston.h5', save_format='h5')
```

The trained model object nn_boston.h5 is saved to generate the counterfactuals.

```
nn = load_model('nn_boston.h5')
score = nn.evaluate(x_test, y_test, verbose=0)
print('Test accuracy: ', score[1])

X = x_test[1].reshape((1,) + x_test[1].shape)
shape = X.shape

# define model
nn = load_model('nn_boston.h5')

# initialize explainer, fit and generate counterfactual
cf = CounterFactualProto(nn, shape, use_kdtree=True, theta=10.,
max_iterations=1000,
                        feature_range=(x_train.min(axis=0), x_train.
                        max(axis=0)),
                        c_init=1., c_steps=10)
```

```
cf.fit(x_train)
explanation = cf.explain(X)
```

The result derived from the counterfactuals can be interpreted as explained in Table 10-4. The owner-occupied units built prior to 1940 is 93.6% and the lower status of the population is 18.68%. In order to increase house prices, the proportion of owner-occupied units built prior to 1940 should decrease by 5.95% and the lower status of the population should decrease by 4.85%.

```
print(f'Original prediction: {explanation.orig_class}')
print('Counterfactual prediction: {}'.format(explanation.cf['class']))
Original prediction: 0
Counterfactual prediction: 1

orig = X * sigma + mu
counterfactual = explanation.cf['X'] * sigma + mu
delta = counterfactual - orig
for i, f in enumerate(feature_names):
    if np.abs(delta[0][i]) > 1e-4:
        print('{}: {}'.format(f, delta[0][i]))

print('% owner-occupied units built prior to 1940: {}'.format(orig[0][5]))
print('% lower status of the population: {}'.format(orig[0][11]))
% owner-occupied units built prior to 1940: 93.6
% lower status of the population: 18.68
```

Conclusion

In this chapter, you explored counterfactual explanations for regression-related problems and classification-related problems. The counterfactual objective is to find the similar data point in the training data that produces a different prediction than the labelled class. The reasoning in counterfactual explanations is if two data points are very similar, then both should have a similar prediction or similar outcome. There should not be different output in the target class. In the diabetes prediction use case, if two people have similar features, then either both of them have no diabetes or both have diabetes. It should not happen that one has diabetes and the other has no diabetes. The existence of different counterfactual information actually creates confusion from an end user perspective, which will lead to lack of trust in AI models. In order to build trust in AI models, it is important to generate counterfactual explanations.

## CHAPTER 11

Contrastive Explanations for Machine Learning

Contrastive learning is a newer approach to finding similar and dissimilar candidate objects in a machine learning pipeline. The contrastive explanation aims to find the similarity between two features to help the prediction of a class. Typical black box models trained on different types of hyper parameters and a bunch of parameters optimized on various epochs and learning rates are very hard to interpret and even harder to reason why the model predicted Class A vs. Class B. The need to generate more explanations so business users can understand the predictions has attracted many developers to create innovative frameworks that can generate value. The contrastive explanation focuses on explaining why the model predicted Class A and not Class B. The reason finding helps the business user understand the behavior of the model. In this chapter, you are going to use the Alibi library for an image classification task using a TensorFlow-based framework.

What Is CE for ML?

In order to understand the contrastive explanation (CE) for machine learning, let's take an example of the loan approval process or credit risk assessment process of a bank. No bank will provide a loan to a risky customer. Likewise, no bank will refuse to give a loan to a non-risky customer. When a loan application or credit application gets rejected, it is not just an arbitrary decision made by someone at the bank. Rather, it's a decision made by an AI model that considers numerous features about a person, including financial history and other factors. The individual whose loan was denied can wonder what aspect determines his loan eligibility, what distinguishes one person from another in terms of loan eligibility, and what element is lacking from their profile, among other things. Similarly, in identifying objects of interest from multiple other images that are available,

© Pradeepta Mishra 2022
P. Mishra, *Practical Explainable AI Using Python*, https://doi.org/10.1007/978-1-4842-7158-2_11

what makes the object of interest different from the rest of the images? The contrastive explanations are the feature differences that distinguish a class from other classes.

Contrastive explanations are like human conversations that help a human have a more engaged conversation. There are two concepts associated with contrastive explanations:

- Pertinent positives (PP)

- Pertinent negatives (PN)

The PP explanation finds the presence of those features that are necessary for the machine learning model to identify the same class as the predicted class. As an example, the income and age of a person determine the net worth of the individual. You want your ML model to identify a class of high net worth individuals from the presence of high income and high age group. This is comparable to the anchors explanations of a machine learning model in several ways. PN is the reverse of PP; it explains the features that should be absent from the record while maintaining the original output class. This is also termed as *counterfactual explanation* by some researchers.

CEM Using Alibi

Contrastive explanations for models help to clarify to the end user why an event or prediction happened in contrast to another. In order to explain the concept of contrastive explanations for a model (CEM) and how it can be implemented through a Python-based library, let's use Alibi. As a first step, you are going to develop a Keras-based deep learning model with TensorFlow as the back end. The following script has various import statements of modules and methods that can be used in developing a deep learning model. CEM is available in the Alibi library under the explainer module.

```
import tensorflow as tf
tf.get_logger().setLevel(40) # suppress deprecation messages
tf.compat.v1.disable_v2_behavior() # disable TF2 behaviour as alibi code
still relies on TF1 constructs
import tensorflow.keras as keras
from tensorflow.keras import backend as K
from tensorflow.keras.layers import Conv2D, Dense, Dropout, Flatten,
MaxPooling2D, Input, UpSampling2D
```

```
from tensorflow.keras.models import Model, load_model
from tensorflow.keras.utils import to_categorical

import matplotlib
%matplotlib inline
import matplotlib.pyplot as plt
import numpy as np
import os
from alibi.explainers import CEM

print('TF version: ', tf.__version__)
print('Eager execution enabled: ', tf.executing_eagerly()) # False
```

When explaining the presence of PP and the absence of PN, it is important to identify and organize relevant features and classify important features from unimportant features. If you have more unimportant features in the model training step, then it really does not matter whether they belong to PP or PN. The unimportant features from the model are not relevant at all. The purpose of showing the MNIST digit classification dataset for the CEM explanation is because many developers and ML engineers are familiar with the MNIST dataset, hence they can relate well to the concept of CEM. The following script splits the data set into a train set and a test set, and a sample image of number 4 is also shown in Figure 11-1:

```
(x_train, y_train), (x_test, y_test) = keras.datasets.mnist.load_data()
print('x_train shape:', x_train.shape, 'y_train shape:', y_train.shape)
plt.gray()
plt.imshow(x_test[4]);
```

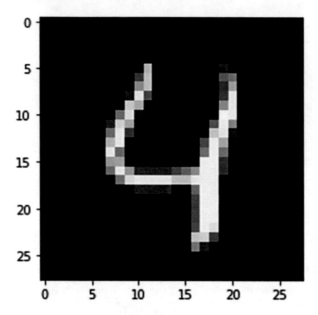

Figure 11-1. *Sample image for digit four*

You are going to develop a classification model. As a next step, you need to normalize the features in order to speed up the deep learning model training process. So you divide the pixel values by the highest pixel value (255).

```
x_train = x_train.astype('float32') / 255
x_test = x_test.astype('float32') / 255
x_train = np.reshape(x_train, x_train.shape + (1,))
x_test = np.reshape(x_test, x_test.shape + (1,))
print('x_train shape:', x_train.shape, 'x_test shape:', x_test.shape)

y_train = to_categorical(y_train)
y_test = to_categorical(y_test)
print('y_train shape:', y_train.shape, 'y_test shape:', y_test.shape)

xmin, xmax = -.5, .5
x_train = ((x_train - x_train.min()) / (x_train.max() - x_train.min())) *
(xmax - xmin) + xmin
x_test = ((x_test - x_test.min()) / (x_test.max() - x_test.min())) *
(xmax - xmin) + xmin
```

The following script shows the steps for creating a convolutional neural network model:

- The input dataset is a 28x28 pixels shape.

- The convolutional 2D layer applies 64 filters and a kernel size of 2, with padding as the same and a rectified linear unit as an activation function.

- After applying the convolutional layer, max pooling needs to be applied in order to generate abstract features that can be consumed by subsequent layers.

- Dropout is usually applied in order to restrict the model from being overfitted.

- There are three layers of convolutional 2D filters followed by a max pooling layer and a dropout layer applied to reduce the dimensions of the data.

- The objective of applying the convolution and max pooling is to arrive at a layer with less neurons that can be used to train a fully connected neural network model.

- If the data needs to be flattened to change the shape, then the dense layer, which is a fully connected neural network model, is applied.

- Finally, the softmax layer is applied in order to generate the class probabilities with respect to each digit class.

- At the compile step, you need to provide the categorical cross entropy as a loss function, adam as an optimizer, and accuracy as the metric.

```
def cnn_model():
    x_in = Input(shape=(28, 28, 1)) #input layer
    x = Conv2D(filters=64, kernel_size=2, padding='same',
        activation='relu')(x_in) #conv layer
    x = MaxPooling2D(pool_size=2)(x) #max pooling layer
    x = Dropout(0.3)(x) #drop out to avoid overfitting

    x = Conv2D(filters=32, kernel_size=2, padding='same',
        activation='relu')(x) # second conv layer
```

```
x = MaxPooling2D(pool_size=2)(x) #max pooling layer
x = Dropout(0.3)(x) #drop out to avoid overfitting

x = Conv2D(filters=32, kernel_size=2, padding='same',
activation='relu')(x) # third conv layer
x = MaxPooling2D(pool_size=2)(x) #max pooling layer
x = Dropout(0.3)(x) # drop out to avoid overfitting

x = Flatten()(x) # flatten for reshaping the matrix
x = Dense(256, activation='relu')(x) #this is for Fully Connected
Neural Network Layer training
x = Dropout(0.5)(x) # drop out again to avoid overfitting
x_out = Dense(10, activation='softmax')(x) #final output layer

cnn = Model(inputs=x_in, outputs=x_out)
cnn.compile(loss='categorical_crossentropy', optimizer='adam',
metrics=['accuracy'])

return cnn
```

The convolutional neural network model summary is shown in a tabular view below. In the model training step, you need to provide the batch size and the number of epochs. Then you can save the trained model object as an h5 format.

```
cnn = cnn_model()
cnn.summary()
cnn.fit(x_train, y_train, batch_size=64, epochs=5, verbose=1)
cnn.save('mnist_cnn.h5', save_format='h5')
```

In order to generate meaningful CEM explanations, you must ensure a model with great accuracy or else the CEM explanations will lack consistency. Hence it is advisable to first train, fine-tune, or search for the best model that produces at least 85% accuracy. In the current example, the model accuracy on a test dataset is 98.73%, so you can expect meaningful CEM explanations.

```
# Evaluate the model on test set
cnn = load_model('mnist_cnn.h5')
score = cnn.evaluate(x_test, y_test, verbose=0)
print('Test accuracy: ', score[1])
```

In order to generate CEM explanations, you need a model object that classifies the input data into a specific class. The CEM tries to generate two possible explanations:

- Tries to find the bare minimum amount of information that must be present in an input, which is sufficient enough to generate the same class classification. This is called PP.

- Tries to find out the absence of minimum information in the input data, which is sufficient enough to prevent the class prediction from changing. This is called PN.

The pursuit of finding the minimum information that possibly can change the prediction or help in staying with a prediction is generally the most important feature value from the input dataset. The matching of input data with an abstract layer generated from the data is used to identify the present or absence of minimum information. The abstract layer is called the autoencoder. For an image classification problem, it can be a convolutional autoencoder. The autoencoder is trained by using the input data in the input layer as well as in the output layer. The model is trained to exactly predict the same output as input. Once the input and output match, then the innermost hidden layer in the neural network model weights can be derived as autoencoder values. These autoencoder values help in identifying the minimum information availability in any input dataset. The following script shows how to train an autoencoder model. It is a neural network model. It takes the 28x28 pixels as input and produces 28x28 pixels as output.

```
# Define and train an Auto Encoder, it works like a principal component
analysis model
def ae_model():
    x_in = Input(shape=(28, 28, 1))
    x = Conv2D(16, (3, 3), activation='relu', padding='same')(x_in)
    x = Conv2D(16, (3, 3), activation='relu', padding='same')(x)
    x = MaxPooling2D((2, 2), padding='same')(x)
    encoded = Conv2D(1, (3, 3), activation=None, padding='same')(x)

    x = Conv2D(16, (3, 3), activation='relu', padding='same')(encoded)
    x = UpSampling2D((2, 2))(x)
    x = Conv2D(16, (3, 3), activation='relu', padding='same')(x)
    decoded = Conv2D(1, (3, 3), activation=None, padding='same')(x)
```

```
    autoencoder = Model(x_in, decoded)
    autoencoder.compile(optimizer='adam', loss='mse')

    return autoencoder

 ae = ae_model()
ae.summary()
ae.fit(x_train, x_train, batch_size=128, epochs=4, validation_data=(x_test,
x_test), verbose=0)
ae.save('mnist_ae.h5', save_format='h5')
```

The summary of the model shows the architecture and the total number of trainable parameters. The trainable parameters have updated weights in each iteration of the model. There are no non-trainable parameters. Once the autoencoder model is ready, then you can load the model object into a session. Using predict function on the test set, you can generate decoded MNIST images. The output from the following script shows that the test images exactly match the generated images using the autoencoder function, which means your autoencoder model is quite robust in generating the exact output. The autoencoder model has two parts: encoder and decoder. The role of the encoder is to transform any input into an abstract layer and the role of the decoder is to reconstruct the same input from the abostract layer.

Comparison of an Original Image vs. an Autoencoder-Generated Image

You can compare the original image from the training set with the autoencoder-based generated model image set in Figure 11-2. What you can see from the images is that the autoencoder-generated model exactly matches with original image. Since this is an example dataset, the matching is very close; however, for other examples a good amount of training is required in order to generate such close images. A well-trained autoencoder model will be very helpful for generating the contrastive exxplanations.

```
ae = load_model('mnist_ae.h5')

decoded_imgs = ae.predict(x_test)
n = 5
plt.figure(figsize=(20, 4))
for i in range(1, n+1):
```

```
    # display original
    ax = plt.subplot(2, n, i)
    plt.imshow(x_test[i].reshape(28, 28))
    ax.get_xaxis().set_visible(False)
    ax.get_yaxis().set_visible(False)
    # display reconstruction
    ax = plt.subplot(2, n, i + n)
    plt.imshow(decoded_imgs[i].reshape(28, 28))
    ax.get_xaxis().set_visible(False)
    ax.get_yaxis().set_visible(False)
plt.show()
```

Figure 11-2. *Comparison of images generated by the AE model vs. the original image*

The first line shows the actual images from the first record of the test dataset and the second row shows the autoencoder-generated predicted images.

```
ae = load_model('mnist_ae.h5')

decoded_imgs = ae.predict(x_test)
n = 5
plt.figure(figsize=(20, 4))
for i in range(1, n+1):
    # display original
    ax = plt.subplot(2, n, i)
    plt.imshow(x_test[i].reshape(28, 28))
    ax.get_xaxis().set_visible(False)
    ax.get_yaxis().set_visible(False)
    # display reconstruction
    ax = plt.subplot(2, n, i + n)
```

```
    plt.imshow(decoded_imgs[i].reshape(28, 28))
    ax.get_xaxis().set_visible(False)
    ax.get_yaxis().set_visible(False)
plt.show()
```

Figure 11-3. *Pertinent negatives explanation*

The above script shows the display and reconstruction of the same image (Figure 11-3) which is displayed below as 5 (Figure 11-4).

```
idx = 15
X = x_test[idx].reshape((1,) + x_test[idx].shape)
plt.imshow(X.reshape(28, 28));
```

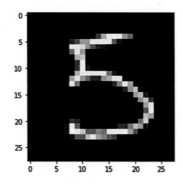

Figure 11-4. *Original image display for digit 5*

```
# Model prediction
cnn.predict(X).argmax(), cnn.predict(X).max()
```

The CNN model predicts the input as 5 with 99.95% probability (Table 11-1).

Table 11-1. *CEM Parameter Explanations*

Parameter	Explanations
Mode	PN or PP
Shape	Input instance shape
Kappa	Minimum difference needed between prediction probability for the perturbed instance on the predicted class as the original instance, and the maximum probability on the other classes in order for the first loss term to be minimized
Beta	Weight of the L1 loss term
Gamma	Weight of the autoencoder loss term
C_steps	Number of updates
Max iterations	Number of iterations
Feature_range	Feature range for the perturbed instance
Lr	Initial learning rate

The following script shows a pertinent negative prediction from the explanation object generated from the sample instance X. The pertinent negative analysis tells you that some important features are missing from 5; otherwise, it would have been classified as 8. That missing information is the minimum information that keeps the 5 class prediction different from the 8 class prediction. Figure 11-5 has 8 overlaid on number 5.

```
mode = 'PN'  # 'PN' (pertinent negative) or 'PP' (pertinent positive)
shape = (1,) + x_train.shape[1:]   # instance shape
kappa = 0.  # minimum difference needed between the prediction probability
for the perturbed instance on the
            # class predicted by the original instance and the max
              probability on the other classes
            # in order for the first loss term to be minimized
beta = .1  # weight of the L1 loss term
gamma = 100  # weight of the optional auto-encoder loss term
c_init = 1.  # initial weight c of the loss term encouraging to predict a
              different class (PN) or
```

```
                # the same class (PP) for the perturbed instance compared to
                  the original instance to be explained
c_steps = 10  # nb of updates for c
max_iterations = 1000  # nb of iterations per value of c
feature_range = (x_train.min(),x_train.max())  # feature range for the
perturbed instance
clip = (-1000.,1000.)  # gradient clipping
lr = 1e-2  # initial learning rate
no_info_val = -1. # a value, float or feature-wise, which can be seen as
containing no info to make a prediction
                # perturbations towards this value means removing
                  features, and away means adding features
                # for our MNIST images, the background (-0.5) is the
                  least informative,
                # so positive/negative perturbations imply adding/
                  removing features

# initialize CEM explainer and explain instance
cem = CEM(cnn, mode, shape, kappa=kappa, beta=beta, feature_range=feature_
          range, gamma=gamma, ae_model=ae, max_iterations=max_iterations,
          c_init=c_init, c_steps=c_steps, learning_rate_init=lr, clip=clip,
          no_info_val=no_info_val)

explanation = cem.explain(X)

print(f'Pertinent negative prediction: {explanation.PN_pred}')
plt.imshow(explanation.PN.reshape(28, 28));
```

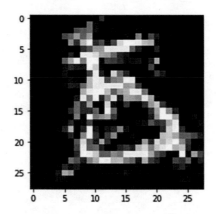

Figure 11-5. *Perntinet negative prediction is digit 8 vs. original image of 5*

A pertinent positive explanation can also be generated for the same digit, 5, which means what features you are absolutely looking for in the image in order to classify the digit as 5. This is called a pertinent positive explanation.

```
# Now Generate pertinent positive
mode = 'PP'
# initialize CEM explainer and explain instance
cem = CEM(cnn, mode, shape, kappa=kappa, beta=beta, feature_range=feature_
        range, gamma=gamma, ae_model=ae, max_iterations=max_iterations,
        c_init=c_init, c_steps=c_steps, learning_rate_init=lr, clip=clip,
        no_info_val=no_info_val)

explanation = cem.explain(X)
print(f'Pertinent positive prediction: {explanation.PP_pred}')
plt.imshow(explanation.PP.reshape(28, 28));
```

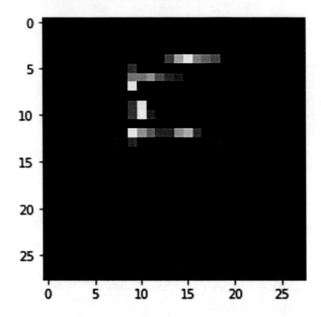

Figure 11-6. *Pertinent positive explanation for number 5*

In the above script you generate the pertinent positive. The pertinent positive explanation states that the pixel values shown in Figure 11-6 are minimally required in order to predict the image as number 5.

CEM for Tabular Data Explanations

For any tabular data (also known as structured data), the rows are the examples and the columns are the features. You can use the same process you followed in the convolutional neural network model above for the example of a simple multiclass classification problem using a familiar IRIS dataset.

```
# CEM for Structured dataset
import tensorflow as tf
tf.get_logger().setLevel(40) # suppress deprecation messages
tf.compat.v1.disable_v2_behavior() # disable TF2 behaviour as alibi code
still relies on TF1 constructs

from tensorflow.keras.layers import Dense, Input
from tensorflow.keras.models import Model, load_model
from tensorflow.keras.utils import to_categorical
```

```
import matplotlib
%matplotlib inline
import matplotlib.pyplot as plt
import numpy as np
import os

import pandas as pd
import seaborn as sns
from sklearn.datasets import load_iris
from alibi.explainers import CEM

print('TF version: ', tf.__version__)
print('Eager execution enabled: ', tf.executing_eagerly()) # False
```

The above script shows the import statements needed in order for the Alibi model to generate the PP and PN explanations.

```
dataset = load_iris()
feature_names = dataset.feature_names
class_names = list(dataset.target_names)

 # scaling data
dataset.data = (dataset.data - dataset.data.mean(axis=0)) / dataset.data.
            std(axis=0)

idx = 145
x_train,y_train = dataset.data[:idx,:], dataset.target[:idx]
x_test, y_test = dataset.data[idx+1:,:], dataset.target[idx+1:]
y_train = to_categorical(y_train)
y_test = to_categorical(y_test)
```

The IRIS model has four features, and the three classes in the target column are setosa, versicolor, and virginica. The first 145 records are the training dataset and 5 records are parked for testing the model. Categorical encoding is required on the target column or the y_train and y_test datasets as the column contains the string values.

The following neural network model function takes the four features as input, and using a fully connected network using the dense function from Keras, a model gets trained. You use the categorical cross entropy as the loss function and the optimizer as the stochastic gradient descent. The batch size for training the model is 16 with 500 epochs. There are a very small number of parameters that are getting trained.

```python
def lr_model():
    x_in = Input(shape=(4,))
    x_out = Dense(3, activation='softmax')(x_in)
    lr = Model(inputs=x_in, outputs=x_out)
    lr.compile(loss='categorical_crossentropy', optimizer='sgd',
    metrics=['accuracy'])
    return lr

lr = lr_model()
lr.summary()
lr.fit(x_train, y_train, batch_size=16, epochs=500, verbose=0)
lr.save('iris_lr.h5', save_format='h5')
```

After training the model, the model is saved as iris_lr.h5. In the following script, you load the trained model object and initialize the CEM function with all the parameters explained earlier in Table 11-1.

```python
idx = 0
X = x_test[idx].reshape((1,) + x_test[idx].shape)
print('Prediction on instance to be explained: {}'.format(class_names[np.
argmax(lr.predict(X))]))
print('Prediction probabilities for each class on the instance: {}'.
format(lr.predict(X)))

mode = 'PN'  # 'PN' (pertinent negative) or 'PP' (pertinent positive)
shape = (1,) + x_train.shape[1:]  # instance shape
kappa = .2  # minimum difference needed between the prediction probability
            for the perturbed instance on the
        # class predicted by the original instance and the max
          probability on the other classes
        # in order for the first loss term to be minimized
beta = .1  # weight of the L1 loss term
c_init = 10.  # initial weight c of the loss term encouraging to predict a
            different class (PN) or
```

```
                    # the same class (PP) for the perturbed instance compared to
                       the original instance to be explained
c_steps = 10  # nb of updates for c
max_iterations = 1000  # nb of iterations per value of c
feature_range = (x_train.min(axis=0).reshape(shape)-.1,  # feature range
for the perturbed instance
                       x_train.max(axis=0).reshape(shape)+.1)  # can be either a
                       float or array of shape (1xfeatures)
clip = (-1000.,1000.)  # gradient clipping
lr_init = 1e-2  # initial learning rate

# define model
lr = load_model('iris_lr.h5')

# initialize CEM explainer and explain instance
cem = CEM(lr, mode, shape, kappa=kappa, beta=beta, feature_range=feature_
          range, max_iterations=max_iterations, c_init=c_init, c_steps=c_
          steps, learning_rate_init=lr_init, clip=clip)
cem.fit(x_train, no_info_type='median')  # we need to define what feature
values contain the least
                                          # info wrt predictions
                                          # here we will naively assume that
                                            the feature-wise median
                                          # contains no info; domain
                                            knowledge helps!
explanation = cem.explain(X, verbose=False)
```

In the above script, the original instance is virginica, but the explanation for the pertinent negative predicts it to be versicolor. Only the difference in the third feature makes the difference in prediction. You can also take the same example for predicting the pertinent positives class.

```
print(f'Original instance: {explanation.X}')
print('Predicted class: {}'.format(class_names[explanation.X_pred]))

print(f'Pertinent negative: {explanation.PN}')
print('Predicted class: {}'.format(class_names[explanation.PN_pred]))
```

```
expl = {}
expl['PN'] = explanation.PN
expl['PN_pred'] = explanation.PN_pred

mode = 'PP'

# define model
lr = load_model('iris_lr.h5')

# initialize CEM explainer and explain instance
cem = CEM(lr, mode, shape, kappa=kappa, beta=beta, feature_range=feature_
          range, max_iterations=max_iterations, c_init=c_init, c_steps=c_
          steps, learning_rate_init=lr_init, clip=clip)
cem.fit(x_train, no_info_type='median')
explanation = cem.explain(X, verbose=False)

print(f'Pertinent positive: {explanation.PP}')
print('Predicted class: {}'.format(class_names[explanation.PP_pred]))
```

In the above script, you explain the pertinent positive predicted class. It is the
virginica class and the actual is also the virginica class. You are creating a visual way
of displaying the PP and PN using the features and results of the CEM model. You create
an expl object and create columns named PN, PN_pred, PP, and PP_pred. You create
a dataframe having the raw data and feature names including the target class. This is
required for data visualization. The Seaborn Python library is used to showcase the PNs
and PPs in a graphical way in Figure 11-7.

```
expl['PP'] = explanation.PP
expl['PP_pred'] = explanation.PP_pred

df = pd.DataFrame(dataset.data, columns=dataset.feature_names)
df['species'] = np.array([dataset.target_names[i] for i in dataset.target])

pn = pd.DataFrame(expl['PN'], columns=dataset.feature_names)
pn['species'] = 'PN_' + class_names[expl['PN_pred']]
pp = pd.DataFrame(expl['PP'], columns=dataset.feature_names)
pp['species'] = 'PP_' + class_names[expl['PP_pred']]
orig_inst = pd.DataFrame(explanation.X, columns=dataset.feature_names)
```

```
orig_inst['species'] = 'orig_' + class_names[explanation.X_pred]
df = df.append([pn, pp, orig_inst], ignore_index=True)

fig = sns.pairplot(df, hue='species', diag_kind='hist');
```

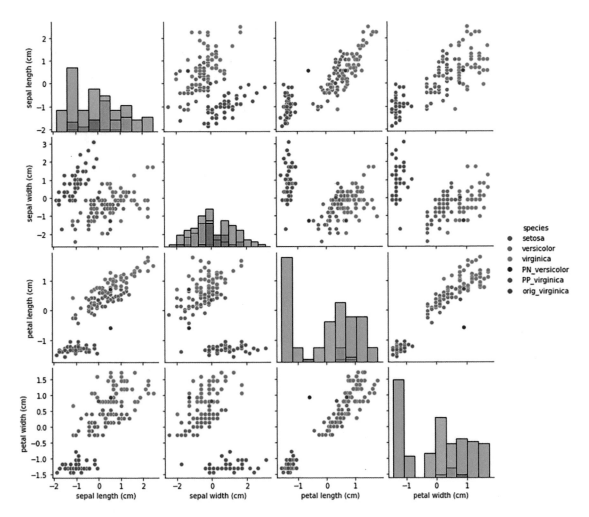

Figure 11-7. *Pertinent Positive and Pertinent Negative visualization*

The contrastive explanations are usually generated by projecting the features into a latent space as abstract features and then considering only the useful features from the feature space for the model to differentiate the target class.

Conclusion

In this chapter, you explored methods and libraries that can establish a contrastive explanation for both an image classification problem where you have MNIST dataset for recognizing handwriting and a structured data classification problem using a simple IRIS dataset. Both the pertinent positives and pertinent negatives are captured from the contrastive explanation module from the Alibi library. This CEM provides more clarity around class prediction and it concludes why a particular class is predicted vs. why it is not predicted.

## CHAPTER 12

Model-Agnostic Explanations by Identifying Prediction Invariance

The invariant terminology taken from the field of mathematics explains that predictions generated by a machine learning model remain unchanged if we intervene with the explanatory variables, given the fact that the model is generated through a formal causal relationship. There is a difference between the causal machine learning model and the non-causal machine learning model. The causal model shows a real cause-and-effect relationship between the response variable and the explanatory variables. The non-causal modal model shows an accidental relationship; the predictions do change many times. The only way to understand the difference between the causal and non-causal models is through explanations. In this chapter, you are going to use a Python library named Alibi to generate model-agnostic explanations.

What Is Model Agnostic?

The term *model agnostic* implies model independence. The explanation of machine learning models that are valid irrespective of model types are called model agnostic. When we explain the inherent behavior of a machine learning model, we typically do not assume any underlying structure of the behavior as displayed by the machine learning model itself. In this chapter, you are going to use model-agnostic explanations to describie the prediction invariance. It has always been challenging from a human

© Pradeepta Mishra 2022
P. Mishra, *Practical Explainable AI Using Python*, https://doi.org/10.1007/978-1-4842-7158-2_12

understanding how a machine learning model works. People always wonder and ask questions about the behavior of the machine learning model. In order to understand the model-agnostic behavior, humans always think they can make predictions about the model behavior.

What Is an Anchor?

Complex models are usually considered as black-box models because it is very hard to understand why the prediction was made. The anchors concept is nothing but finding out the rules. Here the rules mean high precision rules that explain the model behavior, taking into consideration local and global factors. In other words, the anchors are if/then/else conditions that anchor the prediction irrespective of the values of other features.

The anchor algorithm is built on top of model-agnostic explanations. It has three core functions:

- **Coverage**: This implies how often one can change the framework to predict a machine learning model's behavior.

- **Precision**: This implies how accurately humans predict the model behavior.

- **Effort**: This implies the upfront effort required to interpret the model behavior or to understand the predictions generated by the model's behavior. Both scenarios are difficult to explain.

Anchor Explanations Using Alibi

In order to generate anchor explanations for a black box model, you are going to use the Python library Alibi. The following script shows the import statements necessary to explain the concept. You are going to use a random forest classifier, which is also a black box model, as there are a number of trees that generate predictions and the predictions are assembled to produce the final output.

```
import numpy as np
import pandas as pd
from sklearn.ensemble import RandomForestClassifier
```

```
from sklearn.compose import ColumnTransformer
from sklearn.pipeline import Pipeline
from sklearn.impute import SimpleImputer
from sklearn.metrics import accuracy_score
from sklearn.preprocessing import StandardScaler, OneHotEncoder
from alibi.explainers import AnchorTabular
from alibi.datasets import fetch_adult
```

The Alibi library has several datasets in order to generate examples that can be used to explain the concept. Here you are going to use the `adult` dataset; it's otherwise known as the census income dataset available from the UCI machine learning repository. This is about a binary classification model. There are several features that can be used in order to predict the income category and whether it is more than $50K or less.

```
adult = fetch_adult()
adult.keys()
```

The above script brings data to the Jupyter environment. The keys are `dict_keys(['data', 'target', 'feature_names', 'target_names', 'category_map'])`.

```
data = adult.data
target = adult.target
feature_names = adult.feature_names
category_map = adult.category_map
```

The role category map function is to map all the categorical columns or the string columns present in the data.

```
from alibi.utils.data import gen_category_map
```

The categorical map is just a dummy variable mapping because you cannot use the categorical or string variables as they are for computations.

```
np.random.seed(0)
data_perm = np.random.permutation(np.c_[data, target])
data = data_perm[:,:-1]
target = data_perm[:,-1]
```

Before training the model, you randomize the data available in the dataset and use 33,000 records for model training and 2,560 records for model testing or validation.

```
idx = 30000
X_train,Y_train = data[:idx,:], target[:idx]
X_test, Y_test = data[idx+1:,:], target[idx+1:]

X_train.shape,Y_train.shape
X_test.shape, Y_test.shape

ordinal_features = [x for x in range(len(feature_names)) if x not in
list(category_map.keys())]
ordinal_features
```

After the ordinal features have been selected, you can apply the ordinal feature transformer triggered from a pipeline, as follows:

```
ordinal_transformer = Pipeline(steps=[('imputer', SimpleImputer(strategy='m
edian')),
                                    ('scaler', StandardScaler())])
categorical_features = list(category_map.keys())
categorical_features
```

The ordinal features are feature numbers 0, 8, 9, and 10, and the categorical features are 1, 2, 3, 4, 5, 6, 7, and 11. For ordinal features you apply a standard scaler. If there are missing values, you impute by the median values.

```
categorical_transformer = Pipeline(steps=[('imputer', SimpleImputer(strateg
y='median')),
                                        ('onehot', OneHotEncoder(handle_
                                        unknown='ignore'))])
categorical_transformer
preprocessor = ColumnTransformer(transformers=[('num', ordinal_transformer,
ordinal_features),
                                        ('cat', categorical_
                                        transformer, categorical_
                                        features)])
```

For the categorical features, in case of missing values you apply a median imputation technique and perform one hot encoding for the categorical variable transformation. If the categorical variable value is unknown, you ignore the value.

```
Preprocessor
ColumnTransformer(transformers=[('num',
                              Pipeline(steps=[('imputer',
                                             SimpleImputer(strategy='m
                                             edian')),
                                            ('scaler',
                                             StandardScaler())]),
                              [0, 8, 9, 10]),
                              ('cat',
                              Pipeline(steps=[('imputer',
                                             SimpleImputer(strategy='m
                                             edian')),
                                            ('onehot',
                                             OneHotEncoder(handle_
                                             unknown='ignore'))]),
                              [1, 2, 3, 4, 5, 6, 7, 11])])
```

The preprocessor module is now ready for model training. The preprocessor fit function transforms the data set for model training. The random forest model for classification is initialized with 50 trees as the number of estimators. The initialized object is stored in clf. The clf fit function trains the model.

```
preprocessor.fit(X_train)
np.random.seed(0)
clf = RandomForestClassifier(n_estimators=50)
clf.fit(preprocessor.transform(X_train), Y_train)

predict_fn = lambda x: clf.predict(preprocessor.transform(x))
print('Train accuracy: ', accuracy_score(Y_train, predict_fn(X_train)))
Train accuracy:   0.9655333333333334

print('Test accuracy: ', accuracy_score(Y_test, predict_fn(X_test)))
Test accuracy:   0.855859375
```

As a next step, you are going to use or fit the anchor explainer to the tabular data. The tabular anchor has the parameter requirements shown in Table 12-1.

Table 12-1. *Parameter Explanations for Anchor Tabular*

Parameters	Explanation
Predictor	A model object that has the predict function that takes an input data and generates the output data
Feature_names	A list of features
Categorical_names	A dictionary where keys are feature columns and values are the categories for the feature
OHE	Whether the categorical variables are one hot encoded (OHE) or not. If not OHE, they are assumed to have ordinal encodings.
Seed	For reproducibility

```
explainer = AnchorTabular(predict_fn, feature_names, categorical_
names=category_map, seed=12345)
explainer
explainer.explanations
explainer.fit(X_train, disc_perc=[25, 50, 75])
AnchorTabular(meta={
  'name': 'AnchorTabular',
  'type': ['blackbox'],
  'explanations': ['local'],
  'params': {'seed': 1, 'disc_perc': [25, 50, 75]}}
)
idx = 0
class_names = adult.target_names
print('Prediction: ', class_names[explainer.predictor(X_test[idx].
reshape(1, -1))[0]])
Prediction:  <=50K

explanation = explainer.explain(X_test[idx], threshold=0.95)
explanation.name
print('Anchor: %s' % (' AND '.join(explanation.anchor)))
```

```
print('Precision: %.2f' % explanation.precision)
print('Coverage: %.2f' % explanation.coverage)
idx = 6
class_names = adult.target_names
print('Prediction: ', class_names[explainer.predictor(X_test[idx].
reshape(1, -1))[0]])
Prediction:  >50K
```

The explainer.explain object explains the prediction made by a classifier for an observation. The explain function has the following parameters shown in Table 12-2.

Table 12-2. *Explain Function Parameter Values*

Parameter	Explanation
Xtest	New data that needs to be explained
Threshold	Minimum precision threshold
batch_size	Batch size used for sampling
coverage_samples	Number of samples used to estimate coverage from the result search
beam_size	The number of anchors extended at each step of a new anchor's construction
stop_on_first	If True, the beam search algorithm will return the first anchor that has satisfied the probability constraint.
max_anchor_size	Maximum number of features in a result

```
explanation = explainer.explain(X_test[idx], threshold=0.95)
print('Anchor: %s' % (' AND '.join(explanation.anchor)))

Output : [Anchor: Capital Loss > 0.00 AND Relationship = Husband AND
Marital Status = Married AND Age > 37.00 AND Race = White AND Sex = Male
AND Country = United-States
]

print('Precision: %.2f' % explanation.precision)
print('Coverage: %.2f' % explanation.coverage)
```

In the above example, the precision from the model explanation is only 72% and the coverage is only 2%. It can be concluded that the coverage and precision are low due to an imbalanced dataset. There are more less-than-$50K earners than there are greater-than-$50K earners. You can apply a similar anchors concept on the text classification dataset. You are going to use the sentiment analysis dataset in this example.

Anchor Text for Text Classification

The anchor's text function is going to help you get an anchors explanation for the text classification dataset. It can be spam email identification or it can be sentiment analysis. The parameters that can be fine-tuned for generating anchor text are shown in Table 12-3.

Table 12-3. *Anchor Text Parameter Explanations*

Parameter	Explanation
Predictor	Usually a trained model object that can generate predictions
sampling_strategy	Perturbation distribution method, where unknown replaces words with UNKs; similarity samples according to a similarity score with the corpus embeddings; and language_model samples according the language model's output distributions
NLP	spaCy object when the sampling method is unknown or similarity
language_model	Transformers masked language model

The sampling strategies you are going to use are unknown and similarity, because the transformers method is out of scope for this book.

```
import numpy as np
from sklearn.feature_extraction.text import CountVectorizer
from sklearn.linear_model import LogisticRegression
from sklearn.metrics import accuracy_score
from sklearn.model_selection import train_test_split
#import spacy
from alibi.explainers import AnchorText
from alibi.datasets import fetch_movie_sentiment
#from alibi.utils.download import spacy_model
```

The above script imports the necessary libraries and functions from the libraries.

```
movies = fetch_movie_sentiment()
movies.keys()
```

The above script loads the labelled data for sentiment classification.

```
data = movies.data
labels = movies.target
target_names = movies.target_names
```

This includes movies data, the target columns (which are labelled as positive and negative) and the feature names (which are a unique set of tokens from the corpus).

```
train, test, train_labels, test_labels = train_test_split(data, labels,
test_size=.2, random_state=42)
train, test, train_labels, test_labels
```

The above script splits the data into train and test sets, and the following as the train and validation dataset.

```
train, val, train_labels, val_labels = train_test_split(train, train_
labels, test_size=.1, random_state=42)
train, val, train_labels, val_labels
```

```
train_labels = np.array(train_labels)
train_labels
```

```
test_labels = np.array(test_labels)
test_labels
```

```
val_labels = np.array(val_labels)
val_labels
```

```
vectorizer = CountVectorizer(min_df=1)
vectorizer.fit(train)
```

The count vectorizer function creates a document term matrix where the document is represented as rows and the tokens as features.

```
np.random.seed(0)
clf = LogisticRegression(solver='liblinear')
clf.fit(vectorizer.transform(train), train_labels)
```

Logistic regression is used since it is a binary classification problem, with a solver as lib linear. The following predict function takes the trained model object and, given the test data set, makes a prediction:

```
predict_fn = lambda x: clf.predict(vectorizer.transform(x))

preds_train = predict_fn(train)
preds_train

preds_val = predict_fn(val)
preds_val

preds_test = predict_fn(test)
preds_test

print('Train accuracy', accuracy_score(train_labels, preds_train))

print('Validation accuracy', accuracy_score(val_labels, preds_val))

print('Test accuracy', accuracy_score(test_labels, preds_test))
```

The train, test, and validation accuracy is in line.

To generate an anchor explanation, you need to install spacy. You also need to install the en_core_web_md module, which can be done by using the following script from the command line:

```
python -m spacy download en_core_web_md

import spacy
model = 'en_core_web_md'
#spacy_model(model=model)
nlp = spacy.load(model)
```

The AnchorText function requires the spacy model object, hence you initialize the nlp object from spacy.

```
class_names = movies.target_names

# select instance to be explained
text = data[40]
print("* Text: %s" % text)
```

```
# compute class prediction
pred = class_names[predict_fn([text])[0]]
alternative =  class_names[1 - predict_fn([text])[0]]
print("* Prediction: %s" % pred)

explainer = AnchorText(
    predictor=predict_fn,
    nlp=nlp
)

explanation = explainer.explain(text, threshold=0.95)

explainer

explanation

print('Anchor: %s' % (' AND '.join(explanation.anchor)))
print('Precision: %.2f' % explanation.precision)

Anchor: watchable AND bleak AND honest
Precision: 0.99

print('\nExamples where anchor applies and model predicts %s:' % pred)
print('\n'.join([x for x in explanation.raw['examples'][-1]['covered_
true']]))

print('\nExamples where anchor applies and model predicts %s:' %
alternative)
print('\n'.join([x for x in explanation.raw['examples'][-1]['covered_
false']]))
```

Examples where anchor applies and model predicts negative:
the effort is UNK UNK the results UNK honest , but the UNK UNK so bleak UNK UNK UNK hardly watchable .

Anchor Image for Image Classification

Similar to the anchor text, you have anchor image model explanations for the image classification dataset. Here you are going to use the fashion MNIST dataset. Table 12-4 shows the anchor image parameters that need to be explained.

Table 12-4. *Anchor Image Parameter Explanations*

Parameter	Explanation
Predictor	Image classification model object
image_shape	Shape of the image to be explained
segmentation_fn	Any of the built-in segmentation function strings: 'felzenszwalb', 'slic', 'quickshift', or a custom segmentation function (callable) which returns an image mask with labels for each superpixel
segmentation_kwargs	Keyword arguments for the built-in segmentation functions
images_background	Images to overlay superpixels onto
Seed	For reproducing the result

Let's look at the following scripts on generating the anchors image.

```
import matplotlib
%matplotlib inline
import matplotlib.pyplot as plt
import numpy as np
import tensorflow as tf
from tensorflow.keras.layers import Conv2D, Dense, Dropout, Flatten,
MaxPooling2D, Input
from tensorflow.keras.models import Model
from tensorflow.keras.utils import to_categorical
from alibi.explainers import AnchorImage

(x_train, y_train), (x_test, y_test) = tf.keras.datasets.fashion_mnist.
load_data()
print('x_train shape:', x_train.shape, 'y_train shape:', y_train.shape)
```

The training dataset contains 60,000 sample images and the test dataset contains 10,000 sample images. You are going to develop a convolutional neural network model (CNN) to predict the image class and explain the anchors involved. The target class has 9 labels; see Table 12-5.

Table 12-5. *Target Class Description*

Class	Description
0	T-shirt/top
1	Trouser
2	Pullover
3	Dress
4	Coat
5	Sandal
6	Shirt
7	Sneaker
8	Bag
9	Ankle Boot

```
idx = 57
plt.imshow(x_train[idx]);

x_train = x_train.astype('float32') / 255
x_test = x_test.astype('float32') / 255
```

Feature normalization is done by dividing each pixel value by the highest pixel value (255).

```
x_train = np.reshape(x_train, x_train.shape + (1,))
x_test = np.reshape(x_test, x_test.shape + (1,))
print('x_train shape:', x_train.shape, 'x_test shape:', x_test.shape)

y_train = to_categorical(y_train)
y_test = to_categorical(y_test)
print('y_train shape:', y_train.shape, 'y_test shape:', y_test.shape)
```

The CNN model is typically used to predict the image classes. It has a convolutional two-dimensional filter to better recognize the pixel values, followed by a max pooling layer (sometimes it is average pooling and sometimes it is max pooling) in order to prepare the abstract layer. The drop-out layer is designed to control any overfitting problem that may arise in the model prediction.

```python
def model():
    x_in = Input(shape=(28, 28, 1))
    x = Conv2D(filters=64, kernel_size=2, padding='same',
    activation='relu')(x_in)
    x = MaxPooling2D(pool_size=2)(x)
    x = Dropout(0.3)(x)

    x = Conv2D(filters=32, kernel_size=2, padding='same',
    activation='relu')(x)
    x = MaxPooling2D(pool_size=2)(x)
    x = Dropout(0.3)(x)

    x = Flatten()(x)
    x = Dense(256, activation='relu')(x)
    x = Dropout(0.5)(x)
    x_out = Dense(10, activation='softmax')(x)

    cnn = Model(inputs=x_in, outputs=x_out)
    cnn.compile(loss='categorical_crossentropy', optimizer='adam',
    metrics=['accuracy'])

    return cnn

cnn = model()
cnn.summary()

cnn.fit(x_train, y_train, batch_size=64, epochs=3)

# Evaluate the model on test set
score = cnn.evaluate(x_test, y_test, verbose=0)
print('Test accuracy: ', score[1])
```

The superpixels provide the anchors explanation in the image classification example. Hence, in order to identify the core feature, you can use an anchors image.

```python
def superpixel(image, size=(4, 7)):
    segments = np.zeros([image.shape[0], image.shape[1]])
    row_idx, col_idx = np.where(segments == 0)
    for i, j in zip(row_idx, col_idx):
        segments[i, j] = int((image.shape[1]/size[1]) * (i//size[0]) + j
        //size[1])
    return segments

segments = superpixel(x_train[idx])
plt.imshow(segments);
predict_fn = lambda x: cnn.predict(x)
image_shape = x_train[idx].shape
explainer = AnchorImage(predict_fn, image_shape, segmentation_
fn=superpixel)

i = 11
image = x_test[i]
plt.imshow(image[:,:,0]);

cnn.predict(image.reshape(1, 28, 28, 1)).argmax()

explanation = explainer.explain(image, threshold=.95, p_sample=.8, seed=0)

plt.imshow(explanation.anchor[:,:,0]);

explanation.meta

explanation.params

{'custom_segmentation': True,
 'segmentation_kwargs': None,
 'p_sample': 0.8,
 'seed': None,
 'image_shape': (28, 28, 1),
 'segmentation_fn': 'custom',
 'threshold': 0.95,
 'delta': 0.1,
```

```
'tau': 0.15,
'batch_size': 100,
'coverage_samples': 10000,
'beam_size': 1,
'stop_on_first': False,
'max_anchor_size': None,
'min_samples_start': 100,
'n_covered_ex': 10,
'binary_cache_size': 10000,
'cache_margin': 1000,
'verbose': False,
'verbose_every': 1,
'kwargs': {'seed': 0}}
```

Conclusion

In this chapter, you looked at a tabular data example using the adult dataset, the IMDB movie review dataset for sentiment analysis, and the fashion MNIST dataset for an image classification example. The anchors function is quite different for tabular data, textual data, and image data. In this chapter, you worked on examples of explaining the image classification and prediction, text classification and prediction, and the image classification using an explainer from Alibi as the new library.

## CHAPTER 13

Model Explainability for Rule-Based Expert Systems

Rule-based systems are relatively easier to explain to end users because rules can be expressed as if/else conditions. Indeed, at times there are multiple if/else conditions. Expert systems are deterministic in nature and very accurate, because they are driven by well-established rules and conditions. The need for explainability arises when multiple rules either conflict or are combined in such a way that it is difficult to interpret. In the field of artificial intelligence, an expert system is a program designed to simulate a real decision making process. Expert systems are designed to solve complex problems by simple reasoning and are represented as if/else/then conditions. Expert systems are designed to act like an inference engine. The role of an inference engine is to make decisions. Sometimes expert systems are simple, like a decision tree, and sometimes expert systems are very complex. Complex expert systems require a knowledge base. Sometimes these knowledge bases are an ontology, which is a form of a body of knowledge, through which a particular rule can be framed and inferencing can be done.

What Is an Expert System?

The knowledge base is the reasoning store through which the if/else conditions of an expert system operate. In any traditional computer program, reasoning and logic are embedded in the script, making it impossible for anyone other than technology specialists to understand the reasoning. The goal of a knowledge-based system is to make the decision making process explicit. With the knowledge base, the objective of the expert system is to explicitly show the rules in a format that is intuitive, self-explanatory,

© Pradeepta Mishra 2022
P. Mishra, *Practical Explainable AI Using Python*, https://doi.org/10.1007/978-1-4842-7158-2_13

and easily understood by the decision makers. The ontology is a formal representation of classes, subclasses, and superclasses. The entities are linked or associated through some common properties. The relations can be concepts, associations, and other meta-properties. The ontology classification helps maintain the formal structure of the knowledge base on which an expert system works.

Any expert system requires two components:

- **A knowledge base**: The formal structure that is called an ontology

- **An inference engine**: Either a rule-based system or a machine learning-driven system.

An inference engine uses two different forms of reasoning to arrive at a decision rule:

- Forward chaining

- Backward chaining

Backward and Forward Chaining

Figure 13-1 explains the forward chaining process. The abstract features can be extracted from the base features and a final decision can be arrived at using the abstract features.

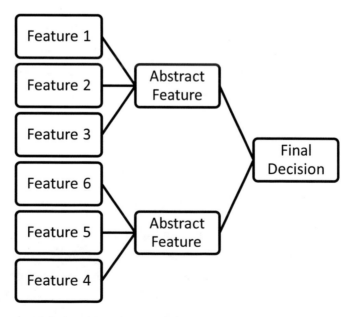

Figure 13-1. *Forward chaining*

The forward chaining method explains what happens to the decision. Suppose in a structured data problem you have features. The features have their own values. The combination of if/else conditions leads to the abstract feature formation. The abstract features lead to the final decision. If someone wants to verify how the final decision is made, it can be traced back. The inference engine follows the chain of if/else conditions and derivations to reach a conclusion about the decision. In the similar manner, we can explain the backward chaining in Figure 13-2.

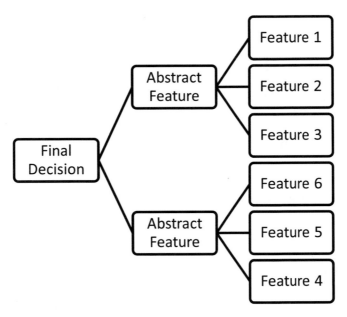

Figure 13-2. *Backward chaining*

The logic followed in backward chaining is to understand why a certain decision is being made. The decision engine of an expert system tries to find out the conditions that led to the decision, as an example, spam email or not spam email. Here the possibility of having a certain token either led to spam or not is of interest to the decision engine.

Rule Extraction Using Scikit-Learn

Rules explanation using a decision tree-based model, where the churn prediction can be explained based on the usage history of the customers in a telecom churn dataset, is shown using the Python scikit-learn library. In order to explain the rule creation and extraction process, let's look at a telecom churn prediction dataset, where predicting the probable churn customers in advance gives an advantage to the business when having

conversations with them, understanding their concerns, and hence trying to retain them.
Customer retention is less costly than customer acquisition. The training dataset has
been already preprocessed where the categorical column states are transformed into one
hot encoded columns. Similarly, there are other categorical features such as area code,
international plan status, voice email plan, and number of customer service calls, which
are transformed into one hot encoded features.

```
import pandas as pd
df_total = pd.read_csv('Processed_Training_data.csv')
```

After reading the data into a Jupyter notebook, you can see the first five records by
using the head function. The first column is a serial number; it has no value, so you can
remove it.

```
df_total.columns
del df_total['Unnamed: 0']
df_total.head()
```

The following script separates the target column as the Y variable and rest of the
features as the X variable:

```
import numpy as np
Y = np.array(df_total.pop('churn_yes'))
X = np.array(df_total)
```

```
from sklearn.model_selection import train_test_split
from sklearn.metrics import confusion_matrix, classification_report
```

```
xtrain,xtest,ytrain,ytest = train_test_split(X,Y,test_size=0.20,random_
state=1234)
xtrain.shape,xtest.shape,ytrain.shape,ytest.shape
```

```
import numpy as np, pandas as pd, matplotlib.pyplot as plt, pydotplus
from sklearn import tree, metrics, model_selection, preprocessing
from IPython.display import Image, display
```

For a visualization of a decision tree in a Jupyter environment, you need to install the
pydotplus library.

```
!pip install pydotplus
```

To start, you can train a simple decision tree model and extract the rules and visualize the rules. You can get into complex models such as random forest classifiers or gradient boosting-based classifiers, which train the model by using numerous amount of trees as defined by the user (100 trees to 10000 trees, but not limited to those two numbers). Identification of rules in ensemble models also can be derived using another library named RuleFit, which is out of scope for this book due to the installation and stability from a library availability point of view. I have included the rule extraction based on a conditional threshold and confidence level using the anchors explanation from the Alibi library in Chapter 12.

```
dt1 = tree.DecisionTreeClassifier()
dt1
dt1.fit(xtrain,ytrain)
dt1.score(xtrain,ytrain)
dt1.score(xtest,ytest)
```

The decision tree with the default parameters are initialized and the object is stored as dt1. Then the model training happens using the fit method, and the score function is used to get the accuracy of the model from the training dataset and the test dataset. The training accuracy is 100% and the test accuracy is 89.8%. This is a clear sign of model overfitting. This is because of the parameter in the decision tree classifier, maximum depth. By default it is none, which means the branches of the decision tree will be expanded until all of the samples are placed in the decision tree. If the model is overfitting the data, then the rules extracted from it will also be misleading, sometimes generating false positives and sometimes false negatives. So the first step here is to get the model right. You need to fine tune the hyper parameters in order to produce a better and stable model. Then the rules will be valid.

```
dt2 = tree.DecisionTreeClassifier(class_weight=None, criterion='entropy',
max_depth=4,
                    max_features=None, max_leaf_nodes=None,
                    min_impurity_decrease=0.0, min_impurity_split=None,
                    min_samples_leaf=10, min_samples_split=30,
                    min_weight_fraction_leaf=0.0, presort=False,
                    random_state=None, splitter='best')
```

in this version of the decision tree model dt2, the branch creation algorithm is selected as entropy, the maximum tree depth is set to 4, and some other parameters that could impact the accuracy of a model are also taken into consideration.

```
dt2.fit(xtrain,ytrain)
dt2.score(xtrain,ytrain)
dt2.score(xtest,ytest)

pred_y = dt2.predict(xtest)
print(classification_report(pred_y,ytest))
```

In the second iteration of the model you are able to make the training accuracy and test accuracy come closer, thus removing the possibility of model overfitting. The training accuracy in the second version is 92% and the test accuracy is 89.9%. The classification accuracy as per the model prediction is 90%.

Once you get a better model, you can extract the features from the model in order to know the weights.

```
import numpy as np, pandas as pd, matplotlib.pyplot as plt, pydotplus
from sklearn import tree, metrics, model_selection, preprocessing
from IPython.display import Image, display

dt2.feature_importances_
```

The features_importances_ function shows the scores associated with each feature in impacting the model predictions. The export_graphviz function generates a dot data object, which can be used by the pydotplus library to populate the graphical way of representing the decision tree. See Figure 13-3.

```
dot_data = tree.export_graphviz(dt2,
                                out_file=None,
                                filled=True,
                                rounded=True,
                                feature_names=['state_AL', 'state_AR',
                                'state_AZ', 'state_CA', 'state_CO',
                                'state_CT',
        'state_DC', 'state_DE', 'state_FL', 'state_GA', 'state_HI', 'state_IA',
        'state_ID', 'state_IL', 'state_IN', 'state_KS', 'state_KY', 'state_LA',
        'state_MA', 'state_MD', 'state_ME', 'state_MI', 'state_MN', 'state_MO',
```

```
                'state_MS', 'state_MT', 'state_NC', 'state_ND', 'state_NE', 'state_NH',
                'state_NJ', 'state_NM', 'state_NV', 'state_NY', 'state_OH', 'state_OK',
                'state_OR', 'state_PA', 'state_RI', 'state_SC', 'state_SD', 'state_TN',
                'state_TX', 'state_UT', 'state_VA', 'state_VT', 'state_WA', 'state_WI',
                'state_WV', 'state_WY', 'area_code_area_code_415',
                'area_code_area_code_510', 'international_plan_yes',
                'voice_mail_plan_yes', 'num_cust_serv_calls_1',
                'num_cust_serv_calls_2', 'num_cust_serv_calls_3',
                'num_cust_serv_calls_4', 'num_cust_serv_calls_5',
                'num_cust_serv_calls_6', 'num_cust_serv_calls_7',
                'num_cust_serv_calls_8', 'num_cust_serv_calls_9',
                'total_day_minutes',
                'total_day_calls', 'total_day_charge', 'total_eve_minutes',
                'total_eve_calls', 'total_eve_charge', 'total_night_minutes',
                'total_night_calls', 'total_night_charge', 'total_intl_minutes',
                'total_intl_charge', 'total_intl_calls_4.0',
                'number_vmail_messages_4.0'],
                                        class_names=['0', '1'])
graph = pydotplus.graph_from_dot_data(dot_data)
display(Image(graph.create_png()))
```

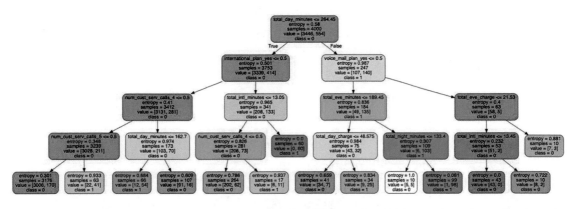

Figure 13-3. *The decision tree object showing the rules from root node to leaf node*

The decision tree starts with the root node and follows the branch creation logic as entropy or the gini formula to create subsequent nodes and finally reaches the terminal node, which is also considered as the leaf node. The entire path from the start of the root node to the leaf node is considered as a rule.

```
from sklearn.tree import export_text

tree_rules = export_text(dt1, feature_names=list(df_total.
columns),decimals=0, show_weights=True)
print(tree_rules)
```

The tree-based rules can also be exported as text so that you can parse the text and integrate it into other applications. The number of rules generated by the decision tree 1 model is many because the model is an overfitted model. So trusting it is erroneous.

This is why you are looking for a better model with a better fit. You want to generate trustworthy rules which are finite in nature so that you can implement them in a production scenario.

```
tree_rules = export_text(dt2, feature_names=list(df_total.
columns),decimals=0, show_weights=True)

print(tree_rules)
|--- total_day_minutes <= 264
|   |--- international_plan_yes <= 0
|   |   |--- num_cust_serv_calls_4 <= 0
|   |   |   |--- num_cust_serv_calls_5 <= 0
|   |   |   |   |--- weights: [3006, 170] class: 0
|   |   |   |--- num_cust_serv_calls_5 >  0
|   |   |   |   |--- weights: [22, 41] class: 1
|   |   |--- num_cust_serv_calls_4 >  0
|   |   |   |--- total_day_minutes <= 163
|   |   |   |   |--- weights: [12, 54] class: 1
|   |   |   |--- total_day_minutes >  163
|   |   |   |   |--- weights: [91, 16] class: 0
|   |--- international_plan_yes >  0
|   |   |--- total_intl_minutes <= 13
|   |   |   |--- num_cust_serv_calls_4 <= 0
|   |   |   |   |--- weights: [202, 62] class: 0
|   |   |   |--- num_cust_serv_calls_4 >  0
|   |   |   |   |--- weights: [6, 11] class: 1
|   |   |--- total_intl_minutes >  13
|   |   |   |--- weights: [0, 60] class: 1
```

```
|--- total_day_minutes >  264
|   |--- voice_mail_plan_yes <= 0
|   |   |--- total_eve_minutes <= 189
|   |   |   |--- total_day_charge <= 49
|   |   |   |   |--- weights: [34, 7] class: 0
|   |   |   |--- total_day_charge >  49
|   |   |   |   |--- weights: [9, 25] class: 1
|   |   |--- total_eve_minutes >  189
|   |   |   |--- total_night_minutes <= 133
|   |   |   |   |--- weights: [5, 5] class: 0
|   |   |   |--- total_night_minutes >  133
|   |   |   |   |--- weights: [1, 98] class: 1
|   |--- voice_mail_plan_yes >  0
|   |   |--- total_eve_charge <= 22
|   |   |   |--- total_intl_minutes <= 13
|   |   |   |   |--- weights: [43, 0] class: 0
|   |   |   |--- total_intl_minutes >  13
|   |   |   |   |--- weights: [8, 2] class: 0
|   |   |--- total_eve_charge >  22
|   |   |   |--- weights: [7, 3] class: 0
```

```
tree_rules = export_text(dt2, feature_names=list(df_total.columns))
print(tree_rules)
```

```
|--- total_day_minutes <= 264.45
|   |--- international_plan_yes <= 0.50
|   |   |--- num_cust_serv_calls_4 <= 0.50
|   |   |   |--- num_cust_serv_calls_5 <= 0.50
|   |   |   |   |--- class: 0
|   |   |   |--- num_cust_serv_calls_5 >  0.50
|   |   |   |   |--- class: 1
|   |   |--- num_cust_serv_calls_4 >  0.50
|   |   |   |--- total_day_minutes <= 162.70
|   |   |   |   |--- class: 1
|   |   |   |--- total_day_minutes >  162.70
|   |   |   |   |--- class: 0
```

```
|    |--- international_plan_yes >  0.50
|    |    |--- total_intl_minutes <= 13.05
|    |    |    |--- num_cust_serv_calls_4 <= 0.50
|    |    |    |    |--- class: 0
|    |    |    |--- num_cust_serv_calls_4 >  0.50
|    |    |    |    |--- class: 1
|    |    |--- total_intl_minutes >  13.05
|    |    |    |--- class: 1
|--- total_day_minutes >  264.45
|    |--- voice_mail_plan_yes <= 0.50
|    |    |--- total_eve_minutes <= 189.45
|    |    |    |--- total_day_charge <= 48.58
|    |    |    |    |--- class: 0
|    |    |    |--- total_day_charge >  48.58
|    |    |    |    |--- class: 1
|    |    |--- total_eve_minutes >  189.45
|    |    |    |--- total_night_minutes <= 133.40
|    |    |    |    |--- class: 0
|    |    |    |--- total_night_minutes >  133.40
|    |    |    |    |--- class: 1
|    |--- voice_mail_plan_yes >  0.50
|    |    |--- total_eve_charge <= 21.53
|    |    |    |--- total_intl_minutes <= 13.45
|    |    |    |    |--- class: 0
|    |    |    |--- total_intl_minutes >  13.45
|    |    |    |    |--- class: 0
|    |    |--- total_eve_charge >  21.53
|    |    |    |--- class: 0
```

Let's explain a rule: if the total day minutes are less than or equal to 264.45, having subscribed to international plans, and the customer makes more than four customer service calls, the person is likely to churn. Conversely, if the person makes less than four customer service calls, keeping all other factors constant, they are not likely to churn. You can explain all other rules in a similar way.

The above examples are derived from the model's behavior, as the model provides the threshold values in determining the decision to identify a churn-or-no-churn scenario. However, the rule's thresholds are defined by the business user or the domain expert who has enough knowledge about the problem statement from an expert system.

The interaction with an expert system can be implemented using natural language processing methods such as developing a question/answer systems. However, the design and development of an expert system requires the following steps:

- Identification of a problem statement

- Finding a subject matter expert in the same domain

- Establishing the cost benefit of the entire solution

Need for a Rule-Based System

The need for a rule-based expert system can be attributed to the following:

- There is not much data to train a machine learning or deep learning algorithm.

- Domain experts frame the rules from their experience, which is based on the truth table they carry. Finding such experts always is a challenge.

- There is a challenge in reproducing the machine learning models or deep learning models as there is a little bit of uncertainty in prediction or classification.

- Sometimes it is hard to explain the prediction decisions generated by the machine learning models.

- Sometimes the machine learning models generate wrong results even if you have trained them with the right procedure; hence there is a need to overwrite the machine prediction with the rule-based outcome.

Challenges of an Expert System

The major challenges of an expert rule-based system for explaining a decision are as follows:

- Too many rules may lead to confusion in explaining the outcome.

- Too few rules may lead to overlooking an important signal.

- You must manage the conflicting rules, and add an alert mechanism for the end user.

- You must find out rules ensembles in identifying a commonality between various rules.

- If two rules lead to the same decision, backward chaining may lead to confusion.

Conclusion

The creation of an expert system is a time-intensive process. This chapter provided a simulated view of how rules can be generated and elaborated for explainability purpose. You learned the approaches, challenges, and needs for a rule-based system. In the real world, major robotics processes are powered by expert rule-based systems. AI models can explain the decisions but control over the actions is limited; hence there is a need for an expert system that often overrides the AI model's decisions whenever they head in an unfavorable direction. Moreover, the rule-based expert system is crucial for computer vision-related tasks. The AI model can be fooled by using some abstract form of an image, but a rule-based system can identify it and recognize the anomalies.

## CHAPTER 14

Model Explainability for Computer Vision

Computer vision tasks such as image classification and object detection are gradually becoming better day by day due to continuous research in improving the accuracy of models, the evolution of new frameworks, and the growing open source community. The results from recent state-of-the-art machine learning models are more promising than half a decade ago, which gives us confidence to expand the horizon of problems by undertaking more complex problems. If we look at the use cases around computer vision, the most prominent are in retail, agriculture, public health, the automobile industry, and the gaming industry. Some of the industries from this list have a legal mandate to use AI responsibly. The European Union is also trying to regulate the application and usage of AI. If the predictions or classifications generated by image classification models go wrong, users will not trust the model and its predictions. It is necessary to understand why the AI model has generated a prediction or classification one way vs. another way. Model explainability shows the end user which particular parts of an image made the model predict class A vs. other classes.

Why Explainability for Image Data?

Images are converted into pixel values. The pixel values are subsequently used as features to train a label that the image best represents. If the AI model generates a wrong prediction/classification, two groups of people are accountable and responsible

© Pradeepta Mishra 2022
P. Mishra, *Practical Explainable AI Using Python*, https://doi.org/10.1007/978-1-4842-7158-2_14

in an organization: the data scientist who built the model and the stakeholder who approved putting the model into production. The wrong classification of image data is due to two reasons:

- The model is unable to consider the correct set of features for prediction. Instead, it picks wrong cues and signals from the data. The right set of features are not taken into consideration while training.

- Not enough training is done to let the algorithm generalize unseen data very well.

Anchor Image Using Alibi

For computer vision tasks such object detection and image classification, you can explain the key features that differentiate an image of a bag from an image of a t-shirt, for example. This can be achieved by using the anchors explanation, which was covered in Chapter 11 of this book. However, the same method can be extended to other computer vision tasks such as fake image identification and possible compromise of the image. The steps are as follows:

- The object detection or image classification model can be trained for each domain, such as famous personalities and popular or common objects.

- If you want to identify the authenticity of another person's image or a cropped image, you can get a prediction, but the probability threshold will be little lower.

- In that case, you can trigger the anchors explanations to learn the key features or the prominent pixels that lead to the prediction.

- In theory, this is fine. In practice, you can verify by using the following super pixel formula.

What the anchors explanation provides are the colors or the contrasting colors that differentiate the image or object from other images. You need to write a function to generate super pixels for any given image.

Integrated Gradients Method

The objective of the integrated gradients approach is to attribute the feature importance score to each of the features used to train the machine learning or deep learning model. You use the gradient descent to update the weights of a deep neural network model. When you reverse the process, you can take the integration of the weights attributing to the feature importance score. Gradients can be defined as a slope of the output with respect to the input features in a deep learning model. The integrated gradients approach can be used to understand the pixel importance in recognizing the correct image in image classification problem. The gradients are typically computed for the output of the class where the probability is highest with respect to the pixel of the input image.

```
import numpy as np
import os

import tensorflow as tf
from tensorflow.keras.layers import Activation, Conv2D, Dense, Dropout
from tensorflow.keras.layers import Flatten, Input, Reshape, MaxPooling2D
from tensorflow.keras.models import Model
from tensorflow.keras.utils import to_categorical
from alibi.explainers import IntegratedGradients

import matplotlib.pyplot as plt
print('TF version: ', tf.__version__)
print('Eager execution enabled: ', tf.executing_eagerly()) # True

train, test = tf.keras.datasets.mnist.load_data()
X_train, y_train = train
X_test, y_test = test
test_labels = y_test.copy()
train_labels = y_train.copy()
```

To explain the working of the integrated gradients approach, let's use the MNIST dataset, which is easy to understand and many people are familiar with it. Table 14-1 explains the parameters of the model.

Table 14-1. *Integrated Gradients Parameters*

Parameters	Explanations
Model	TensorFlow or Keras model
Layer	Layer with respect to which gradients are calculated. If not provided, the gradients are calculated with respect to the input.
Method	Method for the integral approximation. Methods available: `riemann_left`, `riemann_right`, `riemann_middle`, `riemann_trapezoid`, and `gausslegendre`.
N_steps	Number of steps in the path integral approximation from the baseline to the input instance

```
X_train = X_train.reshape(-1, 28, 28, 1).astype('float64') / 255
X_test = X_test.reshape(-1, 28, 28, 1).astype('float64') / 255
y_train = to_categorical(y_train, 10)
y_test = to_categorical(y_test, 10)
print(X_train.shape, y_train.shape, X_test.shape, y_test.shape)

load_mnist_model = False
save_model = True

filepath = './model_mnist/'  # change to directory where model is saved
if load_mnist_model:
    model = tf.keras.models.load_model(os.path.join(filepath, 'model.h5'))
else:
    # define model
    inputs = Input(shape=(X_train.shape[1:]), dtype=tf.float64)
    x = Conv2D(64, 2, padding='same', activation='relu')(inputs)
    x = MaxPooling2D(pool_size=2)(x)
    x = Dropout(.3)(x)

    x = Conv2D(32, 2, padding='same', activation='relu')(x)
    x = MaxPooling2D(pool_size=2)(x)
    x = Dropout(.3)(x)

    x = Flatten()(x)
    x = Dense(256, activation='relu')(x)
```

```python
x = Dropout(.5)(x)
logits = Dense(10, name='logits')(x)
outputs = Activation('softmax', name='softmax')(logits)
model = Model(inputs=inputs, outputs=outputs)
model.compile(loss='categorical_crossentropy',
              optimizer='adam',
              metrics=['accuracy'])

# train model
model.fit(X_train,
          y_train,
          epochs=6,
          batch_size=256,
          verbose=1,
          validation_data=(X_test, y_test)
          )
if save_model:
    if not os.path.exists(filepath):
        os.makedirs(filepath)
    model.save(os.path.join(filepath, 'model.h5'))
```

In order to generate integrated gradients, the target variable specifies which class of the output should be considered to calculate the attributions using the integration approach.

```python
import tensorflow as tf
from alibi.explainers import IntegratedGradients

model = tf.keras.models.load_model(os.path.join(filepath, 'model.h5'))

ig  = IntegratedGradients(model,
                          layer=None,
                          method="gausslegendre",
                          n_steps=50,
                          internal_batch_size=100)
```

The integrated gradient module from `alibi.explainers` is imported, a pre-trained TensorFlow or Keras model is loaded, and then the gradients are generated. There are five different methods of integral approximation, based on the complexity of the image classification. There is no direct rule or way to know which methods work when, so you need to try all of the methods in an iterative manner.

```
# Initialize IntegratedGradients instance
n_steps = 50
method = "gausslegendre"
ig  = IntegratedGradients(model,
                          n_steps=n_steps,
                          method=method)
```

The number of steps you can increase is based on the computational power of the machine and the number of samples in the folder to train a model.

```
# Calculate attributions for the first 10 images in the test set
nb_samples = 10
X_test_sample = X_test[:nb_samples]
predictions = model(X_test_sample).numpy().argmax(axis=1)
explanation = ig.explain(X_test_sample,
                         baselines=None,
                         target=predictions)
```

In order to calculate the attributions for the first 10 images from the test set, you can select the target as predictions and the baseline as none. If you select the baseline as none, it will trigger a black color as a baseline, which is the background color of the image.

```
# Metadata from the explanation object
explanation.meta
```

```
# Data fields from the explanation object
explanation.data.keys()
```

```
# Get attributions values from the explanation object
attrs = explanation.attributions[0]
```

Once you get the attributions, you can show the positive attributions and negative attributions for a target class in a graphical format.

```python
fig, ax = plt.subplots(nrows=3, ncols=4, figsize=(10, 7))
image_ids = [0, 1, 9]
cmap_bound = np.abs(attrs[[0, 1, 9]]).max()

for row, image_id in enumerate(image_ids):
    # original images
    ax[row, 0].imshow(X_test[image_id].squeeze(), cmap='gray')
    ax[row, 0].set_title(f'Prediction: {predictions[image_id]}')

    # attributions
    attr = attrs[image_id]
    im = ax[row, 1].imshow(attr.squeeze(), vmin=-cmap_bound, vmax=cmap_
    bound, cmap='PiYG')

    # positive attributions
    attr_pos = attr.clip(0, 1)
    im_pos = ax[row, 2].imshow(attr_pos.squeeze(), vmin=-cmap_bound,
    vmax=cmap_bound, cmap='PiYG')

    # negative attributions
    attr_neg = attr.clip(-1, 0)
    im_neg = ax[row, 3].imshow(attr_neg.squeeze(), vmin=-cmap_bound,
    vmax=cmap_bound, cmap='PiYG')

ax[0, 1].set_title('Attributions');
ax[0, 2].set_title('Positive attributions');
ax[0, 3].set_title('Negative attributions');

for ax in fig.axes:
    ax.axis('off')

fig.colorbar(im, cax=fig.add_axes([0.95, 0.25, 0.03, 0.5]));
```

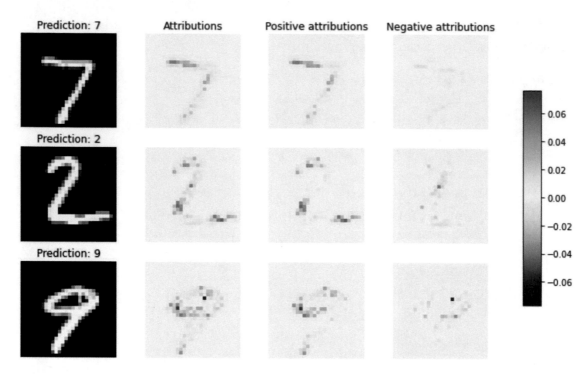

Figure 14-1. *Attributions generated by integrated gradients*

In Figure 14-1, the predicted digits are 7, 2 and 9. The attributions that are positive mostly match the final prediction and the negative attributions are fairly low.

Conclusion

Image attributions are important to explain the reason for a certain image classification. Image attributions can be created using the dominant pixel approach or identifying impacted pixels of the image. This can be useful in certain industries. In manufacturing, it can be used to identify defective products from product images. In healthcare, it can classify kinds of scans and identify anomalies on scans. In all areas it is important to explain why the model has classified a class. As long as you are able to explain the predictions, you will be in a better position to gain the user's trust on the model and thereby you can increase the adoption of AI models in industries to solve complex business problems.

Index

A

B

© Pradeepta Mishra 2022
P. Mishra, *Practical Explainable AI Using Python*, https://doi.org/10.1007/978-1-4842-7158-2

F

G, H

N, O

P, Q

R